Illuminate Publishing

Edexcel GCSE (9–1) Drama
DESIGNING DRAMA
Costume, Lighting, Set & Sound Design

Sue Shewring

Published in 2020 by Illuminate Publishing Ltd,
PO Box 1160, Cheltenham, Gloucestershire GL50 9RW

Orders: Please visit www.illuminatepublishing.com
or email sales@illuminatepublishing.com

© Sue Shewring 2020

The moral rights of the author have been asserted.

All rights reserved. No part of this book may be reprinted, reproduced, or utilised in any form or by any electronic, mechanical, or other means, now known or hereafter invented, including photocopying and recording, or in any information storage and retrieval system, without permission in writing from the publishers.

British Library Cataloguing-in-Publication Data

A catalogue record of this book is available from the British Library.

ISBN 978-1-912820-22-1

Printed by Severn, Gloucester

09.20

The publisher's policy is to use papers that are natural, renewable and recyclable products made from wood grown in sustainable forests. The logging and manufacturing processes are expected to conform to the environmental regulations in the country of origin.

Every effort has been made to contact copyright holders of material reproduced in this book. Great care has been taken by the author and publisher to ensure that either formal permission has been granted for the use of copyright material reproduced, or that copyright material has been used under the provision of fair-dealing guidelines in the UK – specifically that it has been used sparingly, solely for the purpose of criticism and review, and has been properly acknowledged. If notified, the publisher will be pleased to rectify any errors or omissions at the earliest opportunity.

We have made every effort to ensure that website addresses are correct at the time of printing, and links are provided for information only. Illuminate Publishing cannot be held responsible for the content of any website listed or detailed in this book.

Editor: Roanne Charles, abc Editorial
Design and layout and Cover design: EMC Design Ltd
Cover photograph: melnikof at Shutterstock.com.

Endorsement statement

In order to ensure that this resource offers high-quality support for the associated Pearson qualification, it has been through a review process by the awarding body. This process confirms that this resource fully covers the teaching and learning content of the specification or part of a specification at which it is aimed. It also confirms that it demonstrates an appropriate balance between the development of subject skills, knowledge and understanding, in addition to preparation for assessment.

Endorsement does not cover any guidance on assessment activities or processes (e.g. practice questions or advice on how to answer assessment questions), included in the resource nor does it prescribe any particular approach to the teaching or delivery of a related course.

While the publishers have made every attempt to ensure that advice on the qualification and its assessment is accurate, the official specification and associated assessment guidance materials are the only authoritative source of information and should always be referred to for definitive guidance.

Pearson examiners have not contributed to any sections in this resource relevant to examination papers for which they have responsibility.

Examiners will not use endorsed resources as a source of material for any assessment set by Pearson.

Endorsement of a resource does not mean that the resource is required to achieve this Pearson qualification, nor does it mean that it is the only suitable material available to support the qualification, and any resource lists produced by the awarding body shall include this and other appropriate resources.

The author would like to thank specialist consultants without whose knowledgable input this book would not have been possible:

COSTUME — Fi Carrington

LIGHTING AND SOUND — Brent Lees, BCL Lighting Design facebook.com/BCL-Lighting-Design; Info@bcl-lightingdesign.co.uk

SET AND PUPPETRY — Ali McCaw (BA Hons) Theatre Design

CONTENTS

EVERYTHING BUT THE ACTING
Design in drama and theatre ... 5
How to get the most from this book ... 5

HOW YOU WILL BE ASSESSED
Components and assessment objectives ... 7
Practical components ... 8

UNDERSTANDING DESIGN IN DRAMA AND THEATRE
Theatre design ... 10
Understanding stage configurations ... 12

CHAPTER 1 PRACTICAL GUIDE TO SET DESIGN
Introduction to set design ... 16
Two styles of set design ... 18
Research for set design ... 19
How to document your set design ... 20
Understanding your resources ... 25
Sourcing materials for the set ... 26
Health and safety notes for set designers ... 27
Creating your design for the stage ... 28
Technical and dress rehearsals for set designers ... 29
Evaluating your set design ... 30
Set design vocabulary ... 32

CHAPTER 2 PRACTICAL GUIDE TO LIGHTING DESIGN
Introduction to lighting design ... 34
Types of stage lantern ... 36
Understanding your lighting resources ... 38
Angles, colour and intensity ... 40
Special effects in lighting ... 44
Lighting transitions ... 46
Research for lighting ... 47
How to document your lighting design ... 48
Health and safety in lighting design ... 51
Plotting the lighting design ... 52
Rigging and focusing ... 54
Operating the lighting ... 56
Technical and dress rehearsals for lighting designers ... 57
Evaluating your lighting design ... 59
Lighting design vocabulary ... 60

CHAPTER 3 PRACTICAL GUIDE TO COSTUME DESIGN
Introduction to costume design ... 62
Placing costume in history ... 64
Shape and style: what we wear, and why ... 66
Colour and fabric for the stage ... 68
Developing and using your costume resources ... 72
Key process: sewing ... 74
Adapting costume items ... 76
Health and safety in costume design ... 77
Hair and make-up ... 78
How to document your costume design ... 80
Fitting the costume ... 82
Technical and dress rehearsals for costume designers ... 86
Evaluating your costume design ... 87
Costume design vocabulary ... 88

CHAPTER 4 PRACTICAL GUIDE TO SOUND DESIGN
Introduction to sound design ... 90
How to produce sound for the stage ... 92
Research for sound design ... 94
Sourcing, creating and mixing sounds ... 96
Health and safety in sound design ... 99
Special sound effects ... 100
How to document your sound design ... 102
Positioning sound equipment ... 104
Plotting the sound design ... 106
Operating sound equipment ... 108
Technical and dress rehearsals for sound designers ... 110
Evaluating your sound design ... 111
Sound design vocabulary ... 112

CHAPTER 5 COMPONENT 1: DEVISING – A PRACTICAL GUIDE
Your design challenge ... 114
How your design for the devised piece will be assessed ... 116
Responding to stimuli ... 117
Agreeing on your artistic intentions ... 118
Genre, structure, form and style ... 120
Working positively as a group ... 124
Production meetings ... 125
Using rehearsals to develop and refine your designs ... 126
Final rehearsals ... 128
Set Design for the Devised Piece ... **129**
Starting work on the portfolio ... 130
Building ideas ... 131
Contributing to the development of the piece ... 132

Developing the portfolio	134
Producing and documenting your design	135
Completing your portfolio	137

Lighting Design for the Devised Piece — 138
Starting work on the portfolio	139
Building ideas	140
Contributing to the development of the piece	141
Developing the portfolio	143
Producing and documenting your design	144
Completing your portfolio	146

Costume Design for the Devised Piece — 147
Starting work on the portfolio	148
Building ideas	150
Contributing to the development of the piece	152
Developing the portfolio	153
Producing and documenting your design	154
Completing your portfolio	156

Sound Design for the Devised Piece — 157
Starting work on the portfolio	158
Building ideas	159
Contributing to the development of the piece	160
Developing the portfolio	161
Producing and documenting your design	162
Completing your portfolio	164

CHAPTER 6 COMPONENT 2: DESIGNING FOR THE PERFORMANCE FROM TEXT

How your design skills will be assessed	166

Six Steps to Set Design for the Scripted Performance — 168
1 Working on your own with the script	168
2 The design brief meeting and rehearsals	170
3 Revisiting the script	171
4 Confirming your set designs	172
5 The final design meeting	173
6 The completed set design	174
The written explanation for set design	175

Six Steps to Lighting Design for the Scripted Performance — 176
1 Working on your own with the script	176
2 The design brief meeting and rehearsals	178
3 Revisiting the script	179
4 Confirming your lighting designs	180
5 The final design meeting	181
6 The completed lighting design	182
The written explanation for lighting	183

Six Steps to Costume Design for the Scripted Performance — 184
1 Working on your own with the script	184
2 The design brief meeting and rehearsals	186
3 Revisiting the script	187
4 Confirming your costume designs	188
5 The final design meeting	189
6 The completed costume design	190
The written explanation for costume	191

Six Steps to Sound Design for the Scripted Performance — 192
1 Working on your own with the script	192
2 The design brief meeting and rehearsals	194
3 Revisiting the script	195
4 Confirming your sound designs	196
5 The final design meeting	197
6 The completed sound design	198
The written explanation for sound	199

CHAPTER 7 COMPONENT 3: THEATRE MAKERS IN PRACTICE

Introduction to design in the written exam	202
Preparing for the exam	206
Section A: Set design from a director's viewpoint	208
Section A: Set design from a designer's viewpoint	212
Section B: Evaluating a set design in live theatre	218
Section A: Lighting design from a director's viewpoint	222
Section A: Lighting design from a designer's viewpoint	226
Section B: Evaluating a lighting design in live theatre	230
Section A: Costume design from a director's viewpoint	234
Section A: Costume design from a designer's viewpoint	238
Section B: Evaluating a costume design in live theatre	241
Section A: Sound design from a director's viewpoint	244
Section A: Sound design from a designer's viewpoint	248
Section B: Evaluating a sound design in live theatre	253

Glossary	257
Index	261
Acknowledgements	264

EVERYTHING BUT THE ACTING

DESIGN IN DRAMA AND THEATRE

This book is about everything that happens on the stage except for the acting!

Designing Drama will help you to costume actors and give them a set to perform on. It will guide you through the process that fills their world with sound and floods the stage with light.

More than that, you will come to understand how the work of the theatre designer brings the world of the stage to life for the most important people in the theatre – the audience.

Whether you are designing sound for a devised piece of drama, or costume for a scripted one, this book offers practical advice and activities to help you develop your knowledge, understanding and creativity.

If you are a performer at heart, this book will help you to master the knowledge and skills needed to write about design in the exam. You will need a good level of knowledge for all the design elements that exam questions could be about. Performance and design work hand in hand to create the harmonious world of the stage. *Designing Drama* will help you to understand how to be part of this creative process from every angle.

HOW TO GET THE MOST FROM THIS BOOK

Practical guides to design roles

Chapters 1 to 4 are the practical guides to each of the Drama design elements:

- SET
- COSTUME
- LIGHTING
- SOUND

These chapters introduce you to each design role and provide practical guidance, advice and activities to help you through the design process. They will give you a good grounding in your chosen design specialism, enabling you to develop your skills, boost your confidence and explore your creativity.

Drama course content

Refer back to the practical chapters as you move on to the chapters that cover design for each assessed component of the course:

- Component 1: Devising (Chapter 5)
- Component 2: Performance from text (Chapter 6)
- Component 3: Theatre makers in practice (Chapter 7).

Features of the book

In order to highlight important information, activities and assessment objectives, we have included some special features:

FOCUS
A note to summarise the main content of the section.

ASSESSMENT CHECK
Details from the Edexcel specification documents to show you which elements of the assessment criteria the guidance and activities will help you to achieve.

SIGNPOST
These direct you to supporting content from other sections that you are likely to need before you attempt the activities.

TASKS
Activities and exercises to help you learn, practise and develop your design skills.

DESIGN TIPS
Quick ideas, things to remember and helpful tips from professional theatre design.

LOOK HERE
A guide to the most suitable sections of support from other chapters.

This symbol indicates that there is a free download available at www.illuminatepublishing.com. Simply navigate to the product page for this book.

Important technical drama terms are highlighted in **blue** and collected in a Glossary at the back of the book.

We have also included some sample exam questions and example student-style answers. These will give you an idea of the type of questions that will come up in the exam and how some students might have responded.

In addition, the notes are illustrated by diagrams, sketches, plans and photographs to help you visualise the practical elements of theatre that you can achieve as a Drama designer.

HOW YOU WILL BE ASSESSED

COMPONENTS AND ASSESSMENT OBJECTIVES

The three components of the Edexcel GCSE Drama course are:

1 **Devising** (assessed by your teacher)
2 **Performance from text** (assessed by a visiting examiner)
3 **Theatre makers in practice** (written exam).

For these components, the assessment objectives, total marks and percentages of the overall GCSE are:

Component	Assessment objectives and percentages				Total marks	Overall percentage in GCSE
	AO1: Create and develop ideas to communicate meaning for theatrical performance.	**AO2:** Apply theatrical skills to realise artistic intentions in live performance.	**AO3:** Demonstrate knowledge and understanding of how drama and theatre is developed and performed.	**AO4:** Analyse and evaluate their own work and the work of others.		
Component 1: Devising	20%	10%	0	10%	60	40
Component 2: Performance from text	0	20%	0	0	48	20
Component 3: Theatre makers in practice	0	0	30%	10%	60	40

PRACTICAL COMPONENTS

You can work practically as a designer for Components 1 and/or 2, and demonstrate your knowledge and understanding of design in the written exam for Component 3.

Your teacher will assess your work for Component 1, and external examiners will standardise the marking by looking at examples of videos and portfolios.

For Component 2, a visiting examiner will assess your work in performance.

Component 1: Devising

As a designer, you will work as part of a group to create, develop and produce an original piece of drama, devised from a **stimulus**. This is assessed in two parts.

A devised design realisation

This is worth 15 marks and covers AO2. For the choice of the four design roles, you need to produce:

SET
Diagrams, sketches, and **one** actual set for the performance

LIGHTING
Diagrams, documents and use of **at least four** lighting states for the performance

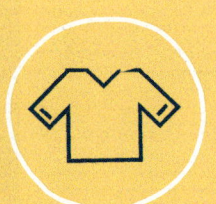

COSTUME
Sketches, documents and completed costumes for **two** characters

SOUND
Diagrams, documents and **at least four** sound cues for the performance.

The portfolio

Your portfolio should cover your creation and development process and your analysis and evaluation of this process. It is worth 45 marks (30 for AO1 and 15 for AO4).

For AO1, your portfolio must include evidence that you have:

- Researched the stimulus and issues arising from this
- Selected, refined and developed your work
- Agreed **artistic intentions**, **genre**, **style** and form
- Made practical explorations.

For AO4, you need to show that you have addressed:

- Communication and development of ideas and designs
- Health and safety issues
- Success and effectiveness.

The portfolio should take the form of:

- 1500–2000 written words, **OR**
- An audio-visual presentation of 8–10 minutes, **OR**
- A combination of 750–1000 words with 4–5 minutes of AV presentation.

Component 2: Performance from text

In your group, you will interpret a playscript. You will prepare and perform **two key extracts** from the text. Your teacher can guide and support you; a visiting examiner will assess you.

This component covers AO2 and is worth 48 marks.

Practical design requirements
For the choice of the four design roles, you need to produce:

- **Set:** **One** set for the performance of **each** extract
- **Lighting:** At least **two** different lighting states for **each** performance
- **Costume:** **One** costume for **each** extract
- **Sound:** At least **two** sound **cues** for **each** performance.

Supporting documents
These are included in your assessment. **For each extract**, you will need to provide the following documents.

Set
- Drawings of the final design that show you have considered actor/audience relationships and health and safety
- A ground plan of the performance space that shows entrances and exits, audience positioning and **stage furniture** (if any).

Lighting
- Plans and a lantern schedule that show you have considered actor/audience relationships and health and safety
- A lighting plot or cue sheet.

Costume
- Final design drawings for one character, including hair, make-up and mask if appropriate, that shows you have considered actor/audience relationships, performer usage and health and safety
- A costume plot or list of costumes and accessories worn by the performer and indications of any changes made during the performance.

Sound
- A source sheet detailing whether each sound cue is original, live or found and which shows that you have considered actor/audience relationships and health and safety
- A cue sheet showing the source, order, length and output of each sound
- The level for every cue.

You must also produce a written explanation of 100–200 words for each extract that outlines:
- How you have **interpreted** the extract
- What you are seeking to communicate to the audience with your design
- Central design concepts.

Component 3: Theatre makers in practice

There is a written exam at the end of the course that lasts 1 hour 45 minutes.

Section A: Bringing texts to life (the study of one performance text)

This assesses AO3 and is worth 45 marks.

As part of Section A, you will be asked to explore the power of a design skill (from a choice of three) from the point of view of:
1. a director
2. a designer.

The questions in this section will relate to an extract from the prescribed text you have studied in lessons. You will be asked to explore the practical ways in which directors and designers create impact and meaning through production and design elements.

Section B: Live theatre evaluation

This assesses AO4 and is worth 15 marks.

Section B gives you the choice of writing about performance or about one element of design from a live theatre production you have seen. You can take 500 words of notes plus sketches you have drawn into the exam with you (but not published photographs).

You will reflect on your experience as an audience member. This will include analysis and evaluation of how production elements combined to create theatre and how successfully you felt this was done.

How You Will be Assessed

> Theatre designers, directors and performers work together to create an artistic vision. Most often, this theatrical vision creates a harmonious world on the stage.

FOCUS
- How design elements enhance theatre.
- A brief guide to the design process.

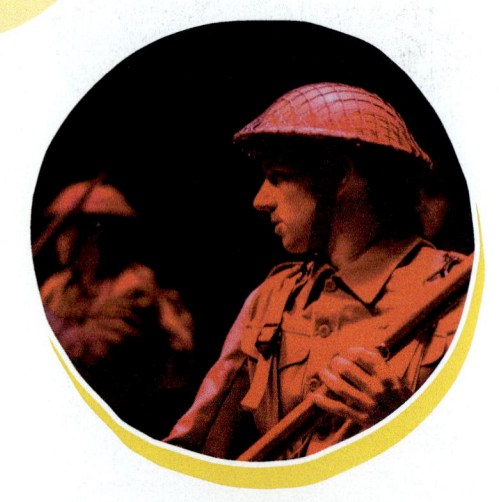

UNDERSTANDING DESIGN IN DRAMA AND THEATRE

THEATRE DESIGN

The focus of this book is design: the theatrical elements of set, costume, lighting and sound. Often known as stagecraft, design covers all the creative, non-performing aspects of staging a theatrical production for an audience.

As a student of Drama, you might have experienced the thrill that comes from putting on a costume or feeling the lights come up on you at the beginning of a scene. While actors wearing simple black outfits can create powerful drama on their own, the integration of performance and theatrical design generally lifts the experience to another, higher, level.

Working in design

Theatre design has evolved over the centuries, and the roles of the designers are as necessary in today's professional theatre as those of director and actor. If theatre design and the technical elements of lighting, sound, costume or set excite you – and you don't mind the travelling that is often involved – careers in the backstage elements of theatre are certainly to be found.

Many colleges, universities and drama schools have courses for designers and technicians that you could investigate to follow on from your Drama courses in school. In addition, the skills required for theatre lighting, costume, make-up and sound apply equally well to the music, television, film and festival industries. These are interesting careers with potentially more employment opportunities compared with acting for example.

> **Fi Carrington, a freelance wardrobe supervisor and costume designer, says:**
>
> *I trained on a theatre costume design course and now do some teaching on a degree course. Most of the students don't have too much difficulty getting freelance work in theatre, film and television.*

The role of design in drama

The role of a theatre designer involves working with a director and other designers to produce workable design ideas for a drama production. There is usually an element of research to be done in relation to the script and historical **periods** and contexts, for example. The designer and director will eventually agree final, budgeted designs and then begin the creation of these in terms of:

- making costumes and sets
- setting plans for rigging, operating and cueing lighting and sounds.

Adaptations to these final designs might be needed as the performance grows closer and issues crop up during rehearsals.

The design process: rehearsal and performance

The technical rehearsal

An important moment in the design process is the technical rehearsal. Here, the performers 'walk' through a complete performance during which they will need to stop, re-perform and skip sections of the play as design details are finalised. This is known as working cue to cue, meaning that each sound and lighting cue is covered and repeated as necessary. This happens until the designers and technicians are confident that the production can run smoothly and maintain the desired artistic intentions. Set and costume changes will also be run through.

Technical rehearsals are notoriously long and taxing for all those involved, but no professional or amateur production can be satisfactorily achieved without one – or sometimes two!

Dress rehearsals

The dress rehearsal is a designer's opportunity to test their design in real time. Lighting and sound designers can practise operating their designs following the script. This means that they can prepare for and then activate their plotted cues. Meanwhile, costume and set designers will often sit in the auditorium with the director, taking notes on what has and hasn't worked well, so that problems can be addressed before the first performance.

Work during the performance

Once a show or run, if there are multiple performances, is underway, there is still work to be done. Costumes have to be cleaned and maintained (although this is done by wardrobe maintenance or dressers in professional theatre). Similarly, sets (including props and set dressings) and technical equipment need to be checked and maintained.

Stage management

In charge of this whole process is the **stage manager**, who co-ordinates all the backstage and technical elements during rehearsals and performances. The stage manager works closely with designers and technicians as well as performers, controlling the production. If you continue your involvement in theatre after your course, stage management is a very important role that could interest you.

Practical design and the exam

Practical components and the written exam are closely related!

- Try to see all your practical work in Components 1 and 2 as preparation for the written exam, where you will have opportunities to use your developing knowledge and skills.
- Even if you are working as a performer for one or both of the practical components, be aware of the design work and opportunities for all the design elements: set, lighting, costume and sound.

TASK I.1

In your next practical drama lesson, where an improvisation or piece of scripted performance is shown, decide on the following in your group:

- What costumes would enhance your performance?
- How could set be used to add meaning and interest to the performance?
- How might you use coloured stage lighting or spotlights to help focus the audience?
- Can you plan one sound cue to emphasise a significant moment in the performance?

Understanding Design in Drama and Theatre

FOCUS
The demands of different staging configurations and their influence on all designers.

ASSESSMENT CHECK
In Components 1 and 2, designs should 'take into consideration performer/audience relationships' and, in Component 3, must 'practically consider use of stage space and spatial relationships, including levels and entrance points'.

Learning about staging configurations is a key part of AO3: 'Demonstrate knowledge and understanding of how drama and theatre is developed and performed.'

UNDERSTANDING STAGE CONFIGURATIONS

Stage space and spatial relationships

All types of theatre designers need to create their designs with close regard to the relationship between acting areas and audience. This relationship will partly depend on how a stage or performance area is arranged.

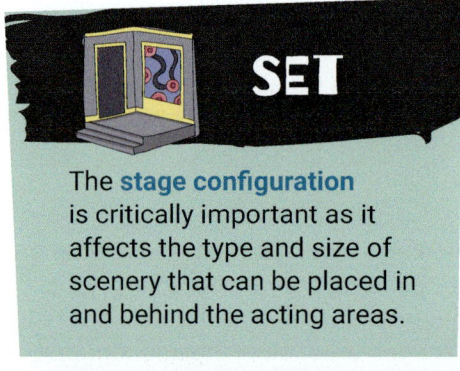

SET
The stage configuration is critically important as it affects the type and size of scenery that can be placed in and behind the acting areas.

COSTUME
Varying amount of detail is required, depending on the proximity of the actors to the audience.

LIGHTING AND SOUND
Staging also affects where lanterns and speakers can be positioned and whether or not projection screens can be used.

You need to be aware of the different types of stage configurations and the advantages they offer and difficulties they present for theatre designers.

Proscenium arch stage

Possible advantages
- Typically Victorian staging: highly appropriate for classical or period plays in a traditional style. Musicals are often staged on prosceniums.
- Creates an intimate acting area.
- Usually includes a small apron area in front of the curtain that can be used for performance during scene changes.
- Gives the audience a sense of peeking into another world.
- Audience seating and/or the stage is often raked to improve sightlines.
- Backdrops, projections and large pieces of scenery work well.
- Straightforward in terms of lighting and sound design.
- Detail in costume and set is not crucial as the audience is at a distance.
- Footlights work well and offer additional lighting angles.

Potential problems
- Sightlines are problematic as the side panels of the arch might obscure parts of the stage for some of the audience.
- Pillared seating areas can also reduce visibility for the audience.
- If the stage is raked, anything on wheels must be wedged or have brakes.
- Many auditoriums have raised circles, which means that some of the audience is distant and almost above the acting area.

The proscenium arch gives a picture-frame effect above and on each side of an end-on stage.

Understanding Design in Drama and Theatre

- Small props are not always easy to see because of the distance between the acting area and the back of the **stalls** or circle.
- Often involves seating part of the audience in raised circles, which means some viewers are a long way from and almost above the acting area while the front row of the stalls is very close. Sound and lighting must be carefully balanced to compensate for this.

End-on stage

Possible advantages

- A neutral stage configuration that lends itself to a range of periods and styles.
- Similar to proscenium arch in that a distinct and separate world can be created.
- Backdrops, projections and large pieces of scenery work well.
- Straightforward in terms of lighting and sound design.

Potential problems

- The distance between the back of the audience and the acting area can be lengthy.
- If the stage is raked, anything with wheels will need to be wedged or have brakes.
- If seating is not raked, sightlines can be a problem.
- Details in costumes and small props might not be seen clearly.

An end-on stage in a small auditorium.

Thrust stage

Possible advantages

- The large apron provides an acting area close to the audience, which helps the audience to feel involved.
- Props and costumes can be detailed.
- The main stage can incorporate large pieces of scenery, projection and backdrops.
- Useful for using different levels, as many thrust aprons include a step.

Potential problems

- Sightlines can be very complex. Audience members on the side banks of seating, for example, will struggle to see action on their side of the main stage.
- No scenery or tall pieces of furniture can be placed on the apron.
- Side-lighting the apron can be problematic as the audience could be dazzled: steep angles are needed.

Timothy Mackabee's award-winning design for *The Odd Couple* at Dallas Theatre Center.

Understanding Design in Drama and Theatre 13

The Railway Children at King's Cross Theatre.

The New Vic Theatre, Newcastle-under-Lyme.

The Dukes Lancaster promenade performance of *A Midsummer Night's Dream*, with Andy Serkis as Lysander. This took place in a local park. Locations included woodland, lawns and next to (and even on) a lake.

Traverse stage

Possible advantages
- The acting area is closer to the audience, creating a more intimate relationship.
- Props and costumes can be detailed.
- The two ends of the acting area can incorporate large pieces of scenery, projections and backdrops, creating different 'worlds' or locations.

Potential problems
- No scenery or large pieces of furniture can be placed on the traverse itself.
- Side lighting can be problematic as the audience can get dazzled: steep angles are needed.
- Costumes need to be detailed at the back too.
- Having audience members directly opposite each other can be distracting.

Theatre in the round

Possible advantages
- The acting area is closer to the audience, which helps the audience to feel involved.
- This configuration allows directors and designers to use the space imaginatively.
- Having performers enter and exit through the corner aisles (close to the audience) can be exciting.
- Props and costumes can be detailed.

Potential problems
- No scenery or large pieces of furniture can be used.
- Lighting is problematic as the audience can be dazzled: steep angles are needed.
- Costumes need to be detailed at the back too.

Promenade theatre

This type of staging is unique. It involves the audience walking (a promenade) from one location to another with the actors. Locations are often outdoors, or in large buildings such as warehouses.

Possible advantages
- Very exciting for both audience and performers.
- Creates a 'we're all in this together' atmosphere.
- Suits productions with outdoor locations.

Potential problems
- The weather!
- Challenging for all design options.
- Considerable health and safety risks.

Understanding Design in Drama and Theatre

PRACTICAL GUIDE TO SET DESIGN

Chapter 1

Introduction to set design — 16

Two styles of set design — 18

Research for set design — 19

How to document your set design — 20

Understanding your resources — 25

Sourcing materials for the set — 26

Health and safety notes for set designers — 27

Creating your design for the stage — 28

Technical and dress rehearsals for set designers — 29

Evaluating your set design — 30

Set design vocabulary — 32

FOCUS
Some tasks to get you thinking like a set designer.

ASSESSMENT CHECK
In beginning your journey as a set designer, you will start to 'use design skills to contribute to and support performances' and gain 'knowledge and understanding of how drama and theatre is developed and performed' (AO3).

DESIGN TIP
Pay attention to your **pre-set**. This can include light and sound too and is seen or heard before the performance begins. It establishes setting and style and lets the audience think, 'I know where we are.'

INTRODUCTION TO SET DESIGN

What is a set designer?
In a sense, you are already a set designer. You probably have opportunities to influence the layout and colour scheme in your bedroom, for example.

Your choices are influenced by practicality, style, comfort and image. An observer might also learn something about you based on the books or games on your shelf or the posters on your wall.

A set designer is very different from an interior designer, however: they think about space from the audience's point of view, not the occupant's. This means that they help to communicate meaning, artistic intentions, style and atmosphere through the **scenery** they design and the stage furniture they select for the stage.

What can you tell about the person who occupies this room? What clues give you those ideas?

How can I design sets as part of this course?
You can opt for set design in either or both of the practical sections of the course. If you choose to work as set designer in Component 1, you will work in a small group to devise a piece of theatre. You will help to develop the piece as a whole, but your specific responsibility will be to design the set.

Component 2 is similar, but you work with a script instead of devising your own drama. As there are two extracts from the same play, you could design a set for one and perform or choose a different design role for the second.

Component 3 is the written exam. When you **evaluate** a performance you have seen, you might have to write about set design. Practical work will give you the knowledge and understanding to write confidently about set in the exam.

How can set design communicate meaning?
We all 'read' peoples, places and situations, but do not always realise it.

TASK 1.1
Study this set for *Blithe Sprit*, then answer the questions, giving specific examples from the set.

1. What room is shown?
2. The play is set in the 1930s. Are there any clues to this? (Look at styles and shapes of **furnishings**, scenery and fabrics.)
3. What seems to be the economic background of the people who live in this house? (Do they seem wealthy? How does the set suggest this?)
4. What **colour palette** is used?
5. What mood or atmosphere is suggested? (Consider, for example, whether colours are light or dark and whether there is clutter or space. Does the set suggest a calm life or hectic one?)

Chapter 1 Practical Guide to Set Design

Creating a location (place)

Location is a key starting point for most set designs. A set designer must be able to design both **interior** and **exterior** locations. The following tasks will help you to explore these in more detail.

Interior spaces

TASK 1.2

1. Look around the room you are in and notice its shape and features.
2. Now imagine it as a theatre set.
3. In a group, discuss what elements you should keep in order to maintain the room's meaning as, for example, a classroom or drama studio.
4. Then share ideas on how you could re-create the space for staging a drama **in the round**. Think about your audience, furniture, scenery, lighting fixtures and flooring.

Exterior settings

TASK 1.3

This scene from *The Woman in Black* uses back projection to place the character outside a mansion.

1. Imagine that you have been asked to create a set design for the same location, but without the use of projection. This means that you would have to place **constructions**, stage furniture and/or **props** on the stage. You could also consider a painted backdrop. You have a small budget of £100–200.

   Use a chart like this to note down items that you could include.

Location set design: Mansion exterior		
Scenery (flats, backdrops, etc.)	**Furniture**	**Props**
		Plant pots.

2. Next, imagine that a set designer has a budget of several £1000s and is designing the same exterior location, for an **end-on** stage configuration. The designer has provided this sketch →

   Work with a partner to give oral feedback to the designer.
   - What do you like about the set design? Why?
   - How could it be improved?

3. Now **you** are the set designer in a school production of the same scene from *A Woman in Black*. It is an end-on stage configuration. Draw and label your own design.

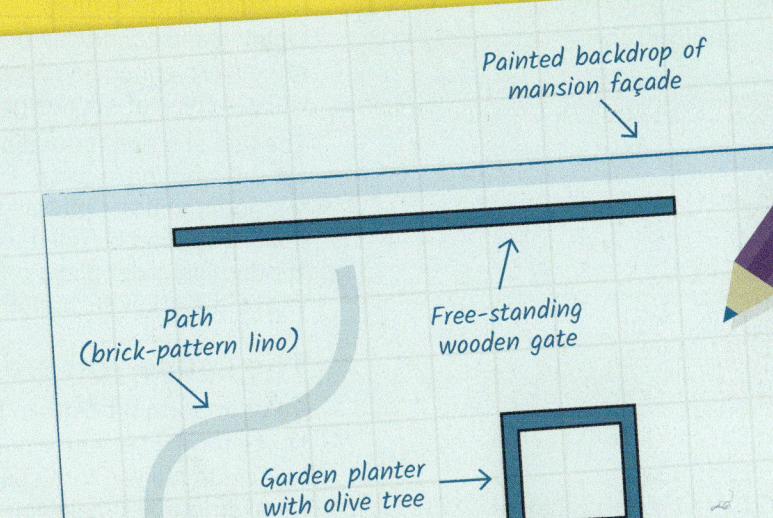

Painted backdrop of mansion façade

Path (brick-pattern lino)

Free-standing wooden gate

Garden planter with olive tree

Chapter 1 Practical Guide to Set Design

FOCUS
Naturalistic and non-naturalistic set designs.

ASSESSMENT CHECK
Analysing choices of set design will help you to 'explore how meaning is communicated through genre, form and style' and 'recognise and understand how theatrical choices are used by theatre makers to create impact.'

TASK 1.4
Study the set, right, for *Crocodile Fever*. Write down three details of the design that make it look like a real kitchen. Remember that set design usually includes large props, furniture, **set dressings**, furnishings and accessories, as well as the 'frame' and 'backdrop' of the space.

TASK 1.5
Write down three thoughts or questions that spring to mind when studying the set on the right. These could be linked to the set itself, the performance or the characters within it.

TWO STYLES OF SET DESIGN

Although there are many ways of categorising types of set design, it is helpful to start with these two basic ideas of **realistic**, **naturalistic** sets and **non-naturalistic** sets. They are clear and recognisable styles, and the choice between the two is one of the first decisions a set designer makes.

Naturalistic sets

A naturalist set could also be described as 'realistic'. It aims for immediately recognisable locations and to make the set appear as natural as possible. The audience does not need to use their imagination to understand the setting, as the **illusion** is complete.

A highly detailed set for *Crocodile Fever* at the Traverse Theatre in Edinburgh.

Non-naturalistic sets

A **representative** or non-naturalistic set might include key items that 'shout' the location within an otherwise **stylised** setting. The set on the right, for example, creates the illusion of a bedroom, but leaves scope for the audience to **interpret** the setting. Lighting and sound can be effective in enhancing meaning with this type of set design.

The use of a non-naturalistic set does not have to be restricted to non-naturalistic texts. They can be used to 'modernise' older plays or 'move' the original location.

The minimalist pre-set for a student production on a thrust stage at the University of Michigan.

The space you are designing for

Other important points in the early stages of set design are the size of the space for the set and what the stage configuration will be. Your teacher will be able to tell you if the performance will be in the drama studio or the hall, for example, and help you with the layout of the acting area and where the audience will sit.

Pay attention to safety issues in your design. It could be very difficult to remove hazards once the set has been constructed.

RESEARCH FOR SET DESIGN

Don't start online! Your first instinct might be to browse the internet, but there is no better place for inspiration and information than the real world.

Ask...

If your set text or devised piece is set in the 20th century, try talking to your family and their friends. You can't beat first-hand experience, and they might have photos.

Visit...

Museums and galleries often have exhibitions linked to particular periods in history. You might get ideas for furnishings and props as well as the set. A visit to a heritage site can be highly inspirational. These places include back-to-back terraces, art deco houses and so on. Take notes and photos, if permitted.

Watch...

There have been some entertaining television documentaries on social history. *Turn Back Time*, for example, placed different families in various historical eras. *A House Through Time* put a modern family in a house that changed to show life from the 19th century to the present day.

Track down some films that are made or set in the period for your drama. Focus on the settings as you watch.

Online research

Use specific key words in your internet searches. Furniture is a good place to start, and 'Ikea 1970s', for example, should bring up some very useful images. A heritage website will also provide inspiration and information.

Just a couple of props and furnishings or pieces of stage furniture will give your set an authentic feel and help to communicate meaning. It is important to reflect the social and economic contexts of your drama.

TASK 1.6

1. Search for '1930s house interior' and choose an image that interests you. (If you want to, narrow down your search by specifying 'working class' or 'art deco', for example.)
2. From it, pick an item or two that you might be able to use in a set.
3. What colours and patterns from the image might also be suitable for your set?

FOCUS

How to start generating ideas for you set designs.

ASSESSMENT CHECK

This research will help you towards AO1: 'Create and develop ideas to communicate meaning for theatrical performance.'

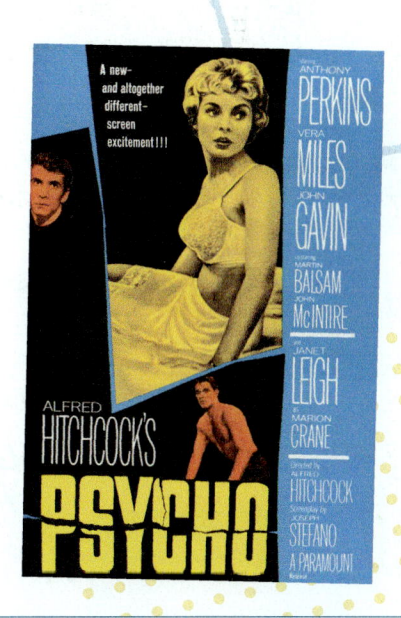

If your design allows it, a print or painting that strongly identifies the period or social context is well worth hanging on a wall. This 1960s film poster adds atmosphere as well as a sense of the period.

Chapter 1 Practical Guide to Set Design

FOCUS
- Clearly presenting your set design as a ground plan.
- Using 3D models to visualise the design.

ASSESSMENT CHECK
These notes will help you to produce the required drawings of the final design and ground plans of the performance space. These will help you towards AO1 and AO2.

HOW TO DOCUMENT YOUR SET DESIGN

Set designers need to produce their designs very early in the process as lighting, in particular, cannot be designed without knowledge of the set. The director and performers also need to lay out the rehearsal area in a way that represents the set.

What documents do I need to produce?

All types of theatre designer must be able to show their design ideas long before their costumes, set, lighting and sound are actually created. Sketches, ground plans and models are useful ways of doing this.

Clear drawings and ground plans are required in your documents for Components 1 and 2. These do not need to be drawn to **scale**, but showing scale on the ground plan, in particular, is very useful. When your set is constructed, the builders will use the ground plan to check measurements.

Set designs are created for a specific space. Produce plans that reflect the size of this space as well as the appropriate stage configuration.

Drawings of the final design

This example draft sketch shows a design idea for Oscar Wilde's Victorian social comedy *The Importance of Being Earnest*. It includes enough detail to base a ground plan on.

- Two portraits are hung at either side of the doors.
- Three **flats** are joined to make a **run** at the back of an end-on stage configuration.
- The centre section is hinged to form outward-opening **French windows**.
- Two more flats are free-standing centre left and centre right.
- Two chairs and a small table stand on the rug.
- A large Victorian-style rug centre stage.

Chapter 1 Practical Guide to Set Design

Find out the exact size of the area you are designing for. Then you can work out a realistic size for the scenery you are placing in it.

Let's say that your stage area for an end-on configuration is: 5 metres wide by 4 metres deep.

- You have allowed 1 metre behind the run of flats at the back so that the doors can open outwards. This means the acting area will be 5 metres wide and 3 metres deep.
- The two outer flats at the back are going to be 1.5 metres wide. The centre one will be 2 metres wide to include the opening doors.
- You are going to make your **free-standing flats** 1 metre wide (2 metres high works well).
- The rug is 2 metres square, laid at an angle.
- A net/voile curtain does not appear on the sketch, but will be added to the ground plan.

Ground plans

A ground plan is a bird's eye view. If you are looking straight down you would see width and depth, but not height. It should represent the performance space, 'including entrances and exits, audience positioning and stage furniture (as appropriate)'.

The information and sketch on the previous page can be transformed into a ground plan at 1:20 scale, below.

Use an ordinary metal rule to create a 1:20 scale: 5cm on the plan represents 100cm (1 metre) on the stage. Simple annotations and a key help to make details clear.

DESIGN TIP
Keep a tape measure handy!

LOOK HERE
See page 215 for advice on including levels in your design.

DESIGN TIP
Some theatre designers use a scale of 1:25. Choose a scale that is most suitable to you.

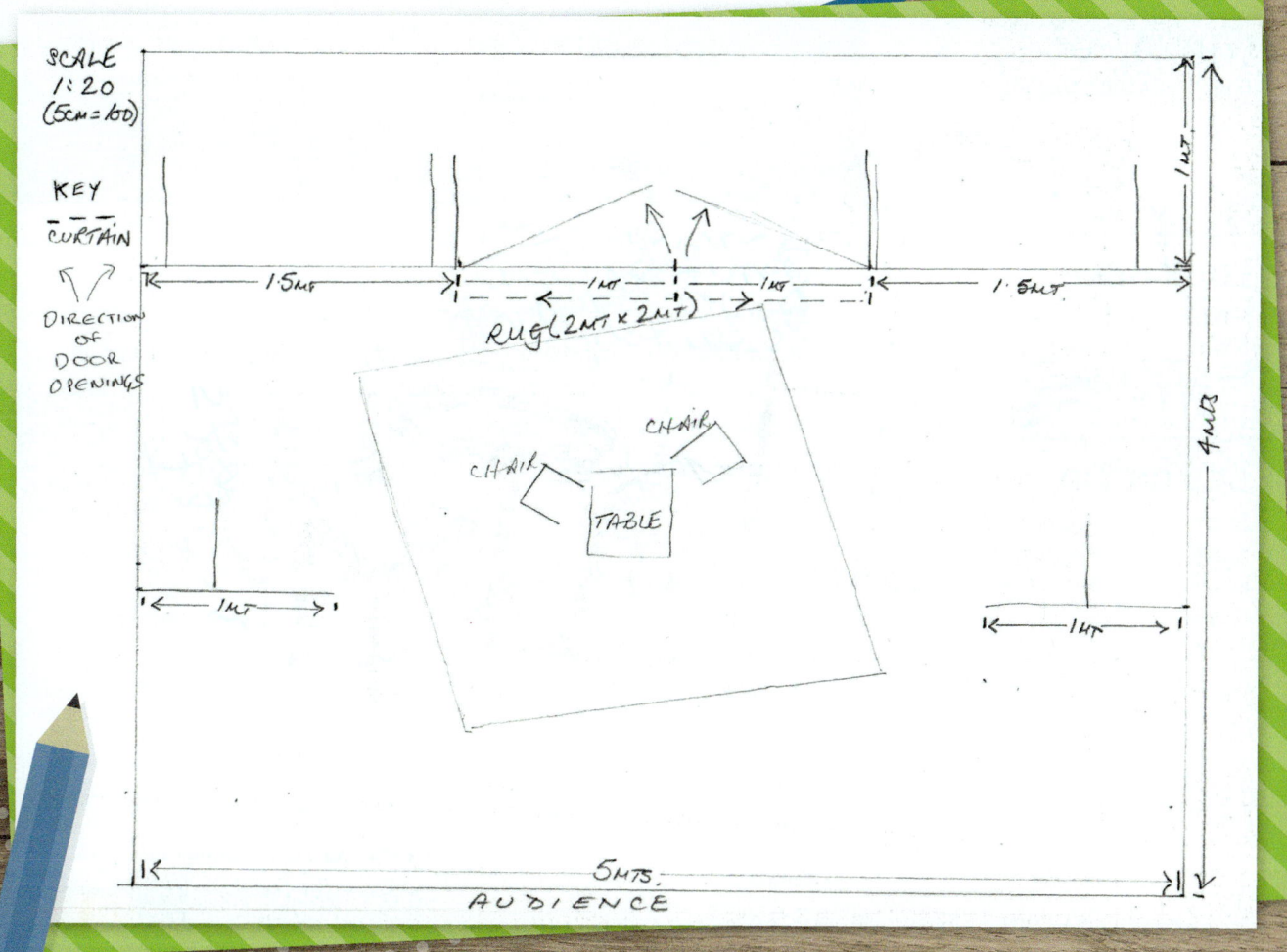

> ## TASK 1.7
>
> **Drawing a ground plan**
>
> 1. Sketch a **simple** set design for the play you are working on.
> 2. Measure the performance area in whole or half metres. (Anything else will be complicated to use on a ground plan.)
> 3. List the dimensions (measurements) of the stage area and the width and depth of all items of scenery to be included.
> 4. Go on to draw a 1:20-scale ground plan of your design.
> 5. Add annotations, such as 'rug', main measurements and a key that explains any symbols you use. Note the scale here too.
> 6. Share your sketch and ground plan with a group member. If they can't understand them, note where the difficulties are, and try again!

3D models

A model of the set for *Kindertransport* at Coventry Belgrade Theatre by Juliet Shillingford.

You are not required to make models, but they are an excellent form in which to show your set designs. Models are widely used because:

- they allow the director and performers to visualise the set clearly
- free-standing parts of the model can be moved around during design meetings, aiding discussion and decision making
- they give valuable information to the set builders.

If you choose to make a 3D model of your set, you might need:

- ○ Paper, pencils, paints and small brushes
- ○ Collage items (magazines and so on)
- ○ Foam board
- ○ Plasticine
- ○ Lolly sticks
- ○ Cardboard
- ○ Plywood offcuts
- ○ Scraps of light weight fabrics
- ○ Glue sticks
- ○ Electrical tape
- ○ Sculpting tools
- ○ Dressmakers' pins
- ○ Cotton reels (about the right scale for tables)

LOOK HERE

Follow the checklist in 'Health and safety notes for set designers', page 27.

DESIGN TIP

Start gathering useful modelling materials as soon as you begin the design process.

White card models

These 3D models are relatively quick and easy to make because they are not detailed. You simply use cardboard. They allow you to experiment with, for example, positioning flats. Moving elements of the model around enables you to see what effects are created in terms of entrances and exits, for instance.

The photographs below show **white-card** elements of a set design for *Hansel and Gretel*. The maker has experimented with positioning the **book flats** in different positions.

DESIGN TIP

Include an 'actor' that can be moved around the 'set'. This is very helpful in understanding the space for various scenes. (At 1:20 scale, you could make your figure 7cm tall.)

These book flats have been made from 10cm-square sheets of card, scored and folded to be free-standing. They are at 1:20 scale. The textures are experiments with origami paper, fabric and string for a non-naturalistic forest effect.

Chapter 1 Practical Guide to Set Design 23

Model boxes

Model boxes are generally made when a designer is fairly certain of their set design. They can be seen as more complete versions of white card models. They can be as simple or as highly detailed as you wish. Some model boxes even include lights!

Detailed models for a set design workshop.

A fairly quickly made model box, developed from the ground plan on page 21.

TASK 1.8

Making a 3D model

1. Choose a design from which to create a model box or white card model. You could use the ground plan from Task 1.7.
2. Gather the materials to work with.
3. Make your model at a scale of 1:20.
4. Take feedback on your model and make the necessary changes if you can.

Chapter 1   Practical Guide to Set Design

UNDERSTANDING YOUR RESOURCES

Materials, tools and equipment

At an early stage of the design process, you should make yourself aware of the materials available for creating the set.

> ### TASK 1.9
>
> Select from the following list the items you would like to use for your set. Then highlight which are available in your school or college.
>
> This will give you a good starting point, but if you think you need further items, add them to the list and begin to think where you could source them.

Building MATERIALS and TOOLS

- Cardboard sheets and boxes
- Large pieces of sturdy cloth such as canvas
- Plywood sheets
- Timber strips
- Staple gun
- Glue gun
- Heavy-duty gaffer tape
- Metal brackets and hinges
- Cable ties
- Drill
- Screwdriver
- Flooring offcuts
- Water-based paint, brushes
- Marker pens
- PVA glue

Human resources

The exam board states that you need to 'be involved in the execution of the design', but 'the ability to manufacture the set is not a specification requirement'. This means that you can get help with the construction of your set.

The most likely source of support is your technology department, especially if topics such as construction and working with resistant materials are on the curriculum. Remember that you need to be closely involved in what is made and how it is constructed. Perhaps a technology teacher or student could construct the set or scenery item while you assist, for you to paint afterwards. Discuss this with your Drama teacher.

You might not even need to build a set. You can hire or borrow items, but you need to be involved with the process, and the **design** of the set must be yours.

> ### TASK 1.10
>
> Arrange to visit the construction rooms of the technology department. Discuss with a teacher:
> - How might they set about constructing a scenery item such as a flat?
> - What materials would they suggest using for your design?
> - What tools and equipment would you need?

FOCUS
Practical aspects you need to know about before you create your design.

ASSESSMENT CHECK
Being aware of the possibilities and limits to your design means that you can:
- 'make appropriate judgements during the development process'
- 'create a clear and practical design with consideration of practical application of materials and production elements.'

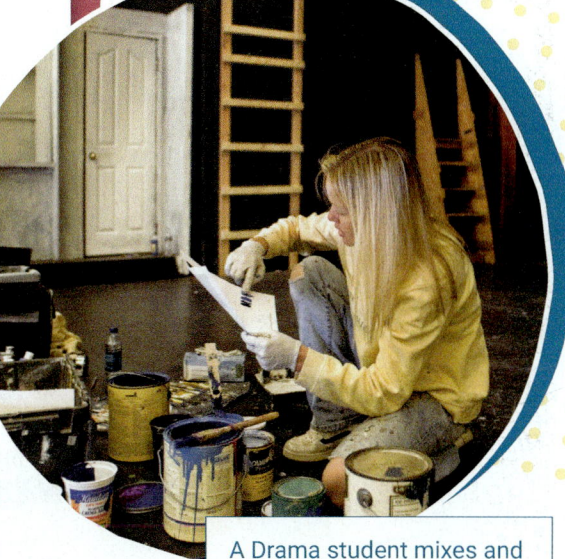

A Drama student mixes and choose paint for her set.

DESIGN TIP
Ask around! There might be a family friend who has a workshop, for example, and a trailer to transport the set to school.

Chapter 1   Practical Guide to Set Design

FOCUS

How to find, recycle or buy the materials for your set and meet your artistic intentions.

ASSESSMENT CHECK

By making considered choices, you are demonstrating skills in: 'making appropriate judgements during the development process.' This stage of design works towards AO1: 'Create and develop ideas to communicate meaning for theatrical performance.'

DESIGN TIP

Be resilient. Tackle problems step by step. If an item is difficult to get, think:

- Can you make a saving elsewhere?
- Could you use a similar but cheaper version?
- Do you really need it?

SOURCING MATERIALS FOR THE SET

Once your set design has been agreed with your group, it is time to think about the actual set.

What do I need and what will it cost?

Keep in mind while designing that you will only have a small amount to spend on your set. Don't buy anything until you know:

- what your budget is
- everything you will need to design and make your set
- where you might get it
- how much it will all cost.

TASK 1.11

Copy and complete a chart like this to keep track of what you need.

Item	Source	Approximate cost
Large pot plant	Borrow from family or friends	None
Backcloth	Pre-painted: hire for 5 days	£100? Too much?
	Make own: canvas and paint	£60? Too much?
	Make own: 2 tarpaulins and paint	£40?
	Make own: sewn-together sheets, rough wooden frame, paint	£30?
	Make own: cardboard boxes taped together	£10? Will they look poor?
	Watered-down PVA as fire retardant	£2
Stage flat	Ply-board sheet from DIY shop	£20
	Rough-cut lengths from wood yard	£5
	Water-based paints and cheap acrylic	£10?
	Watered-down PVA as fire retardant	£2
3ft round table	Borrow	None
Round white tablecloth	Charity shop or make?	£3?

Recycling and borrowing

It is unlikely that you will be able to buy everything needed for your set. Is everything in your design essential? Can anything be changed to something you can borrow or recycle?

Recycling here simply means making an item into something else. For example, you could fix small wheels to a table so that it becomes a trolley. A large scarf can become a tablecloth. A green tarpaulin over a stepladder could be a mountain.

- Find out what is already available in school. Could you borrow a table? Is there an existing stage flat that you can paint over?
- Try pound shops for craft materials and acrylic paint.
- Go to builders' merchants for offcuts.
- Pallets (often free) are useful for timber or even basic furniture.

Health and safety notes for set designers

Taking care of yourselves

You are responsible for the set, so you need to be aware of safety issues around construction, such as the examples below. This applies even if you are supervising others building a set on your behalf.

- ⚠ Follow all instructions and guidance given.
- ⚠ Make sure electrical equipment has an up-to-date PAT (Portable Appliance Testing) certificate.
- ⚠ Check cables and machinery for damage. Make them secure.
- ⚠ Wear safety goggles and gloves whenever necessary.
- ⚠ Some paints and varnishes need to be applied in an airy space. Open windows and wear masks.
- ⚠ Glue and staple guns are popular with set designers: they are quick and effective. Handle all such tools and materials with care and respect.
- ⚠ Use the correct tool for the job.
- ⚠ Store tools and materials neatly and out of the way.
- ⚠ Be aware of what other people are doing around you.

Taking care of performers

On stage, actors need to concentrate on staying in role and immersing themselves in the world of the drama. Your set needs to enhance this world. It must also ensure the performers' safety.

Risks to avoid include:
- ⚠ Trip hazards (rugs, for instance, should be secured with double-sided tape)
- ⚠ Unstable pieces of scenery (brace items with stage weights)
- ⚠ Glass in windows or doors (use Perspex or leave them empty)
- ⚠ Slippery floor finishes (avoid gloss)
- ⚠ Unsuitable access or space for performers with impaired mobility
- ⚠ Large or uneven steps and levels
- ⚠ Unmarked edges of steps (try a textured surface if tape will be seen by the audience).

Making your set fire-safe

Fire regulations for public performances are very strict. (If your show is just for staff and students in school, it is not considered a public performance.) If a prop is always held in a performer's hand, it does not need to be flame proofed. However, any scenery or large prop that is free-standing **must** be made of fire-retardant material or treated to be flame proof. You could:

- ⚠ Buy fire-retardant timber and cloth (effective, but expensive)
- ⚠ Use fire-retardant spray for the fabric parts of your set
- ⚠ Cover painted wood surfaces with water-based matt varnish or watered-down PVA glue (about 5 parts water to 1 part PVA).

FOCUS
Keeping yourself and others safe.

ASSESSMENT CHECK
For both Components 1 and 2, 'Designs should take into consideration performer/audience relationships and any health and safety implications and performer usage.'

FIRE RETARDANT

Chapter 1 · Practical Guide to Set Design

FOCUS

Placing a value judgement on drama is key to Components 1 and 3. These pages will help you to develop the habit of reflecting on your work.

ASSESSMENT CHECK

Essential for AO4 is the ability to: 'Analyse and evaluate your own work and the work of others' in the written exam as well as in your practical work.

LOOK HERE

'Set Design for the Devised Piece' from page 129, has more guidance on the devising process and evaluating as you go through it. See Chapter 7 for more examples of evaluation.

Lord of the Flies by A Theatre Near U.

EVALUATING YOUR SET DESIGN

What is evaluation?

Evaluation is a skill that you will use in many of your GCSE subjects. It is the process of judging something's quality, importance or value. In other words, you give your considered opinion on how 'good' or successful something is when you evaluate it. Evaluation is a valued skill because it requires reflection and reasoning.

When do I evaluate?

You will be reflecting on and assessing the success of your set throughout any designing process.

In Component 1, the most crucial analysis comes after the production, when you evaluate the effectiveness of your contribution to the final performance. A strong ability to evaluate will contribute significant marks to the portfolio, which is a key part of the devising component.

Evaluation is also an essential skill in Component 3, when you **analyse** and form **critical judgements** on the work of other theatre makers.

How do I evaluate successfully?

Evaluation becomes convincing when you build an argument to support your opinions. The way to do this involves giving clear examples. You should aim to use a range of vocabulary for the different evaluations you make because if you always say something is 'effective' it starts to lose its impact.

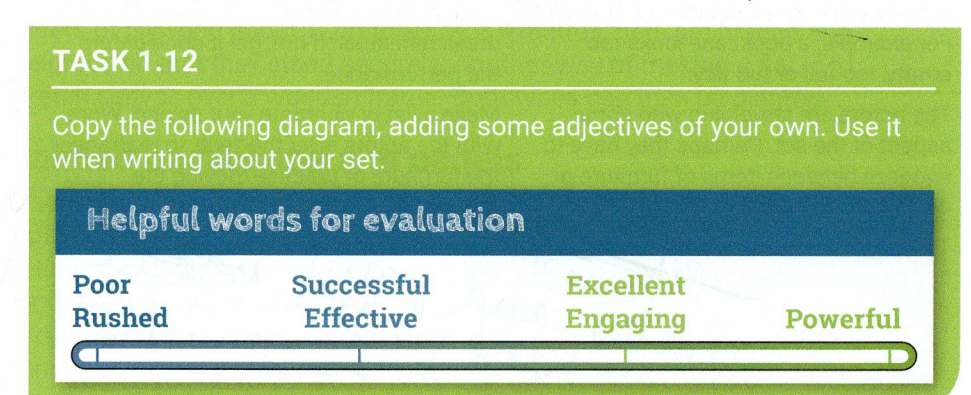

TASK 1.12

Copy the following diagram, adding some adjectives of your own. Use it when writing about your set.

Helpful words for evaluation			
Poor	Successful	Excellent	
Rushed	Effective	Engaging	Powerful

You will be expected to choose a few details from your set and give reasons why you think they were effective in performance. This student has begun to do this as well as using some evaluative words like the ones above:

> I believe that one **powerful element** of my set design was how it **allowed the performers** to use different **levels**. The **moment** when Jack looks down from a height onto Piggy lying on the floor is **a good example of this**. The set **helped to emphasise** the amount of control and power Jack has over Piggy. Also, the set **combined with lighting** in an **engaging** way for the audience...

Chapter 1 Practical Guide to Set Design

Examining the details of your set design

In your evaluation, you will need to make at least three different points with examples that help to illustrate why you have made a particular value judgement.

TASK 1.13

The geometric shapes used consistently throughout this set design are simple to achieve but give flexibility and create a striking effect. (*Brokers* by Tylar Pendgraft performed by the USC School of Dramatic Arts.)

1. Copy and complete your own version of this table (examples are given based on the set design above). These notes will form a solid basis for your evaluative writing.

Set design evaluation			
Design element	**Example / moment in the play**	**Evaluation**	**Reason for evaluation**
Suspended frames	Pre-set and throughout the play.	Engaging. Encouraged audience to ask questions and become involved.	Encouraged the audience to think about uncertainty and things falling. Linked to the theme of the play.
Movable cubes	Scene changes.	Effective in setting scenes quickly and simply.	The fact that the boxes could be easily moved by the actors made it easy and quick to create different locations.
Use of the colour white	The moment when the character became depressed.	Powerful in creating atmosphere and helping characterisation.	The use of white in the set combined with the blue lighting created an atmosphere of emptiness and despair.

2. Once you have made your evaluation into a table like this, turn it into three paragraphs. Remember that you are evaluating. This means that you add a value judgement to an opinion and support it with examples.

Chapter 1   Practical Guide to Set Design   31

SET DESIGN VOCABULARY

Analyse Examine in detail, thinking about parts in relation to the whole.

Backcloth A large piece of canvas or cloth which is often painted with a setting.

Colour palette A complementary set of colours that belong to a group, such as pastel or dark.

Construction Something that has been built (a set for example); the act of building.

Critical judgement Analysing the merits and faults of something to decide its worth or success.

End on A stage configuration that places the audience on one side of an open stage.

Evaluate Give an opinion, a value judgement, backed up with examples and reasons.

Exterior (setting/location) An outdoor space, such as a garden, street or outside a building.

Flat A tall, main piece of scenery that, as its name suggests, generally carries a 2D image.

- **Book flat** Two flats that are hinged along their 'spine'.
- **Free-standing flat** A braced, single flat that can stand anywhere on the set.
- **Run of flats** Two or more flats joined as a length to achieve a wall, for example.

French doors/windows A pair of outward-opening doors often fully glazed, functioning as both windows and doors.

Furnishings Set furniture (sometimes including curtains, rugs and so on).

Illusion Something that is not as it seems; something that is not real, but often gives an impression of reality.

In the round A stage configuration in which the audience encircles the acting area.

Interior (setting/location) An indoor space, such as a kitchen or a school hall.

Interpret Express your own ideas about intended meaning; your choice where there are a number of correct possibilities.

Location The place or setting where action takes place, such as a forest, a bedroom or a park.

Model box A 3D set design, often presented within a box of some sort.

Naturalistic A set, for example, with characteristics of reality; having the appearance of a real place.

Non-naturalistic A set design, for example, that aims not to look like a real place.

Pre-set Features of the drama onstage that are already in place before the audience enters.

Props Short for 'properties' (suggesting ownership): objects that would be owned by a character such as a torch, phone, set of keys.

Realistic A set, for example, that sets out to be like real life (naturalistic).

Representative Something that represents (stands for) something else: for example, a non-naturalistic set that 'represents' and suggests rather than copies real life.

Run Either a rehearsal or read-through of the whole play or the number of times a play will be performed, eg *The Crucible* has a three-week run at this theatre.

Scale The size of something relative to something else.

Scenery Parts of the set that represent locations or surroundings – on cloth or flats.

Set dressings Accessories such as tablecloths, cushions and other decorative items.

Stylised Non-realistic, non-naturalistic, where style features are dominant.

Tarpaulin Large, heavy-duty, waterproof cloth/sheet, usually of woven plastic.

White-card model A simple 3D representation of a set design.

PRACTICAL GUIDE TO LIGHTING DESIGN

Chapter 2

Introduction to lighting design	34
Types of stage lantern	36
Understanding your lighting resources	38
Angles, colour and intensity	40
Special effects in lighting	44
Lighting transitions	46
Research for lighting	47
How to document your lighting design	48
Health and safety in lighting design	51
Plotting the lighting design	52
Rigging and focusing	54
Operating the lighting	56
Technical and dress rehearsals for lighting designers	57
Evaluating your lighting design	59
Lighting design vocabulary	60

FOCUS

- The purpose and power of stage lighting.
- The technical and creative skills in lighting design.

ASSESSMENT CHECK

This section will help you to understand how you can:

- 'use visual elements to create mood, atmosphere and style'
- 'communicate intention and create impact for an audience.'

You are also gaining knowledge and understanding of production and design elements of drama.

INTRODUCTION TO LIGHTING DESIGN

The purpose of stage lighting

At the moment when the house lights go down in the theatre, the lighting designer introduces the audience to the world of the performance. It is as though the audience holds its collective breath ready to enter that world. The first lights that illuminate the stage can create a magical moment. If the lighting design is not right, however, the cast might struggle to grab and keep the audience's attention, and other design elements might not combine well.

Stage lighting can be described as having four main functions:

VISIBILITY
Audience members need to be able to see the actors and the set.

FOCUS
Lighting draws attention to specific areas of the stage.

MOOD
The uses of colour and **intensity** (brightness) have a powerful **atmospheric** affect. These choices can also link to a play's themes and meanings.

LOCATION/SETTING
Similarly, colour choices, intensity and effects (such as a wash or a spotlight) can create a sense of time and place for the audience.

This lighting design is by Nic Farman (with a set by Lily Arnold) for Hornchurch Queens Theatre. It is suitably mysterious and sinister, arousing the audience's curiosity and setting an atmospheric scene for *The Invisible Man*.

TASK 2.1

In a darkened room, experiment with the effects of torchlight. Choose an object in the room and investigate:

- how visible you can make it using a different number of beams
- what size and shape of shadow you can produce
- the different effects produced by front, back and side lighting
- how you can change the atmosphere by using fewer or more torches
- how the **intensity** changes when you move closer or further away.

The power of lighting

A significant difference between lighting a room in your house and lighting the stage is that you should have a blank 'canvas'. Another is that you have considerably more choice of varied and exciting effects. The thinking that determines where you put your desk light and which lightshade you choose is intensified in the role of stage lighting designer as you can use different heights, colours, shapes, shadows and **fades**. You could move suddenly or gradually from one **lighting state** to another and build or reduce intensity of light as the scene demands.

Chapter 2 Practical Guide to Lighting Design

The importance of lighting design

You will find that, as lighting designer, you have a unique power to influence the focus and mood of the audience. You can 'create' sunlight or moonlight, fires and lightning. You can be really creative and your work is an extremely important contribution to a harmonious world for the audience.

Lighting styles

Different genres, styles and forms of performance call for different types of lighting. Bertolt Brecht, for example, often **flooded** the stage with harsh white light. He wanted the audience to be constantly aware that they were watching a play rather than real life. For the same reason, he would keep **lanterns** in full view and sometimes leave the house lights on too.

On the other hand, Konstantin Stanislavski developed a style of theatre that sought realism in every aspect. He used lighting to focus the audience on, for example, an item of set. In today's theatre, **backlighting**, and projections of, for example, clouds would add atmosphere and realism.

DESIGN TIP
The best designers and operators are so skilful that the audience is not consciously aware of the stage lights at all. Unless the designers specifically want them to be...!

TASK 2.2

Watch some different styles and genres of film and/or television. (Here are a couple of example scenes where lighting makes a powerful impact.) Pay particular attention to the lighting effects.

Use the following chart to record what you notice about the effects created.
Include, for example, the use of colours and intensity and the mood of the scene.

Title	Genre	Special effects	Time of day / season of the year / weather	How atmosphere is produced and impact it has
Chicago	Musical comedy/ drama	Overhead **spotlight** picks out the character and creates a halo effect on her blonde hair. She is the star!	Stage conditions – general coverage of blue light on the stage creates a cool effect; the character stands out.	Blue lights in the background with possible use of fog machine help the main character to 'shine'.
Star Wars: The Empire Strikes Back				

How can I design lighting as part of this course?

You can opt for lighting design in either or both of the practical sections of the course. If you choose to work as lighting designer in Component 1, you will work in a small group and help to develop the piece, but your specific responsibility will be to create a lighting design for the performance.

Component 2 is similar, but you will work with a script. As there are two extracts from the same play, you could design lighting for one extract and then perform or choose a different design element for the second.

Component 3 is the written exam. Working practically with lighting will give you the knowledge and understanding to write confidently about lighting in your set text or a performance you have seen.

TYPES OF STAGE LANTERN

Your school or college might have these types of lighting fixture. Each has its own particular purpose.

FOCUS
The different types of lantern and their variety of uses.

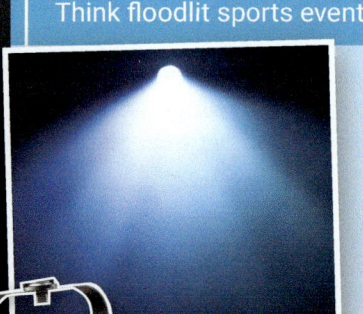

ASSESSMENT CHECK
Learning some of the technicalities of stage lanterns will work towards AO3. You will also be able to use technical vocabulary and show 'understanding of practical application of production elements'.

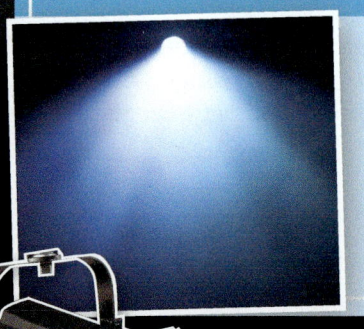

NOTE
Stage lights are called **lanterns** or **lighting fixtures** because **bulbs** are known as **lights** (or **lamps**).

FLOOD
These are basic lanterns, generally with an open or glass front, which produce a wide flood of light. Think floodlit sports events.

Useful for: Lighting large areas of the stage or back cloths: generating a 'flood' of light.

Limitation: The beams' size or shape cannot be controlled.

NB: Where you place and direct these lights is very important as the light will 'spill' everywhere it points.

FRESNEL
Pronounced 'freh-nell', these lanterns have a lens at the front with a 'stepped ring' finish to it.

Useful for: Lighting large or small areas of the stage.

Benefits: The steps on the lens make the light even, making it easy to blend the **focus** of one light to the next.

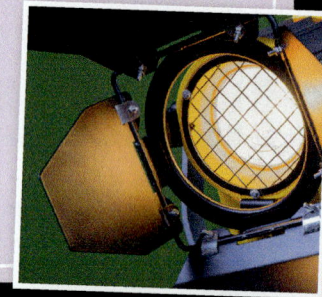

Several fresnels focused onto several areas can light the whole stage evenly (giving general cover).

By moving the lamp closer to or further away from the lens, you can control the size of the beam.

Barn doors (shutters that fit onto the front of the lantern) can control the spread of the beam.

BIRDIES
Birdies are very small lanterns (as small as 12cm). Tiny par cans are the most frequently used type of birdie.

Benefit: Surprisingly bright, they are ideal for hiding on stage or using on the stage edge as footlights.

PAR CANS
These beam lights (lens-less lanterns) get their name from the lamp inside. The lantern itself is simply a '**can**' in which the **par** lamp is contained. The PAR (Parabolic Aluminised Reflector) is a sealed beam unit consisting of a lamp, reflector and lens in one.

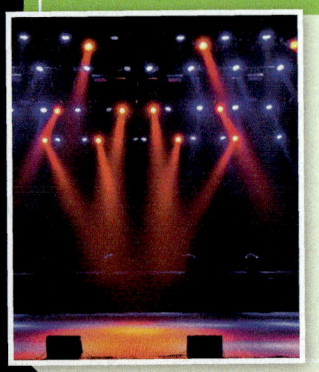

Useful for: Producing a very bright beam, something like a cross between a floodlight and a Fresnel.

Benefits: These lights are excellent for highlighting an area or using with colour filters or gels to produce the bright colourful beams often seen at pop and rock concerts.

Limitation: The only way to change the beam size is either to move the whole fixture, or to physically change the lamp to narrow, medium or wide.

PROFILE SPOT

These versatile lanterns are longer and thinner than floods and spotlights. They also have levers half way down, which are the shutters that control the size and shape of the beam.

Useful for: A soft- or hard-edged beam, produced by moving the lens (not the lamp as in fresnels) forwards or backwards. **Profile** lights with hard edges can create a typical 'spotlight' beam. Alternatively, several profiles focused with a soft edge can overlap for general cover. Profile spots are the type of lantern used to project images with **gobos**.

Benefits: The beam control is generally narrower and more controllable than a fresnel, so a profile spotlight can be further away, while still remaining bright, without 'spilling' light into unwanted areas. The built-in shutters of a profile spotlight mean that barn doors are not needed. They are used to shield areas of the stage that you don't want to light. They can also shape the beam to create a square of light or to focus a tight beam on a particular object or performer.

Follow spot

Follow spots are modified profiles mounted on a tripod and operated manually to track an individual as they move around the stage. You will have seen them used in events such as ice skating.

Gobo

A gobo is a very thin steel plate with a cut-out pattern that fixes over a lens. It is used to project a **silhouette** of images such as trees or windows. The images produced are mainly two-dimensional. The colour is dictated by the colour **filter** or **gel** put in front of the lens. They can produce stunning effects.

LED LANTERN

Many schools are now using theatre lanterns with an **LED** source. The most common is probably an LED par can, but there are now LED floods, profiles and fresnels.

Useful for: The light inside is most commonly made up of red, green and blue LEDs which can be selected or combined to create a variety of colours.

Benefits: LED lights use less power, generate less heat and save on the cost of replacing bulbs and buying colour filters or gels.

Limitations: They can be expensive, and controlling their **colour palette** requires computer software.

AUTOMATED MOVING LANTERNS

Often seen at concerts and large-scale events, moving lanterns are very versatile. They are generally manufactured as profile spots or fresnels.

Benefit: The focus, beam size, gobo and colour are controlled by the software on a **lighting desk** or **console**. The desks usually have libraries of different light fixtures, which enables relatively easy programming and operation, and adds versatility and complexity to a design.

Limitations: They are expensive and require a computerised lighting desk.

Chapter 2   Practical Guide to Lighting Design

FOCUS

Three key components of lighting design.

ASSESSMENT CHECK

This section will help you to 'recognise how theatrical choices are used by theatre makers to create impact' (in AO3).

For AO1 and AO2, you will develop skills in:

- 'using visual elements to create mood, atmosphere and style'
- 'communicating intention and creating impact for an audience'
- 'exploring how meaning is created through production elements.'

DESIGN TIP

Be aware that light bounces off surfaces – particularly light-coloured and shiny ones.

ANGLES, COLOUR AND INTENSITY

Light in the real world

Daylight

Theatre lighting frequently seeks to re-create natural lighting, so begin your design thinking in the real world.

During daylight hours our light source is the Sun. The time of day affects the angle at which the Sun's light hits the Earth. The season and the weather (amount of cloud cover) affect the intensity (brightness) of the sunlight.

TASK 2.7

1. Assuming you are in a room with at least one window, and it is daytime, turn off any artificial lights. Look around you for a minute and note the following:
   - How many sides of the room have portals (windows/doors)?
   - Where can you see bright light? Where does it come from?
   - Where are the shadows? What shape and length are they? Why?
   - How deep (dark) are the shadows?
   - Does the atmosphere vary in the room because of the light? How?
2. Draw a sketch of the room, representing areas of light and shade.

Night-time

When the Sun sets, the Moon and stars create significantly less natural light, so we use artificial light.

TASK 2.8

Thinking about inside and outside:
1. Write down three sources of artificial light.
2. Use them to write two or three sentences about how artificial light has different affects from natural light. An angle-poise lamp, for example, creates a small area of intense white light, whereas a candle creates a dim, flickering warm light.

Think about angle, colour, intensity and atmosphere when comparing natural and artificial light.

Chapter 2 Practical Guide to Lighting Design

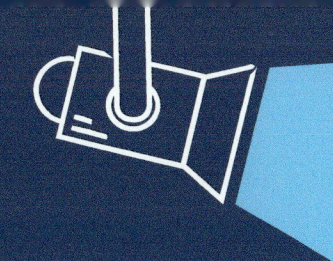

Naturalistic (real-world) lighting on stage

Light in the real world is usually the starting point for stage lighting. (You might explore non-naturalistic effects later.) As the lighting designer, you have a number of tools with which to control light on the stage:

* the number of stage lanterns
* the types of lantern (see pages 36–37)
* where lanterns are positioned (angle and distance)
* the shape of beam produced
* the intensity of the beam projected
* The colour of the beam.

Key lights

There is always a **key light** in the real world. It might be natural sunlight coming through a window, or moonlight, or the artificial light of a desk lamp, for example. A lighting designer will always be aware of the key light and will generally reproduce it on stage with a lantern or group that is more intense than the others. If the light is supposed to be coming from inside the room through artificial lighting, you could show the source of this light, such as a bedside lamp.

Angles

The angle of lighting to suggest sunlight, for example, is also very important. If it was early morning sunlight, would you want your 'sunlight' to come from a steep angle or a shallow one? (How high is the Sun in the early morning?) Side lights at different heights can create the same effect.

Natural light

The key to natural lighting is to re-create the quality that comes with different times of day and weather conditions. There are several shades of warm, straw-coloured gels available that suggest sunlight. You could use cooler blue colours for an overcast day, and paler blues for moonlight.

Lighting in *The Wider Earth* creates ripples, waves and sparkles as well as the naturalistic blue of under the sea.

TASK 2.9

Create a mini world and light it artificially to create the senses of sunlight and moonlight.
1. Use cardboard to create a small scene which includes a cut-out window.
2. Use torches (perhaps on a mini tripod) to experiment with lighting the scene.
3. Try coloured gels to create different times of day and night. You could also consider different weather conditions.

DESIGN TIP

Stage lanterns are very bright. It is crucial that they do not shine onto the audience and dazzle them.

Chapter 2 Practical Guide to Lighting Design

Front-lit, from straight ahead.

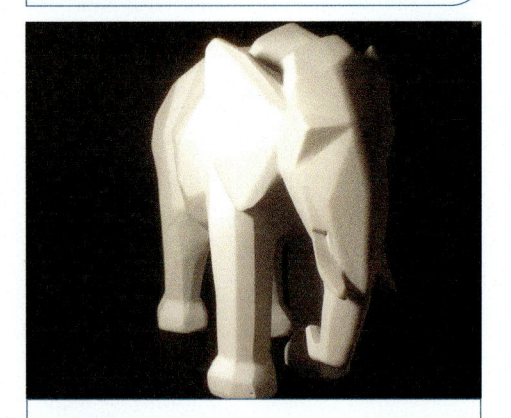

Lit by one light from the front at one side.

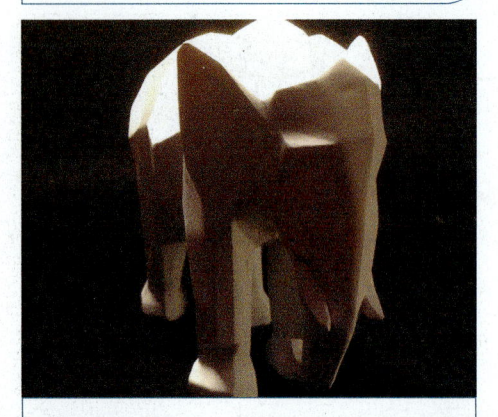

Back-lit.

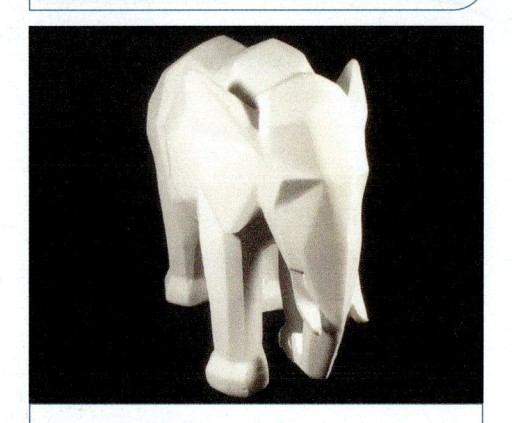

All three lights used equally.

Three-point lighting

Three-point lighting is widely accepted as an ideal starting point for naturalistic lighting. Light coming form only one angle would produce unwanted shadows. So, a second lantern is placed at a 45-degree angle to balance this. In addition, if you only light from the front, the effect is rather flat. To solve this, back light would give a naturalistic, 3D effect.

One of your three lights is the key light. This is likely to be a light that comes from the front, as is the **fill light**, which reduces shadow.

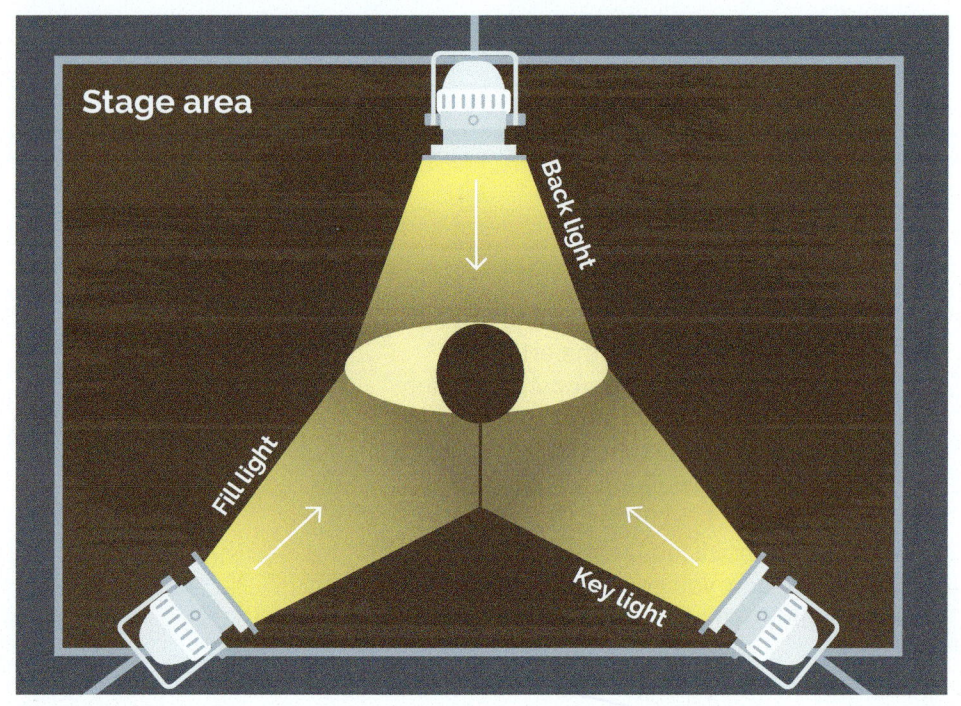

Stage area
Back light
Fill light
Key light

Colour

Colour is one of the most important keys to adding mood and atmosphere to stage lighting. You can see this above, in the explanation of how different colours are used to imitate sunlight and moonlight.

Technical points

White light is produced when a lantern does not have a coloured gel (filter) in front of the lens. In LED lights, white light is produced when all four colours are equally balanced. White light is the brightest light.

Introducing colour is a crucial part of any lighting design. With LED lanterns, you can programme each lighting cue to a specific colour by altering the balance between primary colours (red, green and blue). This versatility means each lantern can project a different colour for every cue if necessary.

Traditional (often older) lanterns use filters or gels to add colour to the beam. Unlike LEDs, each lantern can only be used to project one colour within a single performance. Gels are specially made sheets of thin, transparent, heat-resistant plastic. They are available in a wide range of colours, and can often be bought as a set. Sheets can be cut to fit gel holders that slide into or onto the front of the lantern.

Chapter 2 Practical Guide to Lighting Design

Creative notes

White light is very bright and quite harsh and hard. Simply changing the intensity of the beam is very limiting. To produce more natural or atmospheric effects, you need to add colour.

The following suggestions are starting points for naturalistic lighting.

- Straw gels give a natural sunlight effect.
- Yellows and oranges create a warm, happy atmosphere.
- Pale blue adds a moonlit quality.
- Blues generally create colder and sadder moods.
- Lavenders and lilacs are neutral colours and work well in balancing other colours for a subtle effect.

As a general rule, it is best to use paler colours out front and darker colours from the sides or back of the stage.

Intensity (brightness)

Along with colour, changing the intensity of light is a powerful creator of atmosphere.

The lighting desk gives you as designer control over how bright the beam is (think of household dimmer switches).

Individual lanterns can be made brighter or dimmer using the controls on the lighting desk or board. It is usual to start at 70 per cent and then move up or down to create the effect you want. Be aware that taking the brightness below 20 per cent is likely to give too dim a beam. Coloured filters will also affect the power of a lantern's beam, with darker colours creating a significantly dimmer light.

DESIGN TIP
Always remember to consider coloured lighting alongside set and costume to avoid disrupting the desired overall effect.

LOOK HERE
You will find more information about colour in 'Special effects in lighting' on the following pages.

TASK 2.10
Watch a short interior scene from a TV drama or film in which lighting is important. Concentrate on the effect of lighting in the scene and note the following.

- How intense does the light seem to be, in percentage terms?
- Do the light sources seem natural, artificial or a mixture?
- What angle is the dominant light coming from?
- What colour(s) does the lighting designer appear to be using?

A typically shadowy scene as Eleven takes a call in *Stranger Things*.

Chapter 2 Practical Guide to Lighting Design 43

FOCUS

Different lighting effects and how they might be created.

ASSESSMENT CHECK

Here, you will develop your ability to:
- 'apply design skills effectively within the context of a performance'
- 'communicate intention and create an impact for an audience.'

These will help you towards AO1: 'Create and develop ideas to communicate meaning for theatrical performance.'

DESIGN TIP

Modern LED lights are a good option for lighting designers. They are very useful for practical effects. You could, for example, adapt a bicycle headlight, adhesive cupboard lights or the flashing lights designed for pet collars!

SPECIAL EFFECTS IN LIGHTING

What are special effects?

All theatre lighting has a powerful effect. It can be difficult to separate special effects (or specials) from other lighting states and there are no strict rules. Generally speaking, special effects (FX or SFX) are those that have a very specific, short-term purpose in a theatre performance.

The Rocky Horror Picture Show at the Winnipesaukee Playhouse combines performer spotlights and LED lanterns with the naturalistic lighting (such as the chandeliers) from the room created by the set. (Lighting design by Matthew Guminski.)

In the scene above, for example, overhead spotlights create four distinct areas. They have the effect of isolating each performer. If this lighting effect was only used once or twice during a production, it would probably be 'special'. If it was used frequently, however, it would be the production's typical spot lighting state.

TASK 2.11

1. In the script or devised piece you are currently involved in, identify a moment that might be enhanced by a special effect. (This could be a **practical effect**, or one involving a spotlight that uses a particular angle, colour or gobo.)
2. What effect do you want the special effect to have on the audience? How could you create the effect?
3. If possible, test your ideas. How does the special effect influence meaning, mood, style or characterisation?
4. Take a photograph and make notes to remind yourself of what you have achieved.

Chapter 2 Practical Guide to Lighting Design

Practical special effects

These effects are closely linked to the performers, who generally operate or wear them. Examples include:

- a camp-fire flame made of a battery-operated red light, switched on by an actor
- an 'oil' lamp with a flickering LED candle in it, again operated by the actor
- a light on a costume or at the end of a fairy wand.

Using key lights with special effects lighting

In the illustration below, a key light is used alongside the practical special effect of a camp fire to complete the illusion. The key light illuminates the face of the performer because the practical effect is not bright enough. A key light like this could be positioned at the front of the stage or at a low level in the wings to shine up onto the actor's face.

In this production of *Harry Potter and the Cursed Child*, the actors have practical battery lights on their wands, which they can turn on and off themselves.

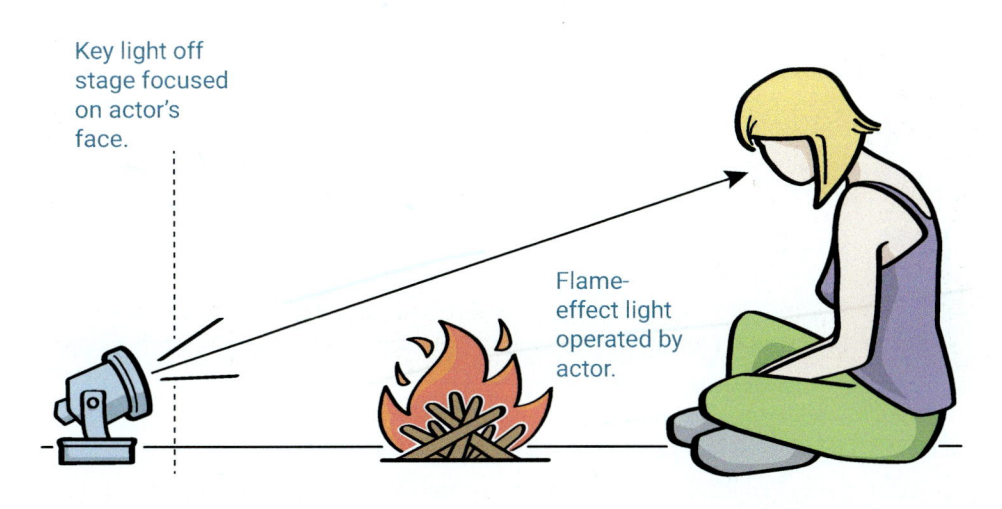

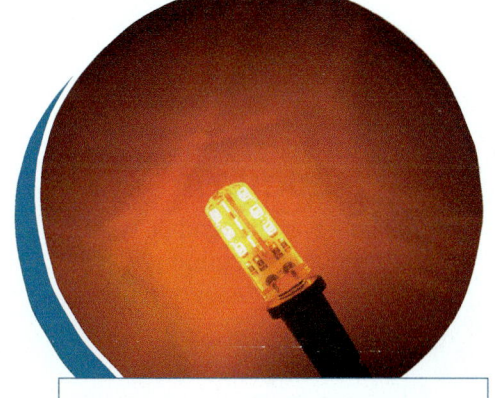

Key light off stage focused on actor's face.

Flame-effect light operated by actor.

This small fire-effect bulb can be used to simulate orange flames and embers with a flicker-effect control.

The opposite of key lighting is fill light, which is often softer. It could be another, less bright, light source, or it could come from general light reflected off surrounding walls, for example.

Naturalistic special effects

Naturalistic effects reproduce particular lighting that you might find in real life, and that the characters in their world would be able to see. Examples include:

- a lightning strike, which can be produced by quickly flashing a white floodlight. (This would be enhanced by an accompanying sound effect!)
- a disco effect, which could be created with LED lanterns or by manually flashing red, blue and green filtered spotlights. (Of course, it is also possible to use an automated moving lantern or a mirror/disco ball.)

Non-naturalistic special effects

These are the weird and wonderful, supernatural types of effect and could include, for example:

- the use of red and green filters combined with a fog machine to suggest an alien planet
- a slowly pulsing red spotlight focused on a character who is being aggressively questioned.

This production of *The Tempest* uses red, green and blue lighting together with an eerie set design and translucent costume to present the other-worldly nature of the island.

Chapter 2   Practical Guide to Lighting Design

FOCUS
The critical skill of how to move from one lighting cue to the next.

ASSESSMENT CHECK
This design skill is included in AO2: 'Apply theatrical skills to realise artistic intentions in live performance.'

DESIGN TIP
A seven-second cross-fade would be a good place to start your experiments.

LIGHTING TRANSITIONS

What is a lighting transition?

In your own home, you simply switch a light on or off: you move from darkness to light and vice versa at the flick of a switch. You might have some rooms with dimmer switches, allowing you to gradually increase or decrease the light's brightness.

In the theatre, in a more sophisticated way, a lighting designer can use the lighting desk to control the speed at which each lantern is made dimmer or brighter. This is known as a **transition**.

Types of transition

Snap
As the name suggests, a snap transition is a sudden movement of lights from on to off or vice versa.

Cross-snap
The sudden movement from one lighting state to another.

Fade
In lighting terms, this means making the lights gradually brighter and dimmer with a high degree of control.

Cross-fade
The gradual movement from one lighting state to another. This is achieved by simultaneously dimming one lighting state and brightening another until one is fully down and the other is fully up.

Choosing which type of transition to use

The more gradually you fade or cross-fade, the less aware the audience will be of the transition. This creates a calmer atmosphere. At the end of a performance, you might fade the lights to **blackout** over about five seconds to give the audience time to recognise that the performance is over. A slow fade to black also gives the audience time to reflect on what they have just seen.

On the other hand, a snap or cross-snap transition has a startling effect. It might jolt the audience and make a sharp contrast to the previous scene.

TASK 2.12

Harold Pinter's play *The Caretaker* includes a long speech in which a man reveals his life story. It is not a happy one. This is the stage direction:

> During Aston's speech the room grows darker. By the close of the speech only Aston can be seen clearly. Davies and all the others objects are in the shadow. The fade down of the light must be as gradual, as protracted [drawn out] and as unobtrusive as possible.

Work with a partner to discuss:
- Why was this detailed stage direction about lighting given?
- What effect might it have on the audience?

The stage darkens around Daniel Mays as Aston in *The Caretaker* at The Old Vic.

RESEARCH FOR LIGHTING

Assessing additional lighting needs

As you progress with your lighting design, you will identify what additional resources you need, if any. In addition to basic equipment such as lanterns and safety bonds, you might find that you need, for example:

- gel sheets in specific colours
- gobos
- filter and/or gobo holders for lanterns
- small LED lights to use as part of a special effect.

Budget

Once you have an idea of the costs of these items, present this to your teacher. If your teacher agrees that these things should be bought, you will be given a small budget. Once this has also been agreed in your group's design meetings, you need to stick to it.

Finding the best deal

It is well worth shopping around for the best-value products. The internet will be the place for much of what you are looking for. Local pound shops and charity shops, however, might be a cheaper source of some practical effect components, such as bicycle lights.

Alternatively, you might be able to borrow or hire items like gobos and their holders from a local theatre. If so, make sure that their accessories fit your equipment.

Battery-operated bicycle safety lights can be useful in special effects.

TASK 2.13

Find good sources – in terms of choice, availability and stock – of:
- a colour filter (gel) sheet
- a B-sized gobo of a window
- a replacement lamp (bulb) for a 1kw fresnel.

FOCUS
Finding and costing additional items to complete your lighting designs.

ASSESSMENT CHECK
This research and decision-making helps to show that you are 'making appropriate judgements during the development process'. You should also begin to analyse and evaluate 'ideas explored and research undertaken'.

A gobo over a precisely directed light can have a striking effect.

DESIGN TIP
Make sure you know exactly what you need before you begin shopping.

Chapter 2   Practical Guide to Lighting Design   47

FOCUS

Examples and guidance to help you prepare the diagrams and charts you need.

ASSESSMENT CHECK

'Creating a clear and practical design' and showing 'confident and accomplished use of appropriate drama terminology' will be demonstrated in your design documentation.

LOOK HERE

There is guidance on compiling and using a cue sheet on pages 52–53.

LOOK HERE

A detailed example of a lighting cue sheet for *Hansel and Gretel* is available on the *Designing Drama* product page at illuminatepublishing.com.

HOW TO DOCUMENT YOUR LIGHTING DESIGN

What documents do I need to produce?

You need to create a detailed **cue sheet**, **lighting plan** (rigging diagram) and schedule (list of all the equipment you have used).

These diagrams and charts can look complicated, but the advice on these pages will help you to complete excellent documents.

In this 3D lighting model, three-point lighting adds visibility and atmosphere to a practical lighting effect.

Why do I need to create these documents?

Plans and cue sheets provide lighting technicians with plans to follow. Even if a designer were to do all the technical work themselves, they could not carry in their heads all the information needed to rig and operate. Lighting charts and plans serve the same purpose as ground plans and model boxes do for set designers.

The documents you draw up will help you practically as well as going in your portfolio and being shown to the examiner who watches the scripted performances.

The lighting plan and schedule provide details of the lanterns and their accessories, along with a plan of where they are rigged. The plan should include a key that explains any symbols used in it.

The cue sheet contains details of every lighting change. It contains all the information needed to operate the lighting in performance.

The equipment and its location

You can only group and rig your lanterns once you know the lighting states and effects required and on which areas of the stage. So, you will already have marked your lighting ideas on the script. You might even have an early version of a cue sheet.

If you are working on a devised piece, you will already be becoming clear about all the lighting states and special effects that you are setting out to achieve.

As you get closer to rigging, you will need to produce finished versions of the following documents.

> **TASK 2.14**
>
> Practise drawing up each type of document as you go along with your design, so that you are confident by the time you are working on an actual production.
>
> Work through all of the types of document detailed here in the order they appear.

The lighting schedule

You can organise details of all the lanterns, gobos, barn doors and so on in any way you want.

Types and quantities of lanterns

A simple list like the one below is fine.

LIGHTING SCHEDULE: HANSEL AND GRETEL

Type of lantern	Quantity
Fresnel	11
Par can	2
Profile spotlight	11

SIGNPOST

Complete Task 2.3 on page 38 first to check what resources you have. There is no point creating a lighting design for 28 lanterns if you only have access to 18!

LOOK HERE

If you are devising, go through the stages in 'Lighting Design for the Devised Piece', beginning on page 138.

DESIGN TIP

You could create a similar document to colour count to give details of gobos used.

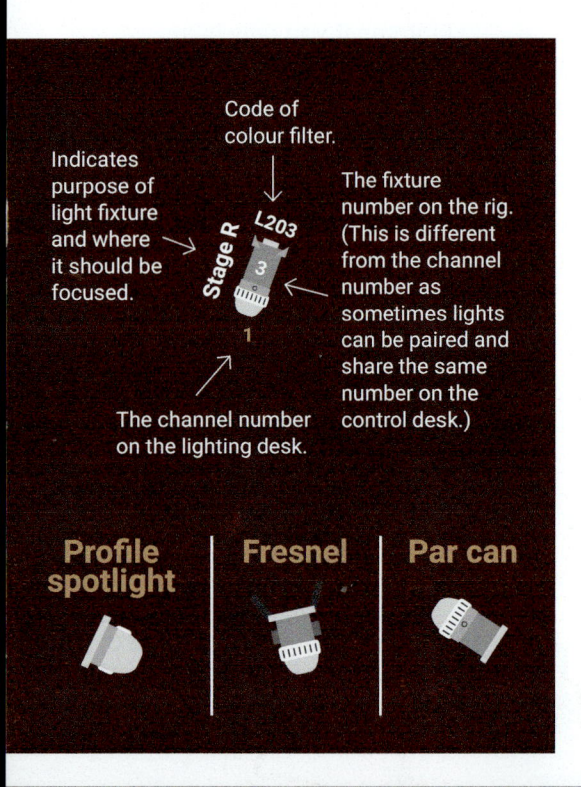

Indicates purpose of light fixture and where it should be focused.

Code of colour filter.

The fixture number on the rig. (This is different from the channel number as sometimes lights can be paired and share the same number on the control desk.)

The channel number on the lighting desk.

Profile spotlight

Fresnel

Par can

Accessories

Here is an example of a **colour count** (using Lee brand filters). It records the different gels used, the size of the colour frames they fit into and how many gels of each you will need. In other words, how many lanterns each colour is going to be used in.

Show	*Hansel and Gretel*
Venue	*Main Hall*

Colour code	Name	Type (of frame)	Count (number of gels required)
L020	Medium Amber	7.5" colour frame	1
L117	Steel Blue	10" colour frame	2
L132	Medium Blue	7.5" colour frame	2
L201	Full CT Blue	7.5" colour frame	2
L203	¼ CT Blue	7.5" colour frame	8
L770	Burnt Yellow	7.5" colour frame	3

The lighting plan

This document (a detailed example is given below) can contain a great deal of information. The most important is the type of lantern and where it is to be positioned on the rig.

The key to the plan

This tells the reader what the symbols and numbers on the lighting plan mean. Yours could be simpler than this one, on the left, which also shows some different lantern types.

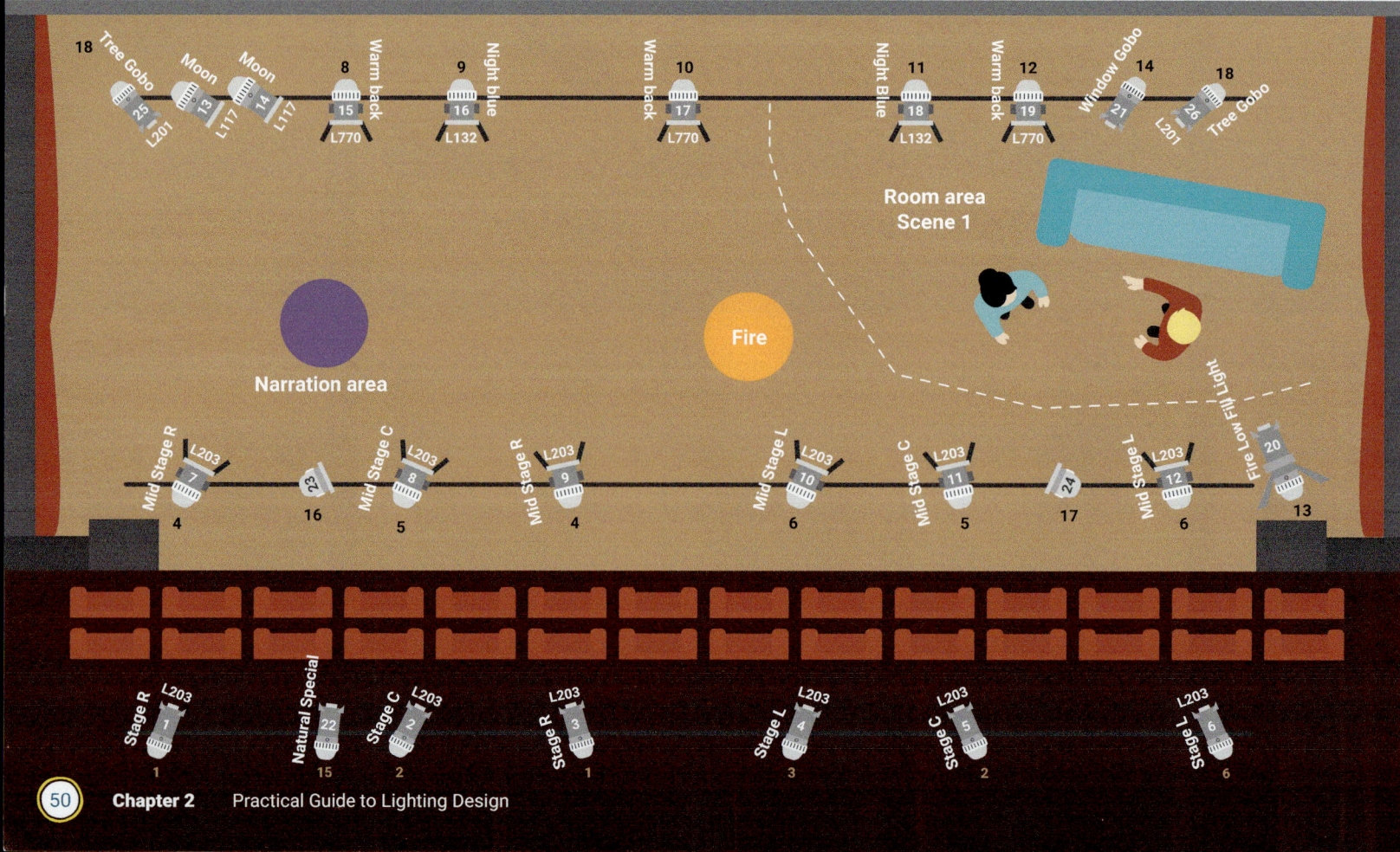

Chapter 2 Practical Guide to Lighting Design

HEALTH AND SAFETY IN LIGHTING DESIGN

Any activity that involves electricity and hanging heavy objects above people's heads needs to be treated with a great deal of care. Stop and think about the risks for a moment!

> If I'm not allowed to rig lights, why do I need to know about health and safety?

The exam board does not want you to take on much responsibility for your own and other people's safety when it comes to lighting. Your school must not allow students to put themselves or others at risk either.

However, there are good reasons why you still need to know about it:

- Everyone bears some responsibility for the safety of their environment. If people look out for potential dangers, the better it is for everyone.
- Assessing risks and avoiding hazards is part of being a responsible member of the group.
- You are expected to show your knowledge and understanding of health and safety issues.
- If you progress to make your living in this field, you need to consider health and safety issues and how to tackle them.

Take notes on any risks and hazards you encounter in your practical work. As well as making sure that they are attended to by an adult, you could mention them in your portfolio if you design lighting for Component 1.

Using your common sense

Many dangerous situations can be avoided when people are sensible. Here are some basic issues to be aware of before your lights are set up.

Hazards	Safety measures
Loose electrical cables	Tape them down or cordon off the area.
Damaged cables or electrical items	Report the problem immediately to someone in authority.
Lack of or out-of-date PAT (electrical safety) test label	
Having the wrong tool for a job, such as a knife instead of a screwdriver	Find out what the right tool is and make sure it is available and used.
Working at height	See 'Rigging and focusing', pages 54–55.
Unsecured lanterns or fixtures on the lighting bars	Make sure no one is underneath. Ask a suitable person (not yourself!) to attach a safety bond (cable).
Hot lanterns and gobos	Wear safety gloves.

FOCUS

This section offers potentially life-saving information!

ASSESSMENT CHECK

Throughout Components 1 and 2, you 'must be aware of any health and safety considerations and implications.' It forms part of your Component 1 portfolio.

This is also covered in AO3: 'Demonstrate knowledge and understanding of how drama and theatre is developed and performed.'

FOCUS
- The stage at which your lighting design really comes together.
- Creating a lighting cue sheet, which is essential for running a show's lighting and required for assessment.

ASSESSMENT CHECK
Achieving the important goal of the cue sheet means that you 'understand the practical application of production elements in performance'.

You can also use your cue sheet to 'analyse and evaluate decisions made and the rationale behind them.'

LOOK HERE
Check how you might use transitions by revisiting page 46.

DESIGN TIP
Remember the requirements that your design should indicate at least **four** lighting states in Component 1, and at least **two** in Component 2.

PLOTTING THE LIGHTING DESIGN

Fixing your cues

In this book, we are using the term **plotting** to mean the act of setting the lighting for every part of the production. The cue sheet should record details of every lighting cue decided. If you have lighting software, record each cue digitally, as you go along.

You will need to make several decisions for each cue, including:
- which lanterns are used
- how bright they should be
- what colours (if any) are needed
- whether any special effects are required
- the type and length of transitions.

Conditions for successful plotting

- Enlist a helper! If you can, invite a younger student who is already involved or interested in lighting to be your assistant – they will be learning too. Your assistant can walk around the acting area so that you can see the effect of your work clearly.
- Choose a quiet time. There is no point trying to plot during a rehearsal or when people need the main (house) lights on.
- Collect everything you need, including:
  - the annotated script or scene list
  - your lighting-rig plan
  - a task light (such as an angle-poise lamp)
  - a template for your cue sheet.

These lanterns could be grouped by colour, for example, or by the area of stage they are illuminating.

Grouping individual lanterns

The first stage in plotting is likely to be putting lanterns into groups. Creating groups means that you can quickly bring up and mix your lighting states.

A group of lanterns is several lights working together to give a particular look, such as **general cover** or warm colours; to light a specific area of the stage (DSL for example), create a special effect (sfx) and so on.

You could also group lanterns by their position on the rig, such as those at the front lighting bar, **sidelights** and so on.

A lantern could be in more than one group, and you will often use more than one group at a time.

Chapter 2 Practical Guide to Lighting Design

Identifying and documenting lantern groups

You will need your lighting plan and script (or detailed performance notes).

TASK 2.15

1. Go through your script and identify the **distinct** groups in your design. Aim for the building blocks. You might find it useful to group by area on the stage or colour, tone, special effects, for example.
2. Give each group a number. You are likely to have between four and ten groupings. Limit the number to the amount of master **channels** on your lighting desk.
3. Select a group to start on. Use your lighting desk to bring up individual lanterns in that group. Keep experimenting until you are happy. You could also make some lights brighter or dimmer to achieve the balance you like.
4. Write down the channel numbers of all the lanterns in the group. Add intensity levels as a percentage as necessary. (F means 'full': 100%.) For example:

Lantern groupings

Group 1: General cover	Group 2: DSL (house interior)	Group 3: sfx (camp fire)
3 (F)	3 (70%)	Key light – 6 (variable %)
5 (70%)	8 (F)	
11 (F)	21 (40%)	

> **DESIGN TIP**
> Make separate notes on **why** you are making decisions. These will help you to **analyse** and **evaluate** your design.

Creating your lighting cue sheet

This document is your ultimate guide to operating the lighting for your production. It plots precisely which groups are in use for each cue along with their intensity and the timings involved.

TASK 2.16

1. Lay your script, groupings chart and a cue sheet template around your lighting desk. If you have software for storing your cues, bring it into action.
2. Starting at the beginning of the show, work through the production cue by cue and scene by scene to build and chart each lighting state.
3. Check that cue numbers are clearly and correctly marked in your script so that the operator can track approaching cues. You could add '6a' and '6b' and so on later, if needed.
4. Continue to fill in your cue sheet until you have plotted the entire production.

> **DESIGN TIP**
> Note that blackouts are a cue in themselves. So are all transitions.

> **LOOK HERE**
> A detailed lighting cue sheet and template are available on the *Designing Drama* product page at illuminatepublishing.com.

One of the more basic lighting desks from Zero 88. You might have more sophisticated equipment, but this sort of model is simple to operate.

Chapter 2   Practical Guide to Lighting Design

RIGGING AND FOCUSING

FOCUS
The method by which lanterns are positioned and focused.

ASSESSMENT CHECK
You are expected to 'supervise the rigging, focusing and operating' of your lighting design. These skills and knowledge will help you towards AO2: 'Apply theatrical skills to realise artistic intentions in live performance.'

This process takes its name from the rig, which, in this case, is the construction of bars from which the lanterns are suspended.

PREPARATION

Complete the checklist on page 182.
⇩
Gather all your resources.
⇩
Check your rigging diagram.
⇩
Set up your lighting desk.
⇩
Switch on the dimmer rack.

Steps for safe and successful rigging

NB: Lanterns should be checked before rigging by a qualified person.
NB: Nobody should be underneath the rig when lanterns are being mounted.
Check that all climbing equipment can be secured and 'guarded'.
Check that all the lantern attachments, such as barn doors, gels, gobos and the safety bond work properly and are secure.

The sequence for rigging lanterns is:
1. Hook over bar and tighten wing nut.
2. Attach safety bond.
3. Point the lantern towards the area you want to light.
4. Adjust shutters and barn doors.
5. Plug in the lantern, wrapping any extra cable loosely around the bar.

DESIGN TIP
These rigging notes are for your information as you supervise the process. (You will not be rigging the lights yourself.)

Chapter 2 Practical Guide to Lighting Design

Focusing

Focusing involves fine-tuning a lantern's beam size, shape and spread.

Each lantern needs to be adjusted so that it lights the required area precisely. You might want a tight, round spotlight to pick out an individual actor. Alternatively, you might focus a group of lanterns for a subtle wash of light. For this effect, look to make the edges of the beams very soft.

You need a minimum of two people, but three are better. Ideally, one will rig and focus; one brings up the working light on the desk and the third moves around the performance area as the subject for the lighting so that the focusing effect can be seen.

A technician needs the following equipment, so provide them if you can:

- **an adjustable wrench** (to tighten and loosen nuts)
- **heat-resistant gloves** 
- **a small torch or headlamp** 
- **a tool belt or pouch** 

To focus a lantern, the following actions might be required:
- Moving shutters or barn doors
- Inserting or removing coloured filters and gobos (Gobos get very hot!)
- Moving lenses backwards or forwards.

House lights need to be off and one lantern needs to be focused at a time. Some lights can be brought up together to test their combined effect.

DESIGN TIP
You will nearly always want to light the performer, not the floor!

LOOK HERE
Use the information on pages 40–43 to guide your positioning and focusing.

DESIGN TIP
Try to get rigging and focusing correct first time to avoid having to get the people and equipment together again and doing tasks more than once.

Chapter 2   Practical Guide to Lighting Design

LIGHTING DESIGN VOCABULARY

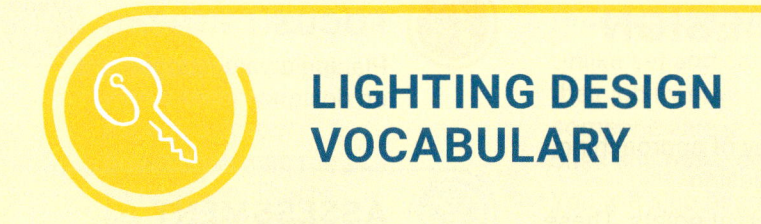

AML (automated moving lantern) Operated digitally, these lanterns can swivel and tilt.

Analyse Examine in detail, thinking about parts in relation to the whole.

Atmospheric A sound, for example, that creates a strong feeling or mood.

Backlight/backlighting Lighting that comes from the back of the acting area.

Barn door A metal attachment that slides into the front of a lantern, with hinged flaps to control the beam.

Birdie A miniature lantern ideal for hiding in small parts of a set or along the front edge of the stage.

Blackout A moment when all the lights are dimmed, often suddenly.

Channel A number given to a lantern that corresponds to a number on the lighting board or desk.

Colour count A record of the number of gels of each colour required.

Colour palette A complementary set of colours that belong to a group, such as pastel or dark.

Cross-fade Fading up one lantern or group while fading down another.

Cue sheet A list of cues along with timings.

Cue to cue Going through a play from one sound or lighting cue to the next, missing out the parts in between.

Digital Using computer technology. Digital lighting desks, for example, are programmed using software.

Dimmer/Fader A way of controlling the intensity (brightness) of the light. These are often manual or digital sliders.

Dimmer rack The control centre for changing the intensity of each channel.

Evaluate Give an opinion, a value judgement, backed up with examples and reasons.

Fade A gradual increase or decrease.

Fill light Working with a key light, fill light is less intense (bright) and is often used to lessen shadows.

Filter/gel A piece/sheet of coloured plastic/resin that fits at the front of a lantern to change the colour of the beam.

Flood A type of lantern that produces a wide spread of light; a broad cover of light.

Focus Adjust the angle and beam size of a lantern so that it lights the exact area required

Fresnel A type of lantern that is good for lighting large areas and which blends easily with other fresnels or spotlights to create a wash of light.

Gel See **Filter**.

General cover Lanterns that provide overall lighting to the acting area.

Gobo A metal cut-out plate that fits in front of a lantern and casts a shadow shape onto the stage (such as a tree outline, window frames and so on).

Intensity The brightness of lighting. Intensity is generally measured as a percentage (such as 60%).

Key light The main, strongest, most intense light, designed to copy the main light source (natural or artificial) in the real world.

Lamp The technical name for a light bulb.

Lantern The technical term for a lighting fixture that contains a light source, such as a lamp.

LED (Light Emitting Diode) Lighting fixtures that use less energy and create less heat than other types of lantern. LEDs are the most popular type of fixture in professional theatres.

Lighting desk/board/console The means of operating the lighting, with channels, dimmers and faders.

Lighting fixture A stage light unit.

Lighting plan The diagram that shows where the lanterns are hung on the rigging.

Lighting state The term used to describe the way a lantern or group of lanterns is used on the stage. For example, a particular lighting state could create a moonlit effect.

Manual Operated by hand as opposed to digitally.

Naturalistic A set or lighting effect, for example, with characteristics of reality; having the appearance of a real place.

Non-naturalistic A set or lighting design, for example, that aims not to look like a real place.

Pace The speed with which lighting effects transition from one to the next.

Par can A type of lantern that produces a very strong beam of light.

Plotting The process of creating a cue sheet to show choices of what light effect happens when and where.

Practical effect A lighting effect that is operated or worn by a performer.

Profile spotlight A versatile lantern that can be used to create tight spots of light or bigger areas as required.

Rig The bars that lanterns are hung on.

Safety bond/cable/chain The metal chain or cable that attaches the lantern to the rigging.

Sidelight Light that shines from the side of the stage, perhaps from the wings.

Silhouette The dark shape of a person or object against a lighter background.

Snap A sudden change such as a blackout.

Special effect A lighting effect that has a specific purpose, such as a colour wash to suggest a flashback.

Spotlight A type of lantern that can create a tight circle of light or a larger, softer-edged one.

Three-point lighting A method that shines light from three different directions to give good coverage.

Transition A change between lighting states, such as a snap or a fade.

PRACTICAL GUIDE TO COSTUME DESIGN

Chapter 3

- Introduction to costume design — 62
- Placing costume in history — 64
- Shape and style: what we wear, and why — 66
- Colour and fabric for the stage — 68
- Developing and using your costume resources — 72
- Key process – sewing — 74
- Adapting costume items — 76
- Health and safety in costume design — 77
- Hair and make-up — 78
- How to document your costume design — 80
- Fitting the costume — 82
- Technical and dress rehearsals for costume designers — 86
- Evaluating your costume design — 87
- Costume design vocabulary — 88

FOCUS
The importance of costume design.

ASSESSMENT CHECK
As you gain awareness and understanding of costume choices, you are:
- 'using visual elements to create mood, style and atmosphere'
- 'communicating intention and creating impact for an audience.'

TASK 3.1
1. Take a few moments to look at the people around you and what they are wearing. Apply the three bullet-point questions above to each person and put yourself in their shoes.
2. If you can, try this task in a range of locations, such as a park and a café. Build up a picture of each person. What other clothing do you imagine they have in their wardrobe?

INTRODUCTION TO COSTUME DESIGN

Everyday costumes
At least once every day we all use costume design skills. When you open your drawer or look in your **wardrobe**, you are choosing clothing to suit your day. Consciously or otherwise, you might be thinking:
- Am I going to be outside much and what will I be doing?
- How do I feel and what image do I want to project?
- Do I just want to be comfortable or do I want to make an impression?

Everyday make-up
Some people wouldn't leave the house without make-up. For others, they wear it for an evening out or not at all. Make-up also has strong cultural and religious meanings for some communities.

There are numerous reasons why make-up can be important, including:
- sharing your culture and identity
- boosting confidence
- helping you to feel older or younger.

How should a character be made-up and costumed?
When you design costumes for the stage, you are making decisions for a character rather than for yourself, but you can start with the same three questions above. Then go on to ask yourself these more specific questions:

- What fashions and fabrics would be available given the period of history in which the play is to be staged?
- How interested is the character in clothes and make-up?
- To what extent do they care about how they look? To what extent can they afford to care?
- How does their occupation (or lack of it) influence their clothing and make-up choices?
- Does the character have any particular personality traits that might influence their choices? (Are they vain? Do they tend to feel anxious?)
- Does the character undergo a journey through the play, or a transformation? How could that be communicated through costume and make-up?

Chapter 3 Practical Guide to Costume Design

Using costume to enhance meaning

As a costume designer, you have the power to influence how an audience perceives a character before they speak or move. Your design input might immediately inform the audience that a character is a pilot in the Second World War, for example, or an impoverished child in the 1960s.

Stylistic and artistic collaboration

Reflecting the context – such as historical and economic signs – is crucial in design. At the same time, a costume designer needs to work in harmony with other designers and the director to achieve the stylistic and artistic intentions of the drama. This might mean, for example, working within a particular **colour palette**, designing a costume that allows an actor to safely climb part of the set, or working with the lighting designer to ensure that your **fabric choices** will be appropriate under particular stage lights.

Costume and the actor

Costuming and make-up are very important for the actor as they help them to portray the character. Costumes also need to be comfortable enough for the actor to move freely. Costume designers will often provide **rehearsal costumes** that help the actor to behave like the character.

Removing or putting on potentially 'fiddly' garments, such as jackets, scarves and headwear, need to be practised and timed in the rehearsal room.

How can I design costumes as part of this course?

You can opt for costume design in either or both of the practical sections of the course. If you choose to work as costume designer in Component 1, you will work in a small group devising a piece of theatre. You will help to develop the piece as a whole, but your specific responsibility will be to create two costume designs for the performance.

Component 2 is similar, but you will work with a script. As there are two extracts from the same play, you could design costume for one and then perform or choose a different design role for the second.

Component 3 is the written exam. When you **evaluate** a performance you have seen, you might have to write about costume design. Practical work will help you to write confidently about costume and make-up in the exam.

Research

Even if you are creating a contemporary (modern) world for the stage, you will still need to complete research so that your design:

- suits the personality of the character
- reflects the right economic and social contexts.

For period costumes, remember that many museums have a fashion and clothing section. Study clothing from different centuries and decades.

Also browse the internet, fashion magazines, history books and crafting and sewing magazines. Look for clothing worn by a particular type of person during the historical period of your drama piece.

TASK 3.2

Watch a few minutes of an unfamiliar television drama or film that happens to be on. Focus on one character's costume:

- What historical period is represented?
- What social and economic conditions are being suggested?
- What can you tell about the character's personality?

DESIGN TIP

Find out early on whether actors have health issues with particular fibres or make-up ingredients, so that you have time to explore options.

TASK 3.3

Ask your teacher if you can bring in some rehearsal costumes for a practical performance lesson. Afterwards, discuss how the use of rehearsal costumes affected the performance.

DESIGN TIP

Keep downloaded and bookmarked resources in a research folder on your computer. Keep magazine pages and so on in your paper folder. If you design for Component 1, these will go in your portfolio.

FOCUS

A short history of clothing to give you a starting point for including authenticity in your design work.

ASSESSMENT CHECK

This section provides useful background for your set text study and your understanding of its 'social, historical and/or cultural contexts'.

PLACING COSTUME IN HISTORY

Professional costume designers understand the relationship between historical period, including today, and clothing. What people wear is largely dictated by the society and time that they live in.

Before the 19th century

Pre-industrialisation, fabrics were limited to woven cotton, linen and wool for most people. Poorer people would typically wear **natural**, undyed clothes, and **styles** were broadly modest, simple and functional. If you were wealthy, however, you might be clothed in silk, taffeta and satin. These fabrics could be plant-dyed using beetroot, berries and onion skins, for example. Fashion played a significant role for those that could afford it. At the highest level of society, there were certain fabrics that only royalty wore, such as purple velvet, gold fabric and certain types of fur.

Similarly, the use of make-up has an interesting history and is used differently across the world. Very pale skin, for example, was desirable in Europe for several hundred years up until the 20th century.

A re-creation of Elizabethan hair (wig) and make-up by Alanna Sadler.

The mid 19th century onwards

The industrial revolution of the 19th century paved the way for a broader range of materials. As textile factories were built in Britain and other industrialising countries, the speed and ease of fabric production increased, which meant that a wider section of the population could add variety to their clothing.

The first sewing machines were developed around the 1830s, gradually leading to the **mass-produced** clothing of today. As home sewing machines became popular too, ordinary people were able to copy the fashions that they saw the wealthy enjoying.

In the early 20th century, the chemical industry began to produce man-made dyes, along with fabrics such as polyester and nylon that added stretch to clothing. **Textured** fabrics such as corduroy and polyester also developed from this period.

Some periods, such as the 1920s and 1960s, saw iconic fashion and make-up styles including cloche hats and mini-skirts.

> **TASK 3.4**
>
> Look at the labels in some of your own clothing. What is the fabric made up of? Can you find out where some of the more unusual materials might have been produced?

> **TASK 3.5**
>
> These photographs of 1940s Hollywood film star Ava Gardner show her without and with costume make-up.
> 1. Write a short paragraph describing her 'look' in each picture.
> 2. Think of at least three adjectives to describe what her made-up look is saying about her character (for example, powerful).

Chapter 3 Practical Guide to Costume Design 65

FOCUS
Some of the factors that affect clothing choices.

ASSESSMENT CHECK
Here, you begin to 'recognise and understand how theatrical choices are used to create impact.' You should also begin to see how costume can contribute to communicating meaning through genre and style.

SHAPE AND STYLE: WHAT WE WEAR, AND WHY

Some of the most distinctive aspects of costume design are shape or **silhouette** and style.

Historical period

Certain times can be identified by typical clothing styles. Fashion and the availability of fabric are the major influences when it comes to shape, which might include skirt and trouser length, neckline, and so on. Oversized flared cords or jeans, for example, place a costume in the late 1960s to early 1970s.

TASK 3.6

Look through magazines, shops and your own clothes for distinctive shapes or styles of cut. What features stand out (in terms of outline, sleeves, leg shape and length, fullness, silhouette)?

Social economics

A person's ability to update and maintain their wardrobe depends largely on the amount of income they are prepared to spend on clothes. Historically, only wealthier members of society could buy more than just essential garments. Today, many people shop widely and frequently for clothes.

For several decades, brand names have been an important influence on purchasing, and favoured brands command a high price tag. Displaying brand names in prominent positions on clothes can be seen as a **status symbol**.

TASK 3.7

Compare the cost of a branded item of clothing with a similar one from a high street retailer.

Assess the difference in quality in terms of styling, fabric and construction.

Chapter 3 Practical Guide to Costume Design

Goth fans pose at a music festival.

Identity and image

Clothing and make-up are often expressions of our character and personality and many periods of history are dotted with notable **subculture** fashions, such as punk or mod, that consciously show the wearers as followers of that style or culture. These are often linked to other areas of popular culture or art, such as music and film.

Suitability

There are two main factors that determine clothing choice in terms of suitability.

- Someone's occupation and way of life will affect what they wear in particular situations. It needs to be practical and functional.
- Body shape and confidence levels can play their part when people think about what suits them.

TASK 3.8

Design a new uniform for **one** of the following (male or female):

- manual council worker, such as a refuse collector
- primary school pupil
- supermarket checkout assistant.

Consider suitability, socio-economic factors and identity.

Chapter 3 Practical Guide to Costume Design 67

> **FOCUS**
> What to consider when choosing costume material.

> **ASSESSMENT CHECK**
> Exploring costume choices will help you to 'recognise and understand how theatrical choices are used to create impact' and work towards AO3: 'Demonstrate knowledge and understanding of how drama and theatre is developed and performed.'

COLOUR AND FABRIC FOR THE STAGE

Selecting colours, patterns and materials

There are eight main considerations for costume designers when selecting which colour and type of fabric to use.

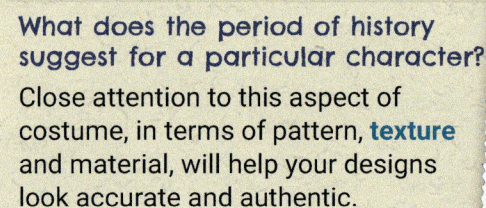

1 What does the period of history suggest for a particular character?
Close attention to this aspect of costume, in terms of pattern, **texture** and material, will help your designs look accurate and authentic.

Paisley patterns were introduced into Britain from India in the 18th century.

2 What **colour palette** is the **set designer** working with?
In the harmonious world of the stage, a unified colour theme is likely to be desired. This does not mean you have to use the same colours as the set, but you might want them to blend or have a complementary use of bold, muted or primary colours.

3 Do the **artistic intentions** of the theatre piece call for any **symbolic use of colour**?
A **stylised** drama might call for all black or all white costumes with the addition of a meaningful colour, such as red to suggest the theme of danger or violence. **Monochrome** (shades of black and white only) can be used for entire sets or costume designs and can be full of impact. Such designs have a clarity and lack of complication that could also be used alongside one or more characters being dressed in colour to emphasise them. White is very effective under coloured lights.

White often has connotations of purity and innocence, while we might associate black fabric with death or evil. Purple has links to royalty and wealth.

A play with opposing groups, such as the Capulets and the Montagues in *Romeo and Juliet*, might use an element of colour coding.

4 **Warm colours** and **cold colours** are often associated with personality types and make an impact on the audience, although they might not be particularly conscious of it.
Warm colours, such as shades of red, orange and yellow, suggest a bold, strong and confident person. Cold colours, such as shades of blue and grey, can suggest a more distant or withdrawn type of person.

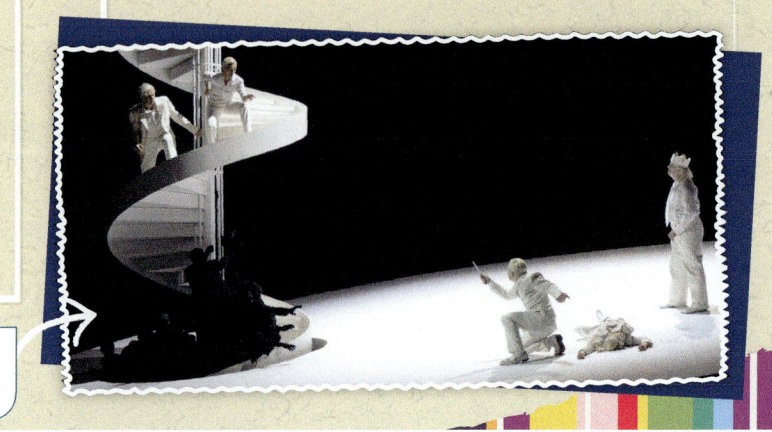

This modern production of Hamlet *in Berlin uses all-white costumes and an all-white set.*

Chapter 3 Practical Guide to Costume Design

5 Even in everyday life, the appearance of coloured fabric varies in different lighting conditions, but the intensity of stage lighting takes this to another level.

A new white shirt can be glaring under white stage lights, so costume designers might knock back the brightness by running the garment through a washing machine with other items a couple of times or dye it off-white.

Coloured lights can neutralise or drain the colour from fabric. This is particularly true with subtle tones and you should always work alongside the lighting designer to test the appearance of your fabrics before you finalise your designs.

Aguecheek's bright yellow jumpsuit in *Twelfth Night* looks its best under 'neutral' lighting.

6 We all have different skin-tones, and costume designers might take account of this when they select colours for their actors. Pale skins, for example, often do not blend particularly well with yellow.

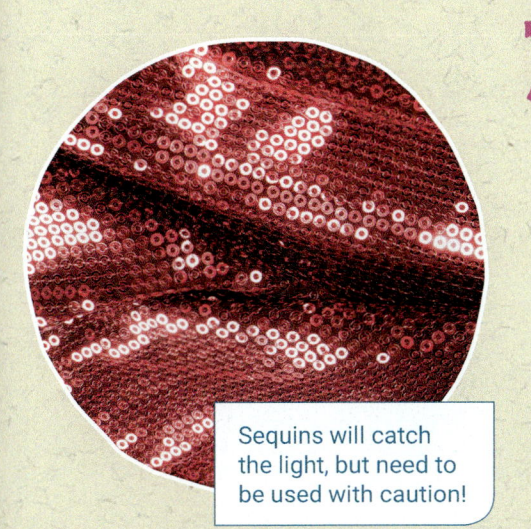

7 Mood, atmosphere and the feel of the play or character affect colour choice for costume designers. A tragic play might call for darker, more muted shades, while bright colours might suit a comedy. Professional directors are notorious for telling designers that something doesn't match the feel of their production. A design might be described as 'too fluffy' or 'not sharp enough', which the costumier has to interpret in terms of changing the shape or colour scheme of costumes.

Sequins will catch the light, but need to be used with caution!

The brightly coloured costumes in *Dream Girls* reflect the upbeat mood of the production.

8 Combinations of colours are an important consideration. Putting two shades of red next to each other, for example, tends to cancel out the tones and gives just one effect. Natural and synthetic fabrics of the same colour will appear differently under stage lights.

ASSESSMENT CHECK

You are using the key skill of interpretation here as you 'develop ideas to communicate meaning for performance.' This is directly assessed in Component 1, and interpretation is also a crucial aspect of the other assessment objectives.

TASK 3.9

1. Choose a character from a play that you have been studying.
   - Would you costume this character in warm or cool colours? Why?
   - Does the historical context of the play suggest particular types of fabric, styles and patterns and make-up?
2. Sketch a quick costume design. Bear in mind the points above, as well as suitability in terms of characterisation. Add notes on hairstyle and make-up, if appropriate.

Selecting fabrics for stage costumes

In the modern world, there are very many types of material available, and costume designers need to consider a number of factors.

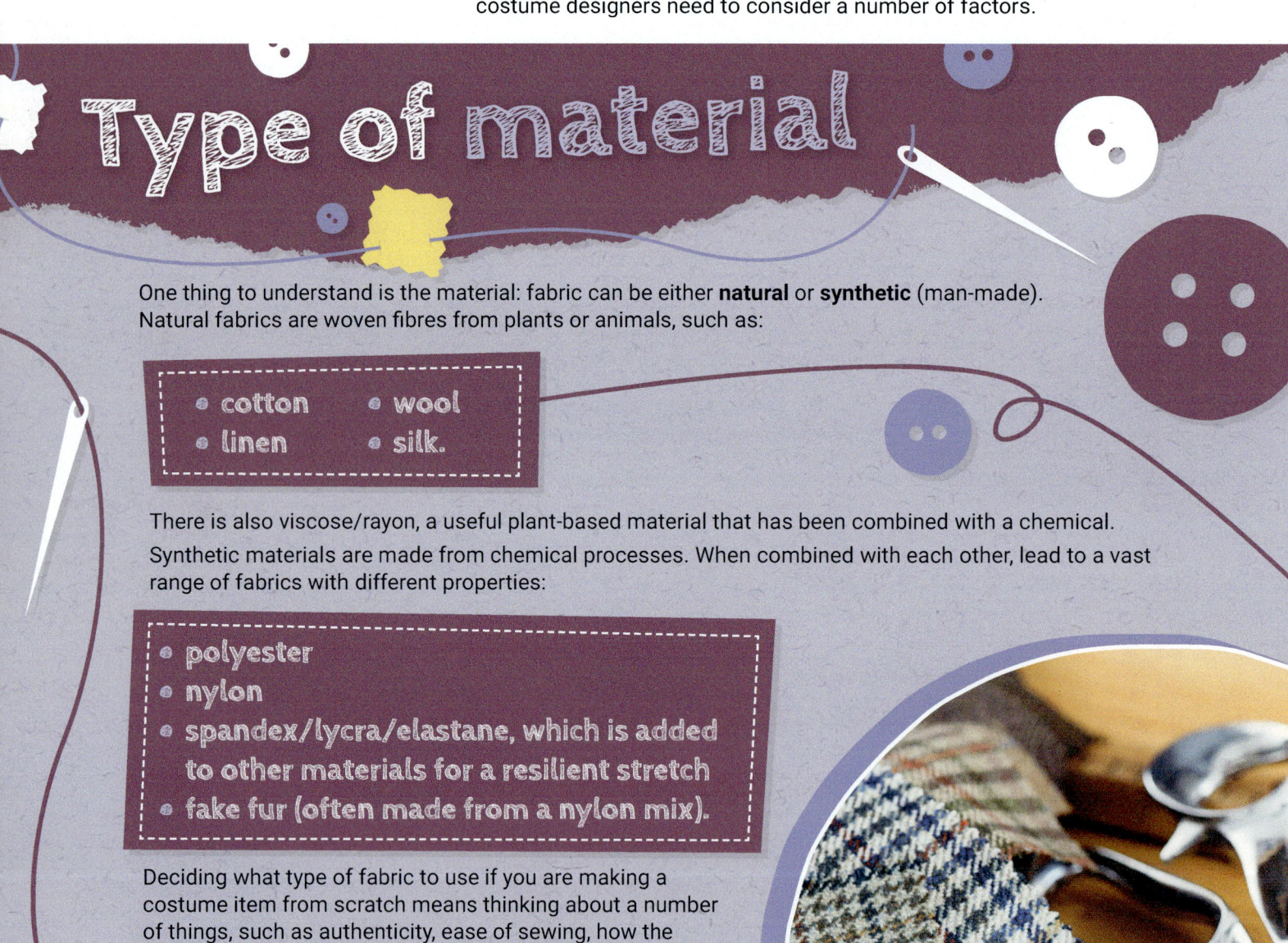

Type of material

One thing to understand is the material: fabric can be either **natural** or **synthetic** (man-made). Natural fabrics are woven fibres from plants or animals, such as:

- cotton
- wool
- linen
- silk.

There is also viscose/rayon, a useful plant-based material that has been combined with a chemical.

Synthetic materials are made from chemical processes. When combined with each other, lead to a vast range of fabrics with different properties:

- polyester
- nylon
- spandex/lycra/elastane, which is added to other materials for a resilient stretch
- fake fur (often made from a nylon mix).

Deciding what type of fabric to use if you are making a costume item from scratch means thinking about a number of things, such as authenticity, ease of sewing, how the fabric moves or drapes and how it will look on stage. The best way to find out if it will suit your character is to get a swatch so you can handle the fabric and test it under stage lights of various colours.

Weight and texture

The **weight** of fabric can be read clearly by the audience. Lightweight, flowing fabrics have more movement. If they are used with lots of fullness, they might give impressions of freedom and wealth.

Flimsy fabrics like this are not hard-wearing and therefore could suggest that the people wearing them do not do much work and can afford for their clothes not to last as long as heavier weight fabrics.

In modern clothing, the time of year and weather is a big hint as to what weight of clothing would be worn, unless it's evening-wear, when anything goes!

Corduroy.

Fabric comes in a wide range of textures such as:
- velvet
- cord
- denim
- coarse-woven
- brushed (including tweed)
- brocade/embroidered
- sequinned
- smooth.

Whether the **finish** of the fabric is dull or shiny affects its appearance significantly. Fabrics with a sheen include:
- satin
- silk
- taffeta (usually made from silk).

Tweed.

These fabrics give the wearer an air of wealth and status, and can be expensive to use in a costume. A cheaper option is to use a synthetic version, or add **embellishments** to less expensive fabric, including:
- braid (narrow, plaited trim)
- sequins (which can be bought in strips)
- bright buttons
- jewellery
- trim, such as a fur collar or lace cuffs.

A fine taffeta dress embroidered with silk flowers.

Braiding on the shoulder of a military dress uniform.

TASK 3.10

Find a simple garment from a charity shop (or use one of your own) and **upcycle** it into a more interesting and attractive version with the use of embellishments. Check the effect of the garment before and after under stage lights.

LOOK HERE

For more on altering and adapting clothing and fabric, see 'Adapting costume items' on page 76.

FOCUS

A basic skill for costume design.

ASSESSMENT CHECK

The practical techniques should help you later to 'apply theatrical skills to realise artistic intentions in live performance' (AO2).

KEY PROCESS – SEWING

At some point in your work as a costume designer you should sew something! This book won't teach you to become a dressmaker, but these pages show you the key process that securely holds one piece of fabric to another. It really is quite easy.

You can make a bag, for example, or simple garment even if you just have some fabric and basic sewing equipment. Sewing machines are quick, but hand sewing works well too. The following are two simple hand-sewn stitches.

TACKING

TACKING temporarily holds two pieces of fabric together loosely so that they can be tried on (carefully) or held in place while you sew them together permanently. It is a long up-and-down stitch that you make with the right (outer) sides of the fabric together.

BACK STITCH uses small stitches with no gaps between them. It is strong, permanent stitching which will hold fabric together securely.

BACK STITCH

MAKING YOUR FIRST PIECE OF COSTUME: A DRAWSTRING BAG

Drawstring bags were popular in Britain from Victorian times until the 1920s, and versions of it are still used today. You could make one for yourself, a friend or as part of a finished costume design.

You can buy the fabric new, but even better for developing your skills as a costume designer, would be to source, from a charity shop or second-hand sale, a garment or home furnishing item with an interesting pattern. Existing buttons or embroidery could be left on for instant embellishment. Of course, choosing and adding your own embellishments would enhance the impact of your bag as well.

Cotton fabric is the easiest to work with as it does not stretch, fray or slip around. Or you could try heavier, textured fabrics, such as velvet, cord or brocade. These bring glamour and interest, but can be more awkward to work with. You could experiment with several fabrics to make a range of bags.

74   Chapter 3   Practical Guide to Costume Design

Method

*Back-stitch steps can also be done on a sewing machine.

You will need

- Approximately half a metre of fabric
- Three-quarters of a metre of narrow ribbon, piping or cord
- Pins
- Needles and thread
- Flexible tape measure
- Steel and/or wooden ruler
- Scissors
- Iron
- A safety pin
- Buttons, sequins, beads and so on (optional)

1. Cut two identical oblong pieces of fabric. Your bag will end up about 4cm smaller, so 18cm by 26cm would give you a make-up bag.

2. Using a hard edge to guide you, such as a steel ruler, iron a 1cm fold onto the wrong side (inside) of the fabric over one short side of each piece of fabric. This will be the top of your bag.

3. Pin the two pieces of fabric, wrong sides together. Leave 5cm unpinned at the top on each side.

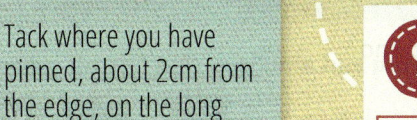

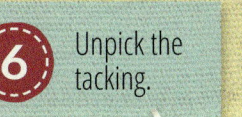

4. Tack where you have pinned, about 2cm from the edge, on the long sides. Remove the pins.

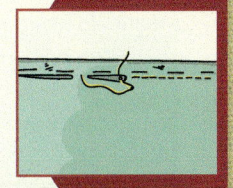

5. Back-stitch next to where you have tacked.

6. Unpick the tacking.

7. Press the **seam** open with the iron. Press up to the top of the bag (the unstitched section).

8. Fold the unstitched sections in half onto the wrong sides.

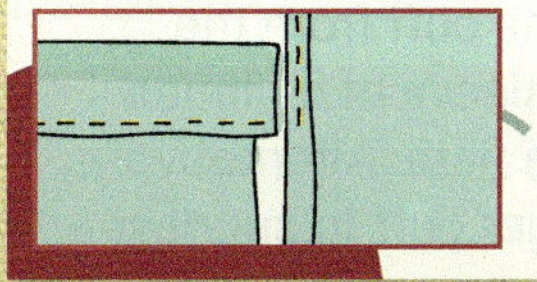

9. Pin, tack and then remove the pins.

10. Back-stitch next to the tacking and remove the tacking. You now have a channel to put your ribbon through.

11. Cut your ribbon in half and attach a safety pin to the end of one piece.

12. Turn your bag the right way out and use the safety pin to thread the ribbon through the channel of one side of the bag.

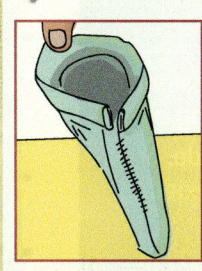

13. Thread the other half of the ribbon through the other channel and press the whole thing.

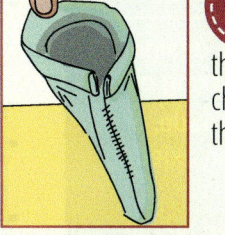

14. Sew on any embellishments, making sure that you fix them to one side of the bag only.

Chapter 3 Practical Guide to Costume Design

FOCUS

The role of hair and make-up in costume design and how you can make your own interpretations.

ASSESSMENT CHECK

This knowledge and understanding should help you towards AO2: 'Apply theatrical skills to realise artistic intentions in live performance.'

HAIR AND MAKE-UP

No costume design is complete without a consideration of hair and make-up.

HAIRSTYLES

Hairstyles need to suit the characters and match the style of the costumes and period of the play. Assess whether you can work with the actor's own hairstyle in relation to the style of the play and the social, economic and cultural context of the character.

It is also important to think about the character's personality and any changes they undergo during the play. Hair that is up in a bun or ponytail, for example, could be let down at a moment in the play as an effective way of showing that a character is relaxing or is distraught, for instance. Putting hair up neatly could indicate an upward change of status.

SPECIAL EFFECTS

Ageing or unconventional looks can be aided with the use of wash-out colour sprays, but it is important not to exaggerate the use of grey unless you are aiming for comedy. Colours might be useful for a fantasy or science-fiction play or as part of an animal costume. Fake facial hair is available, but use it sparingly to avoid causing unwanted humour. Always use specialist adhesive!

Careful use of back-combing adds volume to hair, and products such as gel can smooth and flatten, both of which can significantly change a hairstyle.

If your school or college has a hairdressing department, you might find that teachers and students are keen to be involved. This is extremely helpful for you and can often contribute to those students' coursework.

WIGS

Wigs are very useful for completely changing an actor's hairstyle. A wig can create instant impact when it comes to period plays or creating styles, such as a punk Mohican, that are not easily achievable with the actor's own hair. They can also be cut and coloured as needed. They are fairly cheaply available from specialist stores.

You need to research the look you need and add this to your knowledge of the text and character to arrive at a workable design.

Christopher Ainslie has a completely green costume – including his hair and eyebrows – in his role as Oberon, king of the fairies, from *A Midsummer Night's Dream* (English National Opera).

Make-up

Stage make-up is important for a number of reasons:

- It helps make facial features more visible, which helps the audience to see expressions clearly. Even when a character would not be wearing make-up, a little carefully applied lipstick in one shade darker than the lips accentuates the mouth, and eyes could be lightly lined. A base layer (foundation or powder) can be helpful in reducing shine under stage lights.
- It can help to establish period, setting and character.
- It can suggest significant aspects of a character, such as age or job.

What products should I use?

Everyday cosmetics are fine for use on stage, but always check with actors for any allergies. For more unusual looks, theatrical make-up can be well worth the expense.

As with shapes and styles of clothing and hair, different cultures and periods of history are associated with certain make-up styles. These are easily researched and should form the basis of your designs.

Useful 'extras' include:
- false eyelashes
- temporary tattoos
- stick-on jewels
- nail polish.

Have a good supply of different brushes to obtain good quality, varied effects. Keep them (and everything else you use) very clean!

Special effects

Ageing make-up should be applied carefully and sparingly or it will look comical. A useful tip is to add shading or highlighting to existing laughter and frown lines.

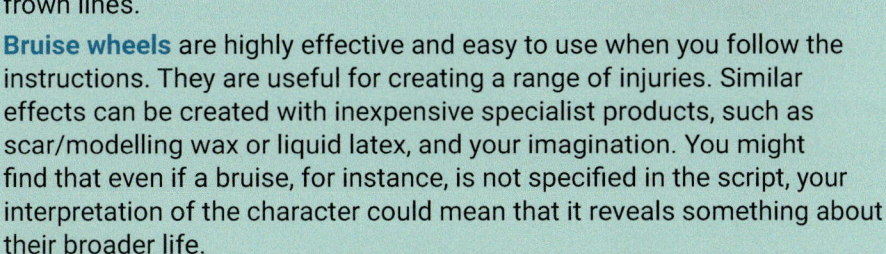

Bruise wheels are highly effective and easy to use when you follow the instructions. They are useful for creating a range of injuries. Similar effects can be created with inexpensive specialist products, such as scar/modelling wax or liquid latex, and your imagination. You might find that even if a bruise, for instance, is not specified in the script, your interpretation of the character could mean that it reveals something about their broader life.

Be very careful with fake blood. It often contains dye that is difficult to remove from skin and fabric. Avoid very cheap products.

LOOK HERE

Try Task 3.5 on page 65 to see how make-up can contribute to characterisation and meaning.

Make sure you follow the health and safety guidance on page 77 when trying out make-up.

TASK 3.12

Draw a detailed hair and make-up design for a character you are currently studying. If you have tools and products available, ask your teacher if you can create the look on yourself or another member of your group.

Chapter 3 Practical Guide to Costume Design

FOCUS
Increasing your confidence in drawing clearly presented designs.

ASSESSMENT CHECK
Improving the quality of your presentation will help you to communicate your artistic intentions in your final designs.

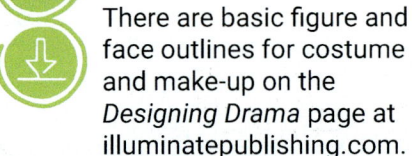

LOOK HERE
There are basic figure and face outlines for costume and make-up on the *Designing Drama* page at illuminatepublishing.com.

TASK 3.13
1. Browse magazines to find a standing, full-length figure of a man or woman. It is ideal if they are in underwear or swimwear.
2. Trace the outline of the figure onto plain paper. You do not need facial features or fingers.
3. On another piece of paper, have a go at sketching the figure freehand. Use short pencil strokes to create lines and curves. Be as basic or detailed as you like.
4. Look at your two versions. Decide which feels most promising and continue with that method. (You can always change your mind later.)
5. If both versions fill you with fear, try a fashion template. There are many online.

HOW TO DOCUMENT YOUR COSTUME DESIGN

All types of theatre designer must be able to show their design ideas long before the costumes, set, lighting and sound are actually created.

Costume design sketches by Alice Smith for Jude and Lynette in *Noughts & Crosses* at Nottingham Playhouse.

You do not need to be good at art to sketch your designs, but you certainly need to include drawn designs when working on your portfolio and in your supporting documents for Component 2.

What documents do I need to produce?
In addition to making or supervising the construction of your costumes, you must produce on paper the final costume designs for:
- two characters in Component 1
- one character per extract in Component 2.

If appropriate you must incorporate hair, make-up and mask considerations.

You must also produce a costume plot or list of costumes and accessories worn by each performer, indicating any changes as appropriate.

How do I create costume designs on paper?
It is entirely up to you whether you work **freehand** or use guides such as templates. Your drawings do not have to be 'pretty': the costume details are the important things.

The first thing to discover is what method of sketching suits you best.

If you choose to draw your designs from scratch, you might find the guidance on the following page helpful.

BODY PROPORTIONS

This guide should help you get the proportion of your figures correct if you are not a confident artist, but prefer to work without a ready-made template. Fashion drawings tend to elongate the body, so you should find that the following ratio is more suitable for costume design.

The head of the figure can be drawn as an oval of any size. Two further ovals underneath will take you down to the waistline, and a further three will take you to the ankles.

Developing your design

Below is a suggested sequence for moving from initial sketches to a finished costume design.

You will need to annotate or redraw your first designs after discussion with other designers and performers, and during and after rehearsals.

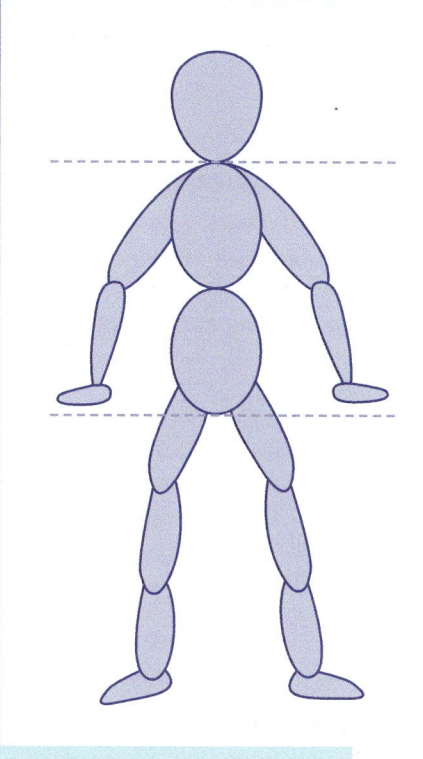

Smaller ovals can be used for hands and feet at the ends of approximated arms and legs.

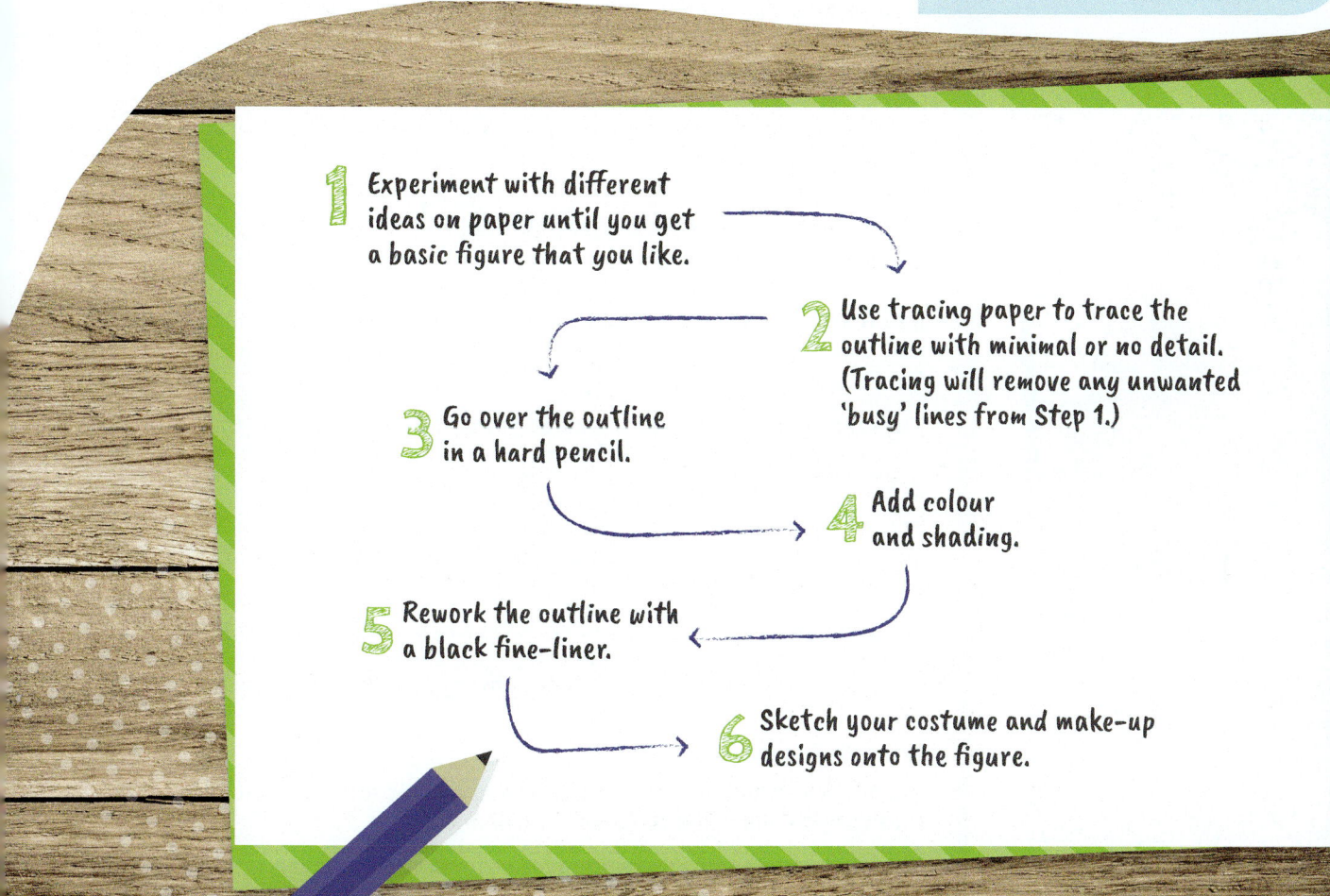

1. Experiment with different ideas on paper until you get a basic figure that you like.
2. Use tracing paper to trace the outline with minimal or no detail. (Tracing will remove any unwanted 'busy' lines from Step 1.)
3. Go over the outline in a hard pencil.
4. Add colour and shading.
5. Rework the outline with a black fine-liner.
6. Sketch your costume and make-up designs onto the figure.

FOCUS
Ensuring your costume fits and looks its best.

ASSESSMENT CHECK
Adjusting and fitting costumes shows that you are 'making appropriate judgements during the development process' and 'using and applying design skills to contribute to the performance as a whole' and so 'applying theatrical skills to realise artistic intentions in live performance' (AO2).

FITTING THE COSTUME

Your design needs to be 'refined and dynamic'. An ill-fitting costume will be neither of these.

To put together a costume that fits the performer early on, they need to try it on as you source, make and alter it.

Professionals continuously adjust a costume through a series of fitting sessions with the actor. This might even be right up to the performance.

Darts from the waistband of a skirt give a slim, fitted shape.

THE IMPORTANCE OF A WELL-FITTING COSTUME

Appearance
A badly fitting costume will not show your design as it should be. The silhouette will be altered if the costume doesn't hang properly, for example. Make sure that it is neither too big nor too tight.

Comfort
A badly fitting costume will hinder the actor's movements. The actor needs to be able to breathe, walk, stretch and sit in the costume. There are safety implications here too. An actor also needs a costume that will enhance the posture of their character. A casual item such as a sloppy jumper needs to be fitted to the actor, even if a 'bad' fit is a design choice.

How can I make my costume fit?
Everyone has an individual body shape proportioned in a unique way. This is why one pair of size 16 or 32" jeans will fit you very well, but a pair from another shop will not. You are unlikely to start altering the size of jeans, but it can be quite easy to adjust the fit of most garments for the stage.

The **type of fabric** a garment is made of will influence how you fit it.

Stiff fabric
This won't have much stretch, so you might need to use darts, tucks or gathers to alter the shape and make the garment smaller. Alternatively, a belt could be used to pull an item in.

Could you put a panel in the front or the back to make it bigger? For example, a panel of jersey fabric would give more ease as well as more volume. It could also add interest in terms of texture and colour

Stretchy fabric
Fabric with stretch has more ease of wear and movement. It can hug the figure but allow the actor freedom of movement.

You can try similar fitting techniques as for non-elastic fabric, above. In addition, you can alter the side seams on skirts or trousers and add elastic to necklines and waistbands.

Chapter 3 Practical Guide to Costume Design

COMMON FITTING ISSUES AND HOW YOU MIGHT SOLVE THEM

Avoid attempting to make a radical change to a sourced garment. If it is much too big or too small, get something else! Minor adjustments, however, can be very successful.

All of the following ideas can be achieved without taking a garment apart.

Too long

It is not difficult to reduce the length of everything from hems to sleeves. You could carefully cut away excess fabric and re-hem the garment, as long as the style is not complicated. If the bottom of a dress or skirt is very fancy, you might be able to take it up at the waist. You could add elastic to the bottom of long sleeves or simply fold them upwards.

If the top half of a garment looks saggy, try lifting it at the shoulders by shortening its straps or creating a dart. You need to remember, however, that the armholes will also be lifted and that it won't lie properly if the garment has sleeves. Shoulder pads are a possibility, but they are generally best in science-fiction, fantasy or costumes for the 1950s or 1980s.

Darting the shoulders will lift the arm section of a garment. The darted section of fabric should be wider at the shoulder edge than the neck edge.

Too short

Solving this can be a bit trickier than lengthening garments, but there are a couple of tricks you can try. Add borders or frills to sleeves and/or hems, for example. Simply seam them together on the wrong side. You will probably need to use a different material, so, unless you can find something very similar, choose fabric with a strong contrast (difference) in colour and perhaps texture. If you can add a piece of the same material in another place on the costume, this will give a well-finished look.

TASK 3.14

On the dress above, can you see two other places where the same white material could be added to give a considered, balanced look?

LOOK HERE

'Key process – sewing' on pages 74–75 will show you how to make a seam.

Chapter 3   Practical Guide to Costume Design   83

Too big

First, ask the actor to put on the costume to find out where there is too much fabric. Depending on the style of the garment, you might be able to simply sew in some elastic or add a belt. If so, carefully consider shape and size to ensure the whole costume suits the required period and style.

Another possibility would be to remove fabric by taking in the side seams. However, you can only take in side seams all the way from top to bottom if the garment doesn't have sleeves. If most of the extra fabric is around the waistline, you could try adding diamond-shaped darts on each side of the centre-front and centre-back lines.

The costume designer has added a wide elasticated belt to improve the fit and style of this dress.

A good alternative might also be to add wide pieces of elastic to pull a garment in. This could be done at the back or the sides for a natural look or vertically to add a more stylised effect. You could make a feature of the gathering by adding a button or bow, for example. This would make the gather appear to be a deliberate aspect of the design.

Shirred waistband.

Paperbag waistband.

Tiered waistband.

Fold-down waistband.

Necklines

Necklines can be adjusted and embellished to great effect. This is easier if the garment does not have a collar. You could add elastic, a drawstring or laces to a loose neck or one where you have removed the collar. This kind of technique can be useful for creating a period costume for characters in *The Crucible*, for example.

An infill can solve the problem of a neckline that is too low, as well as improving the appearance. Use lace or a contrasting stiff fabric.

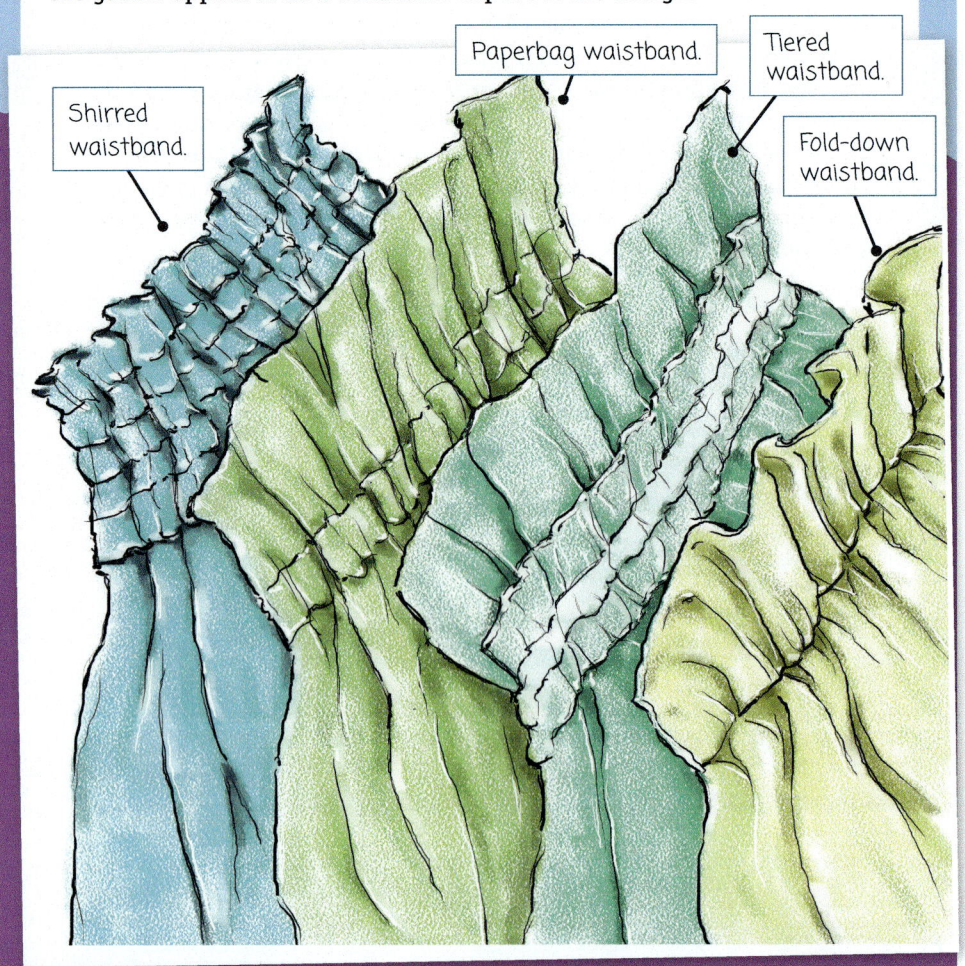

Button extenders can add a little more room and stretch to a waistband.

Frog fastenings change the style of a garment and could give you an extra inch of room.

Too small

It is often more difficult to add fabric than to take it away, but there are tricks that can solve the problem. If a garment pulls at the front because it is too tight, for example, you could move the buttons or change the type of fastening. Button extenders are useful too.

If skirts or trousers are too tight at the waist, you could move a button (or use extenders). If there is not a waistband, you could let out a seam. Another option would be to insert a panel of appropriate shape in a similar or contrasting fabric. You would probably need to cut the garment and use seams to insert extra fabric. Stretch fabrics would give extra ease. It is a good idea to balance the contrast fabric elsewhere on the costume if the panel is visible.

DESIGN TIP

Be adventurous! Costume design is a great opportunity to unleash your creativity.

Underwear matters

If the costume has a fitted silhouette, it is very important to consider what will be underneath it. For a good fit, you need to think about the style of underwear your actors should wear. Adding bra-strap loops to a neckline will keep straps hidden.

You might also need to advise your male actors on the question of briefs or boxers if it could affect the costume!

TASK 3.15

Select a garment that you are thinking of using for your costume. Try it on the actor and experiment with adjusting the fit using some of the techniques above.

Chapter 3   Practical Guide to Costume Design

COSTUME VOCABULARY

Accessories Items such as bags, jewellery and small items that accompany garments.

Allergy Natural or synthetic products that cause adverse reactions to skin etc.

Appliqué A small colourful piece of embroidery – often a picture or pattern – sewn onto an item of clothing.

Back stitch A closely worked stitch done by hand.

Bruise wheel Available from theatre make-up sellers, a palette of yellows, reds, browns and cream make-up, excellent for a range of special effects.

Collaboration Working with others towards a common aim.

Colour palette A complementary set of colours that belong to a group, such as pastel or dark.

Darting Sewing small, tapered folds into a garment to provide shape or otherwise alter the fit.

Embellishments Added extras such as lace, buttons, braids and so on; decorative details.

Evaluate Give an opinion, a value judgement, backed up with examples and reasons.

Fabric choice Considerations such as suitability and effect under lights.

Finish The surface of fabric – usually shiny or dull.

Freehand Drawing something without a tracing or template to guide you.

Mass-produced Made in great numbers, usually in a factory.

Monochrome Black, white and grey only.

Natural In terms of fabric – not man-made. Examples of natural fabric are cotton and wool.

Pattern Design printed onto or woven into fabric, including tartan, paisley, stripes. A paper pattern is the template pieces that guide sewers as they cut cloth out to make into garments.

Rehearsal costumes Practice clothes or shoes that bear some similarity to the final costume.

Run Either a rehearsal or read-through of the whole play, or the number of times a play will be performed (for example, *The Crucible* has a three-week run at this theatre).

Seam The joining of two pieces of fabric on the wrong side.

Silhouette The outline shape of a costume.

Status symbol A possession that is seen to show someone's wealth, social position or sense of style.

Style Distinctive appearance, often typical of a particular person, period or place.

Subculture A cultural trend in society that is not the dominant one, such as goth, punk.

Symbolic use of colour The use of colour to communicate a certain meaning or represent a particular theme or mood.

Stylised Non-realistic, non-naturalistic, where style features are dominant.

Swatch A small sample of fabric that gives an idea of how an item made from it would look and feel.

Synthetic Man-made (fabric).

Tacking A fast, long, hand-made, temporary stitch to hold seams together ready for trying on or for permanent stitching.

Texture The surface feel of fabric, for example. Raised fabrics, such as velvet and cord, have a different texture from smooth ones, such as silk, which are flat.

Upcycle Taking an existing garment and changing it in some way to make something different.

Wardrobe The wardrobe department is where the costumes are produced in a theatre. Alternatively, our wardrobe is the collection of clothes we own.

Weight How heavy or light is the fabric? Does it drape or hang heavily?

PRACTICAL GUIDE TO SOUND DESIGN

Chapter 4

Introduction to sound design	90
How to produce sound for the stage	92
Research for sound design	94
Sourcing, creating and mixing sounds	96
Health and safety in sound design	99
Special sound effects	100
How to document your sound design	102
Positioning sound equipment	104
Plotting the sound design	106
Operating sound equipment	108
Technical and dress rehearsals for sound designers	110
Evaluating your sound design	111
Sound design vocabulary	112

FOCUS

The power of sound in theatrical performance.

ASSESSMENT CHECK

This section develops your ability to 'create and develop ideas to communicate meaning for theatrical performance' (AO1).

You will learn how to use 'aural elements to create mood, atmosphere and style' and start to 'recognise and understand how theatrical choices are used by theatre makers to create impact', which will help you in Component 3.

INTRODUCTION TO SOUND DESIGN

Sound in the real world

Sound is one of the five senses that connect human beings with the world. We hear things in the womb before we are born, and it is generally accepted that hearing is the last sense to fail when we die. Sound is possibly the most evocative sensation.

We are not particularly conscious of many of the sounds that most of us hear every day. Traffic noises, people chatting, bird song, the wind and so on often fade into the background. Our brains filter them out so that we can focus on more important sounds.

Other sound choices, such as our ringtones and the volume of our video games, are very conscious. Similarly, we choose our music to suit our situation and the mood we want to create.

Then there are the sounds that are signals in our life, such as a doorbell, text alert, smoke detector or siren of an ambulance. This kind of sound alerts us to actions that we might need to take.

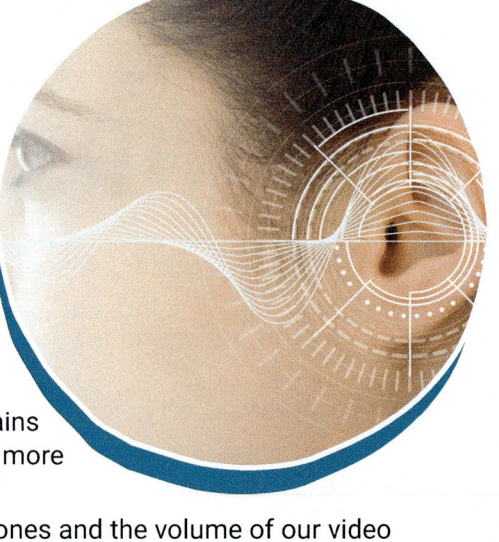

TASK 4.1

1. Take a few moments to listen carefully and identify all of the sounds you can hear right now. Note them in a chart like this one (some examples have been included for guidance.)

Sounds in life		
Closest sound: Computer whirring	**Sound(s) that suggest mood and atmosphere**: Breeze, clock ticking, songbirds, crows…	**Intermittent sound(s)**: Toddler whinging
Most distant sound: Football on playing field (whistle, shouts, ball being kicked)	**Constant sound(s)**: Clock ticking	**Other sounds**: Car door slamming

2. On a scale of 1 to 5, at what level of volume would you place each sound?
3. Finally, try to imagine the blend of sounds you are hearing as a **soundscape** for the stage. What sounds might you take out or add in order to add meaning or atmosphere?

Sound and the stage

In the theatre, the sound designer re-creates many different types of sound to convey meaning and add atmosphere to a production and fit into the harmonious world of the stage. Every sound is included for a reason, including those that help to create location. The sounds feed the imagination of the audience.

Different types of stage sound

There are broadly two types of theatre sound. **Diegetic sounds** are those that seem to come from the world of the stage, such as a scene's background noise, doorbells, music that is put on by an actor, phone ringtones. **Non-diegetic sounds** are those used to add mood and ambience for the audience, such as **atmospheric** sound effects and music. Non-diegetic sounds would not be 'heard' by the characters.

TASK 4.2

Look at this image on the right from *The 39 Steps*. Imagine you are creating a soundscape for it.

1. What sounds would you create? Describe them here.

An atmospheric soundscape	
Diegetic sounds	Non-diegetic sounds

2. For each sound, add a volume level from 1 to 5 to create the blend of sounds that you think is suitable. Think about the atmosphere you wish to create.

3. Using CDs, online sound effects and/or (with permission from your teacher) a smartphone, create a version of your soundscape. Even if you are not able yet to mix the sounds, you will be able to blend at least three.

4. Play your soundscape to others. Note their responses regarding the meaning and atmosphere your blend of sounds create for them.

- Was it what you hoped for?
- What could you change to achieve your desired effect?

Chapter 4 Practical Guide to Sound Design

FOCUS
The different equipment needed to produce stage sound.

ASSESSMENT CHECK
You need to show 'understanding of practical application of materials and production elements in performance.' This is the beginning of AO2: 'Apply theatrical skills to realise artistic intentions in live performance.' It will also help you to 'recognise specific challenges for designers' and 'analyse and evaluate production elements' in Component 3.

DESIGN TIP
If your mixing desk runs from a laptop, check what your operating system provides. Apple has a free version of *QLab*, for example, which enables you to mix and pre-programme sound **cues**.

HOW TO PRODUCE SOUND FOR THE STAGE

Resources for producing sound

Every professional designer needs to understand the mechanics of how sound is produced and most professionals will have significant skills and knowledge. Once you have gained a good understanding of the technical aspects of theatrical sound design, you will be able to unleash your creativity. At GCSE level, it is your design that is assessed, but you need to have sufficient knowledge and understanding to create and transmit sounds for the stage.

As a sound designer, your tools are:

- **sources** of sound (microphones, CDs, **digital** recordings, musical instruments)
- mixing desk (**manual** or digital) and **playback device**
- **amplifier** (produces the signals for the speakers)
- **speaker** (broadcasts the sound).

If we add an 'H' for the person who **h**ears the sound, we can make a mnemonic for the sequence of sound production:

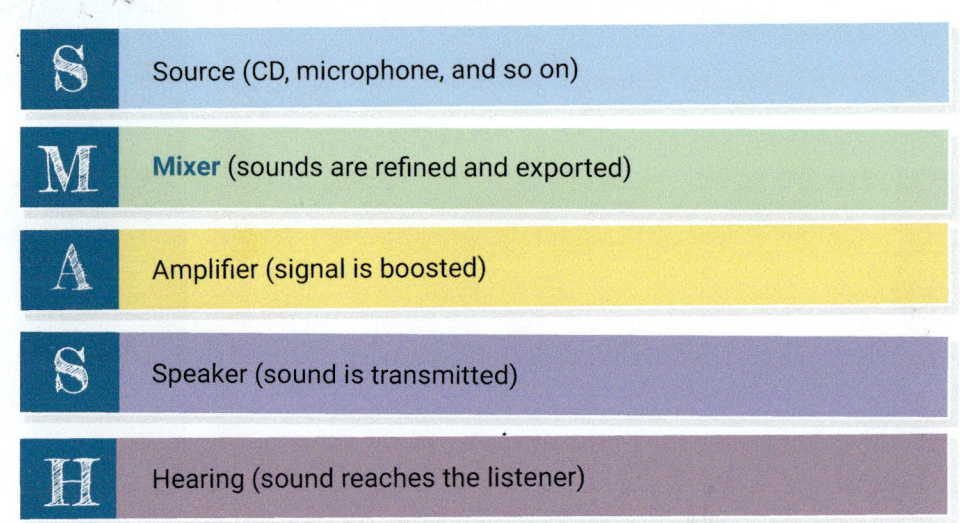

S — Source (CD, microphone, and so on)
M — **Mixer** (sounds are refined and exported)
A — Amplifier (signal is boosted)
S — Speaker (sound is transmitted)
H — Hearing (sound reaches the listener)

Getting to grips with your resources

Experiment with sound technology until you feel confident. It can be quite easy to produce impressive results.

TASK 4.3

Complete this table to take stock of the sound equipment you have available.

Number of speakers, their positions and if they can be moved	Mixing desk: manual or electronic? Number of channels?	Playback device: type and details	Other resources

Chapter 4 Practical Guide to Sound Design

Sound sources

The source of a sound is simply the place where you 'grab' the sound you want. You can find a piece of music, for example, on a CD, online music service or, with the help of microphones, from live instruments or voices.

Mixing desk

As its name suggests, a sound mixer is the device where a designer or technician refines and blends sounds. Digital mixers are more complex than manual ones, but work on the same principles.

If you don't have a mixing desk, sounds can be mixed and edited in software and played through a computer or amplifier during the performance.

> The input section is where the raw sound enters the system. You can then balance the sound. This might be to equalise it (improve tone) and add effects (such as **reverb**). Several channels mean you can mix several sounds.

> Once the sounds have been adjusted, a **fader** is used to set the volume of each sound. Each input can then be routed to one or all of the outputs.

> The output section also has faders. These are where the final volume for the blend of sounds is adjusted. The mixed sound(s) go from here to the amplifier(s).

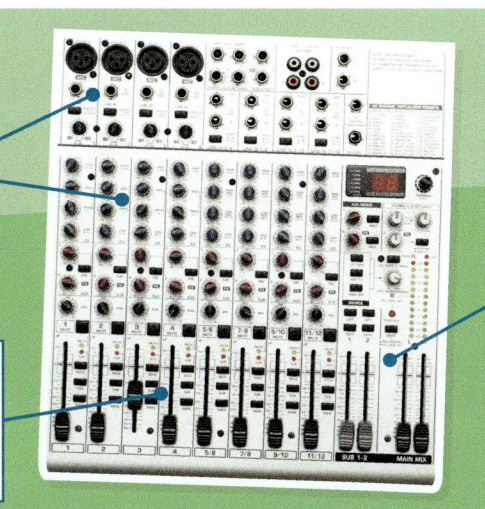

Amplifier

To amplify means 'to make louder or bigger'. In sound design, the amplifier (amp) boosts the signal from the mixing desk to a level where it can be 'read' by the speakers.

Some venues have more than one amplifier. One might connect to the speakers on stage, for example, and another to speakers in the audience.

Speaker

Speakers might be the piece of equipment you are most familiar with. They broadcast sound! Find out early on what speakers you have and whether they are fixed or moveable.

Microphones

In larger spaces, performers sometimes struggle to make themselves heard. This is an issue for sound designers, particularly as you might want to use other sounds under dialogue. In a smaller space, you might not need a microphone, but might want to create specific effects, such as a voice-over.

Radio mics are used in many theatres to amplify actors' voices. Your school or college might have some or can hire them. If so, it is part of your job to make sure they are working and fitted properly.

Floating mics tend to be positioned at the front of the stage. They can be problematic unless used and positioned carefully. They tend to pick up unwanted sounds, such as footsteps on stage.

Hanging mics are suspended above the stage. Again, they will pick up all the sounds on the stage, not just voices.

DESIGN TIP
Store all your sourced sound effects into a computer file in a folder that you can find easily for editing and/or mixing.

LOOK HERE
For more on using sound software, see page 109. For advice on positioning speakers, see page 104.

Chapter 4   Practical Guide to Sound Design   93

FOCUS

Developing ideas and making approximate costings of equipment and materials.

ASSESSMENT CHECK

This element will help you to 'make appropriate judgements during the development process' and further your understanding of 'production elements and theatrical conventions'.

TASK 4.5

Repeat Task 4.4, but search specifically for clips from musical theatre. **Analyse** the sounds using the same table.

RESEARCH FOR SOUND DESIGN

Where can I find inspiration for sound design?

If you are new to sound design, an effective and fun way to learn is to study how the professionals work.

TASK 4.4

1. Search the internet for something like 'best sound design'. It should produce a wide choice of videos and articles to inspire you. They might be mainly about film sound, but the basic ideas are the same. Watch, listen and read, and use your notebook!

2. Now turn away from your screen as you play some film trailers. Listen carefully, using headphones if possible. You should be impressed by the clever use of sound to create mood and atmosphere as well as suggesting location, **genre** and style. One trailer for *La Haine*, for example, ends with the slam of a garage door. It is highly effective!

3. Fill out a version of the following table using two or three different film trailers. (This example is based on *Titanic*.)

Analysis of sound design: film trailers	
Title: *Titanic*	
Use of voice (dialogue, monologue, voiceover)	**Montage** of character voices. Short clips from key moments in film. Chilling shouts and screams gradually increase after ship hits iceberg.
Diegetic sound	Waves. Water gushing into the ship. Hull creaking slowly.
Non-diegetic sound	**Echo** on voices suggests the past. Bells (single chimes) are like ship bells and church bells at a funeral. These bells are at the start and end of the trailer.
Music	Orchestral soundtrack suggests romance, drama and tension at different moments. Use of Celine Dion song is moving.
Impact on audience	Strong sense of genre – Action and Romance comes from music and sound effects. Layering of music, dialogue and effects creates different atmospheres. Excitement, panic and sorrow suggested by varied **pace** and volume.
Useful ideas for my stage sound design	Different volumes and pace of music and sound create different moods. Could I use actors' voices off stage to suggest memories? A simple sound could be repeated at different moments to suggest theme or time passing (motif).

Chapter 4 Practical Guide to Sound Design

Finding the sounds you need

If you need an ambulance siren, you will probably need to look online. There are many websites that provide free sound effects. Others might charge a small fee. There are also sound effects CDs available. Some are general; others specific. Don't buy any until you know just what you need.

There is also the possibility of recording your own effects. For instance, you might not be able to find the exact playground sound effect that you want. You could take out a microphone with a simple recording device (or possibly a smartphone) to record the right sound.

Don't settle for the first effect you find. Select the effect that exactly fits the meaning, mood and style for your drama piece.

TASK 4.6

1. Search 'temple bell sound' on the internet. You should discover many versions that you can listen to without paying for or downloading.
2. Choose one that you think would work well diegetically in a **naturalistic** setting, for example, when a character visits a temple.
3. Now choose another that you might use in a non-diegetic way. For example, to represent a character having an idea.
4. Think about what it was that made you choose each sound. What mood or atmosphere did each effect create?

How do I find technical sound support?

If you are not quite confident yet, or need further help:

Read...
For additional technical information, refer to stage sound books.

Watch...
There are many online videos and guides that should help.

Ask...
Consider your human resources. Are there people in your school who could help? Approach the music department. They are very likely to have staff and students with the skills you need.

Visit...
Local theatres should have a sound specialist. They will probably be keen to share their expertise. Is there a local youth theatre that encourages technicians as well as performers?

Continuous research

Make sure that you visit your group's rehearsals regularly. You are likely to be inspired with new ideas, or note the need for:

- new or different sound effects
- opportunities for performers to be involved with sound effects.

If you discover that your performers do need radio mics, or you want to use floating mics, for example, find out if you can hire them.

ASSESSMENT CHECK

Pinning down the sounds you need shows that you are 'applying theatrical skills to realise artistic intentions in live performance' (AO2) and 'demonstrate knowledge and understanding of how theatre is developed and performed' (AO3).

DESIGN TIP

Always make notes on your research to include in your portfolio or supporting documents. Examiners will be impressed by your ability to go into the community as part of your research.

DESIGN TIP

The more you experiment, the more you will discover. Your knowledge and skills will really develop and improve and you will have plenty to write about in Component 1, for example.

FOCUS
Combining sounds and being adventurous as you put your sound design together.

ASSESSMENT CHECK
Choosing, finding and building sounds are important aspects of 'creating and developing ideas to communicate meaning for theatrical performance' (AO1). You are also beginning to 'apply theatrical skills to realise artistic intentions in live performance' (AO2) and developing 'knowledge and understanding of how drama and theatre is developed and performed' (AO3).

DESIGN TIP
If permitted, you could download suitable software or an app so that a phone or tablet could be used as a recording device.

DESIGN TIP
Listen out for what you don't want to hear! Recording an outdoor sound on a windy day, for example, is pretty much impossible.

Do we have to pay for the music we use?
Your school or college will have its own policy regarding copyright and royalties, and might already have a licence to play your choices of music to the general public. It can be a complicated issue, so make sure you check with your teachers.

SOURCING, CREATING AND MIXING SOUNDS

Can I make my own recordings?
You might want, for example, the sound effect of a bath filling or emptying. It is possible to create it yourself – with a recording device and patience. How authentic it sounds is something you will need to discover! You might end up with something different but magical. Simply taking a recording device out and about with you and recording in different locations can provide very useful sound material. Similarly, experimenting with musical instruments can produce effects that will be unique to your design.

Styles and places
Trying different locations for your effect recordings can produce interesting variations. Recording in a small space like a bathroom will generate a different effect from that in a big, empty space. Experiment to find styles of sound that suit your group's artistic intentions.

Music
You are familiar with where to find the music you like. You might be knowledgeable about different types and styles of music. But, can you select music that will enhance the performance you are involved in?

TASK 4.7

Imagine you are working on a devised piece about the threat of climate change. The **structure** is episodic, and the style is **non-naturalistic**. You need to find a piece of music to use during each scene change. Research three different types of music that might be suitable; then complete the following chart.

Specific music requirement: Scene changes		
Music type	Suggested piece	Notes on meaning and atmosphere
Classical music (Orchestral? Chamber?)		
Modern instrumental (Atmospheric?)		
Contemporary song with lyrics (Try your own ideas here.)		

Chapter 4 Practical Guide to Sound Design

How do I create a particular mood for a scene?

Your sound design is made up of all the individual sounds you source and mix. They must have a sense of belonging together.

Let's suppose that you want non-diegetic sound or some music that will build tension or romance underneath onstage dialogue. This is **underscoring**.

You might find music tracks that are up to 15 minutes long, so you should be able to find a piece suitable for your scene. If you have the right technical equipment (*Audacity*, for example), you can edit tracks to put together particular sections.

DESIGN TIP

If you are searching online for underscoring pieces, try something like 'ambient soundtrack'. Streaming services like Spotify are a good place to start.

MIXING SOUND

Live mixing

Live mixing of sounds occurs in performance. At some point, you will probably want to combine sounds. This is done by bringing up individual channels on your mixing desk so that sounds come in, are added to and are taken out. This is fine as long as you are not setting yourself too many things to do at once. You can set volume levels during the **plotting** process (see 'Plotting the sound design', on pages 106–107).

Pre-recording soundscapes

You could combine a number of sounds onto a single track to make operating easier. If you have sound-mixing software, you will be able to do this quite easily. You could start with some music as your base sound, for example. Then, using timing controls, set sound effects, such as echoing voices and a siren, to come in and go out automatically. You can set the relative volume levels as you go along. Then, come performance time, it is simply a matter of hitting the space bar on your laptop!

TASK 4.8

Experiment with both live and pre-recorded mixing if you can.
- Which method do you prefer? Why?
- Which will be most useful or effective in your performance?

Live sound effects

Does all my sound design have to be recorded?

It is most certainly possible to create **live sound** during the performance. You could play a musical instrument, for example, create thunder with a metal sheet, or ring a real school hand bell.

Depending on the style of your production, the performers could create sound effects as part of your sound design. A **drone**, for example, can be made by the cast, or they could make percussion sounds by tapping different parts of their bodies or costumes. Generally, this kind of sound design suits a non-naturalistic performance style.

In one production of Richard Shannon's play *Sabbat*, performers made whistling noises with their voices and also used an old wind machine to create atmosphere. The audience saw them creating their own sound effects and it had a powerful impact. In this scene, an actor plays hand bells to accompany a song. (Music and sound design by John Biddle.)

ASSESSMENT CHECK

In creating your own sounds, you will show secure 'understanding of the practical application of materials and production elements in performance.'

DESIGN TIP

You, and your performers, will need plenty of practice for live sounds to be successful in the performance.

TASK 4.9

Think about the performance you are working on now or a one you were recently involved in. Find a particular moment in the piece at which a live sound effect could be included.
- Why is that moment suitable?
- What sound effect would you use?
- How would the effect be produced?
- What impact are you trying to achieve?

TASK 4.10

Study the sound design ideas you have so far. Where might a period of silence be effective?

Silence has impact

Silence has a definite place in sound design. In a performance that might be quite full of dialogue, music and sound effects, quietness can make a significant impact. It gives time for the audience to pause and think and, depending where the silence is placed, can be a very effective contribution to mood and atmosphere.

Chapter 4   Practical Guide to Sound Design

HEALTH AND SAFETY IN SOUND DESIGN

Using your common sense

Many dangerous situations can be avoided when people are sensible. Here are some basic issues to be aware of when using sound equipment:

Hazards	Safety measures
Loose or unsafe electrical cables.	Tape them down or cordon off the area. Don't use electric cables outdoors.
Damaged cables or electrical items. Lack of or out-of-date PAT test label.	Report the problem immediately to someone in authority.
Having the wrong tool for a job, such as a knife instead of a screwdriver.	Find out what the right tool is and make sure it is available and used.
Damaging ear drums. This applies to people wearing headphones as well as in the rehearsal and performances spaces.	Check – beforehand – that volume levels are not too loud.
Startling people with sudden, loud sounds during rehearsals. Negative effects of sudden loud noises or loud continuous sound.	Fade sounds in during practice sessions. Warn people if you are about to bring up loud sounds. Monitor sound levels carefully. Post a notice in the show programme or in the performance space as a warning.

FOCUS
Some rules and reminders for keeping yourself and others safe.

ASSESSMENT CHECK
Throughout Components 1 and 2, you 'must be aware of any health and safety considerations and implications.' It forms part of your portfolio.

This is also covered in AO3: 'Demonstrate knowledge and understanding of how drama and theatre is developed and performed.'

DESIGN TIP
In practice, health and safety needs to be your top priority!

Chapter 4 Practical Guide to Sound Design

FOCUS
Adding extra features to your sounds.

ASSESSMENT CHECK
Complexity in your sound design shows that you can 'create an assured design, demonstrating an accomplished ability to employ and combine skills. All aspects of design are highly engaging, dynamic and skilful.' Your experiments and choices help you to 'apply theatrical skills to realise artistic intentions in live performance' (AO2).

SPECIAL SOUND EFFECTS

What are special effects in sound?

As with lighting special effects, it can be tricky to decide what makes a special effect as opposed to a regular sound effect. For now, we will define a special sound effect as one that has additional features such as reverb, echo and **pitch-shift**.

You can add these effects to voices, instruments and other sounds.

Reverb

Reverb is short for 'reverberation'. Sound waves hit surrounding surfaces and we hear the original sound plus its sound reflections. Reverb is always there to some degree, but we don't often notice it. Reverb **is** noticeable when we increase the effect of sound bouncing back to us. This adds depth and fullness to a sound. The sound becomes somehow longer and weightier. It then gradually dies away.

You can record a sound effect in a specific space to affect the reverb acoustically.

TASK 4.11

Take a simple recording device (a phone with a suitable app is fine) to a variety of spaces, such as a cupboard or small bathroom and a large hard-surfaced space such as a sports hall.

In each space, record your voice saying the same thing. You could also take a percussion instrument to experiment with.

- Which space(s) gives you the most reverb?
- Why do you think that is?
- Can you describe what you do and do not like about the special effect created?
- Is there a moment in your devised or scripted piece where it would be useful?

Echo

Echo is another specific quality that can be added to an existing sound effect. Echoes occur when sound bounces off surfaces that are at least 17 metres away from the source of the sound. Echo is different from reverb: the sound has time to repeat rather than blend into the original one.

How do I add reverb and echo?

You can add these effects easily and effectively with the help of technology:
- Digital **sound desks** are likely to have reverb and echo settings.
- *QLab* (the Mac sound programme) and Windows-compatible software, such as *Audacity* and *CSC Show Control*, should have reverb built into them.

Your music department might have a reverb unit you can feed into your mixing desk. Most reverb units have a range of settings, which could include echo.

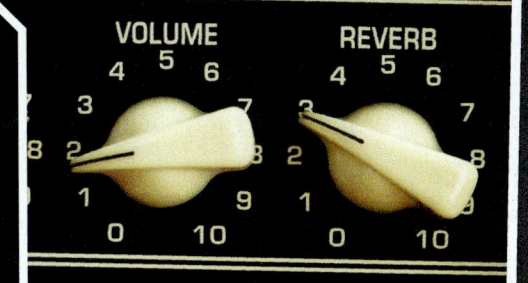

TASK 4.12

Using reverb or echo to add meaning or atmosphere

1 Choose a sound effect from the design you are working on. Alternatively, think of a sound that is rather 'flat', such as a ball thudding onto a rug or long grass.
2 Fill in the following table. (An example has been included to guide you.)

Sound effect	Echo or reverb	Notes on the special effect and meaning or atmosphere
Pre-recorded voice of narrator	Auditorium-style reverb added	• Reverb gave the narrator's voice much more depth. • It sounds more important and more powerful.

This vintage guitar amplifier has a reverb control.

Pitch-shifting

People might think about singers who can't stay in tune when they consider pitch-shifting! There are many uses for this technology, however. You could alter a sound effect, for example, by having three differently pitched versions of the same effect. One would be left at its original pitch. One could be pitch-shifted to 10 per cent below the original, and the third copy could be pitch-shifted to 10 per cent above. The final version – the three mixed together – should have a richer, thicker sound.

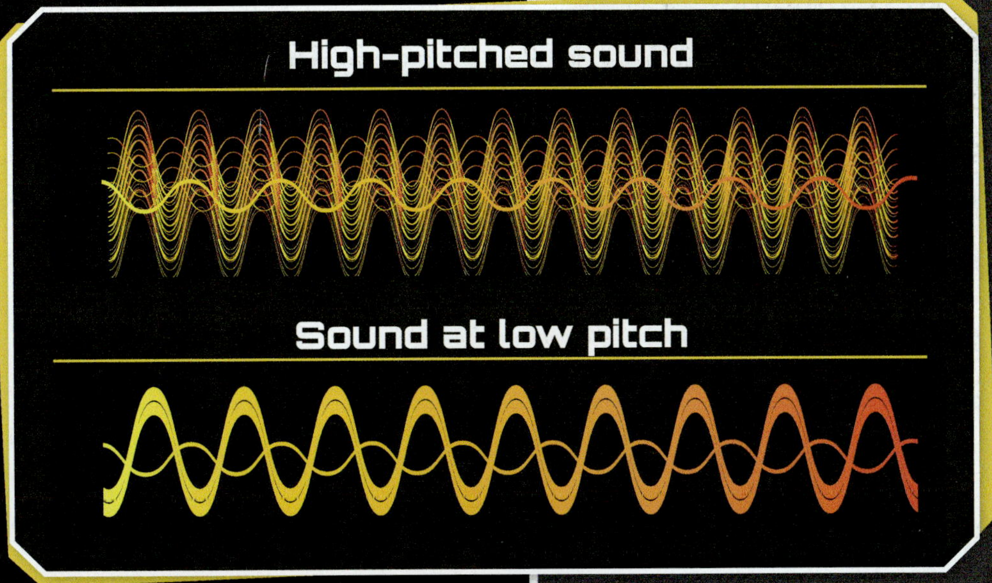

High-pitched sound

Sound at low pitch

TASK 4.13

1 Pick one of the additional special effects in this section (reverb, echo or pitch-shift).
2 Conduct some research and explore the effect in practice on some potential sounds for your design.
3 Create a short presentation for other students who are interested in sound design, or for other members of your performance group. (Your presentation could be live or recorded.) Explain the impressions the different effects should make on the listener.

DESIGN TIP

By experimenting, you will discover what type of special effect lends the right meaning and atmosphere to your sound design.

Chapter 4 Practical Guide to Sound Design 101

FOCUS
Examples and guidance to help you prepare the plans and charts you need.

ASSESSMENT CHECK
'Creating a clear and practical design' and showing 'confident and accomplished use of appropriate drama terminology' is demonstrated well through the documentation needed for sound design.

LOOK HERE
These sound design documents fit the *Hansel and Gretel* extracts in Chapter 6.

TASK 4.14
1. Practise drawing up each type of document as you go along with your design, so that you are confident by the time you are working on an actual production.
2. Work through all of the types of document detailed here in the order they appear.

LOOK HERE
If you are devising, go through the stages in 'Sound Design for the Devised Piece', beginning page 157.

Task 4.18 on page 107 provides detail on how to use your cue sheet when plotting your sound design.

HOW TO DOCUMENT YOUR SOUND DESIGN

What documents do I need to produce?

You need to create a source sheet, which details whether each sound you use is live or a piece of **recorded sound**. You are also required to put forward a **cue sheet**, which shows the source, order, length and output level of each cue.

These plans and tables can look complicated, but the advice on these pages will help you to complete excellent documents.

Why do I need to create these documents?

Source and cue sheets provide the sound operator (whether this is your or a technician) with plans to follow.

The documents will help you practically as well as going in your portfolio and being seen by the examiner who watches the scripted performances.

A sound plan is not essential, but does show you (or anyone else) what speakers are used and where they should be positioned. It should include a key that explains any symbols used in it.

The completed cue sheet and source sheet contain all the information needed to complete the design and operate the sound during the production.

Source sheet

A simple list like this is fine:

Sound	Source
Introduction music	Found
Owl hoots in the distance	Found
Sound montage of wind with occasional owl hoot	Mixed from two found sources
Suspense music underscore	Original
Cockerel crowing in the distance	Found
Gentle wind with birdsong	Mixed from two found sources
Forest effect	Mixed from three found sources
Fire effect	Found
Thunder clap	Found

Cue sheet

You cannot plot the sound for the production until you know what your music and effects are going to be. So, you will already have marked your sound ideas on your script or notes. You might even have an early version of a cue sheet as well as a source sheet.

The key to the sound plan on the following page explains the different types of speaker that are detailed in a cue sheet.

LOOK HERE
A detailed sound cue sheet for *Hansel and Gretel* is available on the *Designing Drama* product page at illuminatepublishing.com.

Sound plan

This diagram is not essential, but will be useful (and should be included in your portfolio if you design sound in Component 1, for example). It shows the positioning and type of speakers to be used in the production.

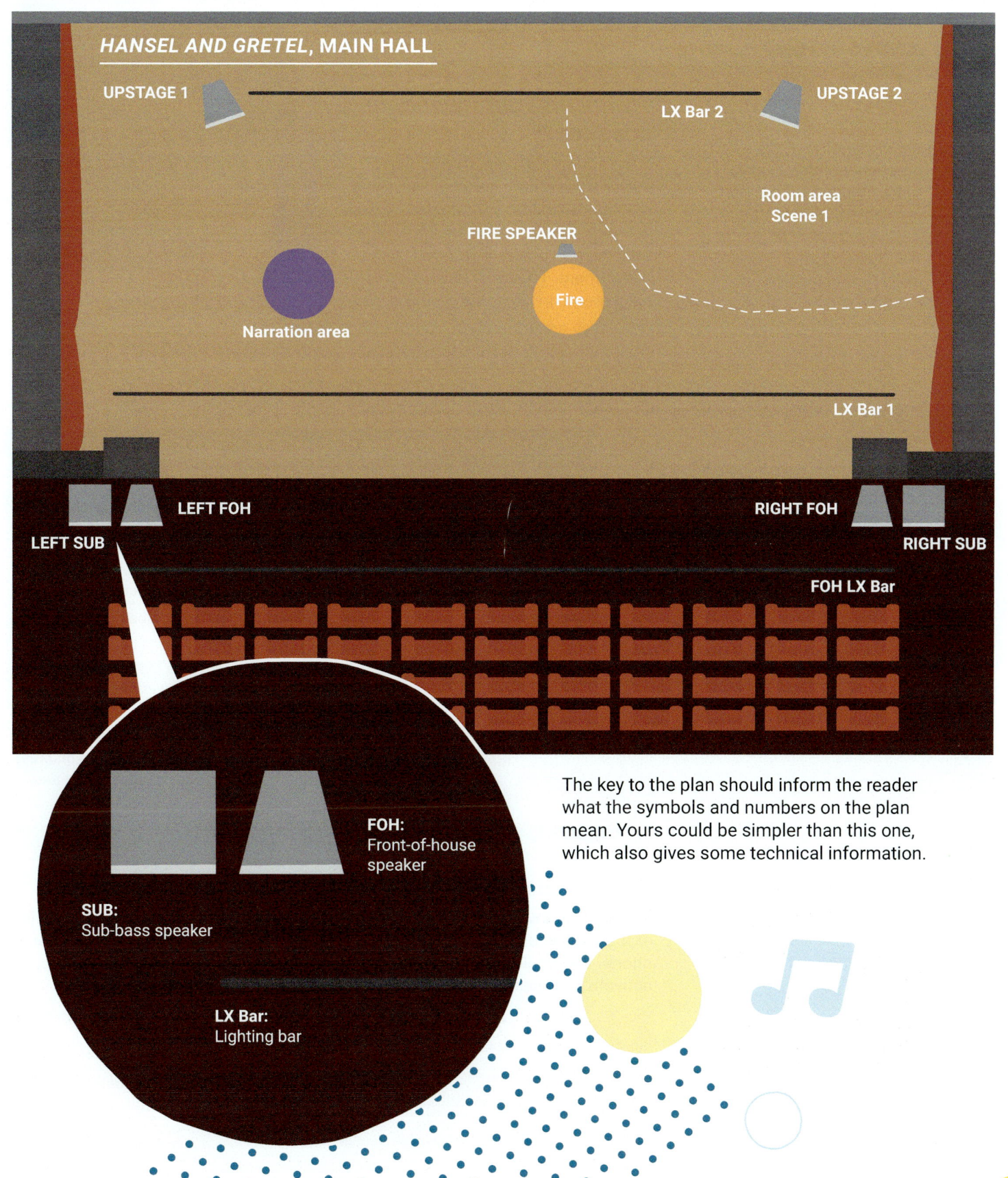

HANSEL AND GRETEL, MAIN HALL

- UPSTAGE 1
- UPSTAGE 2
- LX Bar 2
- Room area Scene 1
- FIRE SPEAKER
- Fire
- Narration area
- LX Bar 1
- LEFT FOH
- RIGHT FOH
- LEFT SUB
- RIGHT SUB
- FOH LX Bar

FOH: Front-of-house speaker

SUB: Sub-bass speaker

LX Bar: Lighting bar

The key to the plan should inform the reader what the symbols and numbers on the plan mean. Yours could be simpler than this one, which also gives some technical information.

Chapter 4   Practical Guide to Sound Design

FOCUS
How to place sound equipment carefully in the performance space.

ASSESSMENT CHECK
This section will help you to gain 'sound understanding of the practical application of materials and production elements in performance'. This is part of AO2, where you must 'apply theatrical skills to realise artistic intentions.'

DESIGN TIP
Add your own notes to the table as you progress with your design.

POSITIONING SOUND EQUIPMENT

An important aspect of your sound design and practical skills is taking care with the placement of your speakers and sound desk.

As a general rule, you would have at least one speaker for each section of the audience.

Where do I put moveable speakers?

If the sound speakers in your performance area are fixed, you need to consider that in your design. It is likely, however, that there will be some speakers that you can position yourself. Ask the music department. The table below indicates ideal placements in common configurations.

Once they are in position, you might need to secure speakers with safety bonds or cargo straps.

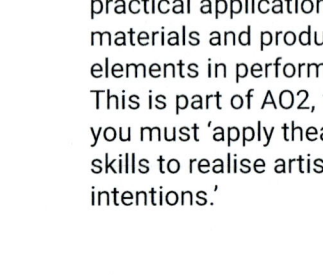

Minimum number of speakers and their positions		
Stage configuration	Position of speakers	Notes
Proscenium arch / end on	Front of stage – left and right	If possible, all speakers should be positioned at ear height for the audience.
Traverse	Facing the audience from the acting area (minimum of 2)	See above.
Thrust	Front and sides of stage (3 in total)	See above.
In the round	All four sides, facing the audience	Ideally, these speakers would be hung discreetly above the acting area.

Are mini-speakers useful?

The short answer is that it depends on your sound design. One good example of their use is on stage as part of a diegetic sound device, such as a radio or phone. You could use a powerful bluetooth speaker that the performers would activate themselves.

TASK 4.15
Draw a plan diagram of your performance space. Pick a simple icon to show the position of your speakers. Be sure to mark the position(s) of the audience too.

Note that 'left' and 'right' in sound usually refers to the audience's right and left, rather than stage left and stage right. (Think about where the sound operator is likely to be.)

Sub-bass speakers produce very low-frequency sounds. They produce the 'thump' in music tracks. They can be useful for sound effects such as thunder.

FOH speakers produce mid- to high-frequency sounds and are the most common type in school halls, for example.

The fire speaker in the plan on page 103 is a small speaker concealed within the fire set on stage and used to make fire crackle sounds. As in lighting, this kind of speaker is called a 'special'.

Is there an ideal place to position the sound desk?

The ideal position for the sound desk is in the audience area. (Why do you think this is?)

In some venues, there is a 'box' at the back of the auditorium where technical equipment is fixed. Sometimes, these have a sliding window that allows the sound operator to hear what the audience is hearing.

The other element to consider is communication with the lighting operator. There are likely to be times when lighting and sound effects should be **synchronised**. If they can't sit near each other, how could the operators for sound and lighting communicate?

TASK 4.16

1. Walk your performance space with your teacher or other human resource. Identify the ideal location for your sound desk and establish whether it is a practical and safe site.
2. When you have settled on the best place for the sound operating equipment, use a simple icon to add to the diagram that you made in Task 4.15. Add a key to your sketch.

Chapter 4 Practical Guide to Sound Design

FOCUS
Creating the cue sheet that will guide you through a performance.

ASSESSMENT CHECK
A cue sheet is a requirement for Components 1 and 2. It will show 'understanding of practical application and production elements' and 'demonstrate an accomplished and comprehensive interpretation of the text, showing sustained and assured support for the performance.'

DESIGN TIP
Don't try to plot the performance until you have sourced your sounds and know where in the performance you are putting them!

DESIGN TIP
Remember that your design should indicate at least **four** sound cues in Component 1, and at least **two** in Component 2.

PLOTTING THE SOUND DESIGN

As sound designer, you are contributing to and supporting a performance as a whole. So, the sound operator needs to be able to run the 'sound show' smoothly and accurately. Plotting the sound and creating the cue sheet makes this possible.

What is plotting sound?

In this book, we use the term **plotting** to mean the act of fixing the sound for every part of the production. The **cue sheet** should record details of every sound cue decided. If you have sound design software, record each cue digitally as you go along.

You will need to make several decisions for each cue, including:

- what the sound is and from where it is sourced
- when it happens
- how loud it is
- how long it lasts (Does it snap off or fade?)
- what sounds are combined (if not plotted in software)
- the type and length of transitions.

Conditions for successful sound plotting

Don't underestimate the amount of time plotting will take. You might need more than one session if the performance is lengthy or complex.

- Make sure you plot sound in the performance space that you will be using!
- Choose a time when you can have the space to yourself. There is no point trying to plot during a rehearsal or when people are talking loudly. Setting volume levels, for instance, requires quiet and concentration.
- Collect everything you need, including:
  - your annotated script and notes
  - sound equipment
  - prepared sound effects
  - a task light (such as an angle-poise lamp)
  - a template for your cue sheet.
- You might also find it useful to ask an assistant to read lines of dialogue and check volume in various parts of the audience areas.

Understanding the terminology of sound levels

Unless you have worked with a sound desk before, you would probably expect that 0 on a fader would mean that the sound was off... In fact, sound is measured in decibels, which is a complex unit using a scale. All you really need to know is that 0 decibels is in fact quite loud.

> **TASK 4.17**
>
> Experiment with the faders on your sound desk, keeping your drama piece in mind. Make notes for yourself or use masking tape to label points on the scales that are quiet, average and loud.

Creating your cue sheet

When you have good sound conditions and clear understanding of both your design and the technology, you are ready to plot the production.

> **TASK 4.18**
>
> 1. Lay your script and a cue sheet template around your sound desk. If you have a software package for storing your cues, bring it into action.
> 2. Starting at the beginning of the show, work through the production cue by cue and scene by scene to build and chart each sound cue. (An example is given to show you how it works.)
> 3. Check that cue numbers are clearly and correctly marked in your script so that the operator can track approaching cues. You could add '6a', '6b' and so on, if needed.
> 4. Continue to fill in your cue sheet until you have plotted the entire production.
>
> **Sound cue sheet**
>
> | Cue number and script page | Cue signal | Sound | Playback device (if more than one) | Level (dB) | Transition | Notes with timings |
> |---|---|---|---|---|---|---|
> | 1 pre-set | House open | Play music | CD player | −10 | | Pre-set from time house is open. Visual. |
> | 2 p1 | Visual – actors walk on | Music off | | All out | Fade out | Over 10 seconds (in time with lighting transition). |
> | 3 p3 | "Come over here!" | Soundscape 1 | Laptop | +6 | Fade up | Over 5 seconds – gradual fade up. |

DESIGN TIP

Take your time with plotting. Continue to check that you are supporting the artistic intentions of the piece. If you miss a cue, add it later, as '3a', for example.

ASSESSMENT CHECK

Here, you are 'applying theatrical skills to realise artistic intentions in live performance' (AO2).

Chapter 4 Practical Guide to Sound Design 107

FOCUS
Making sure everything runs smoothly.

ASSESSMENT CHECK
Rehearsals allow you to:
- 'make appropriate judgements during the development process'
- 'adapt designs in response to rehearsals'
- 'demonstrate the ability to apply design skills effectively within the context of performance'
- 'apply theatrical skills to realise artistic intentions in live performance' (AO2).

LOOK HERE
The notes on pages 108–109 will help you to put everything in place before the tech.

DESIGN TIP
If you are using *QLab* or *SCS*, the software can trigger sound cues as well as lighting ones. This can be very useful if you want to precisely co-ordinate a blackout, for example.

DESIGN TIP
Sound levels vary depending on how full the space is. So, you might need to turn up the volume if you have a full house!

TECHNICAL AND DRESS REHEARSALS FOR SOUND DESIGNERS

The final rehearsals are your chance to check that you have a creative sound design that works well in practice. You might have a lot of equipment to set up, so try to complete this before the technical rehearsal ('tech').

The technical rehearsal

Techs are lengthy because they must allow lighting and sound operators to test their designs. At the same time, the director and other designers are checking that other aspects of the production are working smoothly.

Decide as a group whether to run the performance in full or move from cue to cue, missing out some sections. Make sure that everyone is confident that the process can then be repeated without interruptions.

As sound designer, you are likely to be heavily involved in the tech. If someone else is operating the sound, you need to guide them through the cues and make adjustments to levels, timings of fades and so on.

You will also need to watch the acting area to check the following points.

- Are sound effects and music coming in and going out correctly?
- Is sound that involves the performers managed successfully?
- Is the music long enough to cover scene changes, for example?
- Does the music or sound effect fit the piece as intended?
- Do any vocals in music or effects clash with dialogue?
- Is timing with lighting correct?
- Are any long pieces of underscoring at a suitable level? Should this vary in sympathy with the action?

You (or an assistant) should also move around the audience area to hear volume levels. It is likely that levels and timings will need to change for some cues. Set these as you go along, even if it means holding up the tech for a couple of minutes.

If you or the sound operator are struggling with a technical aspect, ask your group if you can run a cue again. This is the purpose of the tech.

TASK 4.20
1. Update your notebook and script with any issues to be resolved before the dress rehearsal.
2. Arrange some time to work things through with other designers.

The dress rehearsal

The dress rehearsal ('dress') runs through the whole production without interruption. The performers can experience the full show with all the technical elements, but without an audience. You can test that the sound design can be operated successfully and works effectively in performance.

EVALUATING YOUR SOUND DESIGN

Once you are clear about what **evaluation** is and the best way of approaching it, you can focus on assessing the success of your sound design.

Examining the detail of your design

You need to provide a careful evaluation of your design skills demonstrated in performance. The only way that you can do this really well is to give detailed examples.

Whenever you evaluate, you should make at least three different points. These points should be illustrated with specific examples. Each time, you should also explain the reason why you have made a particular value judgement. You should highlight things that could have gone better.

It is very important to compare your finished sound design against your artistic intentions. Check your notes and make sure you include the success of this aspect in your evaluation.

Try not to repeat yourself when you evaluate. Discuss different types of sound and use a wide technical vocabulary.

TASK 4.21

1. Complete a table like this (some examples have been suggested). The notes will provide a solid basis for your evaluation writing.

Design element	Example / moment in the play	Evaluation	Reason for evaluation
Pre-set music	Before the performance began.	Engaging. Helped to create mood and place piece in time.	The music was chosen to put the audience into the right time period and to create the mood we wanted in our artistic intentions for the start of the piece.
Underscoring	The increasingly tense duologue between the two characters.	Atmospheric and contributed to action.	The underscoring track that I mixed included the use of reverb, which added depth. The pace increased as it went along, but was quiet enough for the actors' voices to be heard clearly.
The live sound from the performers	The end of the piece.	Successfully performed. Suited the ending.	As the performers linked hands and moved around the stage, they used their voices to make a humming sound. As they varied pitch and volume, there was a strong sense of their connection. I do wish that it could have been a little louder.

2. Expand your notes into three paragraphs of evaluative writing.

FOCUS
Placing a value judgement on design.

ASSESSMENT CHECK
This part of the design process is the essential element of AO4: 'Analyse and evaluate your own work and the work of others.'

SIGNPOST
Use the evaluation guidance on page 30 before you start.

DESIGN TIP
No process is complete until you reflect upon it. Evaluation is a skill that will be important in all your exam subjects.

SOUND DESIGN VOCABULARY

Amplifier A piece of equipment that produces the sound for the speakers, primarily used to increase volume.

Analyse Examine in detail, thinking about parts in relation to the whole.

Atmospheric A sound, for example, that creates a strong feeling or mood.

Constant sound An uninterrupted sound.

Cue sheet A list of cues with timings.

Cue to cue Going through a play from one sound or lighting cue to the next, missing out the parts in between.

Diegetic sound A sound that the characters would hear within their world, such as a phone ringing.

Digital Using computer technology. Digital lighting desks, for example, are programmed using software.

Drone A constant sound that is often in the background. Drones are often used in non-naturalistic sound effects and are very good for creating atmosphere such as tension.

Echo The effect that occurs when a sound bounces off surfaces.

End on A stage configuration that places the audience on one side of an open stage.

Evaluate Give an opinion, a value judgement, backed up with examples and reasons.

Fade A gradual transition from quiet to loud, or vice versa.

Fader A device to control the volume of a sound.

Floating mic A microphone positioned on the front of the stage.

Hanging mic A microphone suspended above the performance area.

Intermittent sound A sound that is not constant; it comes and goes.

Live sound A sound that is played directly for the audience.

Manual Operated by hand, rather than digitally.

Mixer A device that can change and combine sounds.

Montage A sequence or joining together of sounds to make a new piece of sound.

Naturalistic A set or lighting effect, for example, with characteristics of reality; having the appearance of a real place.

Non-diegetic sound Sound that can be heard by the audience, but would not be heard by the characters (such as atmospheric music to encourage the audience to feel something).

Non-naturalistic A set or lighting design, for example, that aims not to appear like reality.

Pace The speed with which lighting or sound effects transition from one to the next.

Pitch-shifting Altering the pitch of a sound which, when mixed with other differently pitched versions of the same sound, makes it have a richer, thicker sound.

Playback device The means through which recorded sound is played, such as a CD player or smartphone.

Plotting The process of creating a cue sheet to show choices of what sound happens when.

Proscenium (arch) A stage configuration where the audience are where the 'fourth wall' of a room would be – similar to **end on**, but with the addition of a picture-frame effect around the stage.

Radio mic A microphone that is worn by a performer, often taped to the cheek.

Recorded sound Sound that is captured electronically, such as onto a computer file.

Reverb The effect that occurs when sound waves hit surrounding surfaces and we hear the original sound plus its reflections. Adding reverb to a sound makes it longer and weightier.

Snap A quick and sudden transition, such as from loud to silent or a blackout.

Sound desk The means of operating the different sounds.

Soundscape An effect made up of several sounds to give the impression of a city street, for example.

Source Where the sound comes from, such as a computer file. Also used to describe the sound itself, such as a bell ringing.

Speaker The device that transmits the sound. Its volume level can be altered.

Structure The way that something is sequenced, put together or built.

Synchronised Two or more sounds operating at the same time.

Transition Movement between sound cues, such as fade and snap.

Traverse A stage configuration where the audience is in two parts that are seated opposite each other along two sides of the stage.

Underscore Sound (often non-diegetic) that is played quietly while performers are speaking, to add atmosphere.

COMPONENT 1: DEVISING – A PRACTICAL GUIDE

Chapter 5

Your design challenge	114
How your design for the devised piece will be assessed	116
Responding to stimuli	117
Agreeing on your artistic intentions	118
Genre, structure, form and style	120
Working positively as a group	124
Production meetings	125
Using rehearsals to develop and refine your designs	126
Final rehearsals	128
Set Design for the Devised Piece	**129**
Starting work on the portfolio	130
Building ideas	131
Contributing to the development of the piece	132
Developing the portfolio	134
Producing and documenting your design	135
Completing your portfolio	137
Lighting Design for the Devised Piece	**138**
Starting work on the portfolio	139
Building ideas	140
Contributing to the development of the piece	141
Developing the portfolio	143
Producing and documenting your design	144
Completing your portfolio	146
Costume Design for the Devised Piece	**147**
Starting work on the portfolio	148
Building ideas	150
Contributing to the development of the piece	152
Developing the portfolio	153
Producing and documenting your design	154
Completing your portfolio	156
Sound Design for the Devised Piece	**157**
Starting work on the portfolio	158
Building ideas	159
Contributing to the development of the piece	160
Developing the portfolio	161
Producing and documenting your design	162
Completing your portfolio	164

FOCUS
How to pin down the aims and objectives of your devised drama.

ASSESSMENT CHECK
This process helps you to:
- communicate and realise your intentions
- consider the impact that you can make on an audience
- explore ideas that you want to communicate
- collaborate and come to decisions.

Make sure your discussions address the focus of AO1, to 'create and develop ideas to communicate meaning for theatrical performance.'

AGREEING ON YOUR ARTISTIC INTENTIONS

What are artistic intentions in a devised piece?

When you perform or design from a playscript, the content (narrative, characters, setting and so on) are already in place. Your artistic intentions will be how you interpret that script for an audience.

In **devised** theatre, by contrast, your artistic or creative intentions relate to what you want to tell the audience. You might begin with a message or question that springs from your stimulus, for example:
- What can society do to avoid climate catastrophe?
- Why is a sense of community important?
- How can we use social media platforms more positively?

FOLLOWING WARM TRAILS

This metaphorical idea encourages you to trust your instincts when developing ideas. Look for signs that a particular route on the devising trail will lead you to an excellent devised piece. If an idea excites several members of the group, you are probably onto a good thing.

How can our group decide on its aims and objectives?

TASK 5.3
Work together to test some of the group's ideas through drama activities such as improvisations. Make notes on successful points that move you closer to agreeing your artistic intentions.

DESIGN TIP
Revisit your ideas board often while agreeing your artistic intentions. Update it by removing, adding and regrouping ideas.

TASK 5.4
An ideas board is a useful way of bringing ideas together and specifying aims and objectives. More than just a list of ideas, look to include on your board (you could use a pin-board, whiteboard or a large sheet of cardboard):
- the stimulus, its title, or a description of it
- themes, messages and questions that arise from the stimulus
- descriptions, photographs or sketches of dramatic explorations you have found inspiring
- news headlines and articles, for example, that have prompted ideas
- images that have captured your imagination
- initial design ideas – keep that part of your brain firing!

Deciding on your artistic intentions

In addition to generating and sharing ideas, you need to analyse and evaluate this creative process. This will help you to make decisions and assess why they are the best choices.

Time will be limited. Settling on the aims and objectives for your piece should be a relatively quick aspect of the creative process. If your group starts to feel stuck, try the following task.

TASK 5.5

1. One at a time, each member of the group takes one item from the ideas board and puts it on the floor or table.
2. Give yourselves two minutes to arrange the items in priority order. If there is indecision or argument, collect items for further review.
3. Study the result. Sensitively analyse and evaluate the group's decisions and confirm your artistic intentions.

Wording artistic intentions

Once you have agreed on what your artistic intentions are, try the following task as a way of writing them down.

TASK 5.6

1. As a group, write a short paragraph that sums up the theme or message you want to share with your audience.
2. Highlight the most important key words.
3. Use these key words to write a brief, clear aim for your theatre piece.

The following table provides a couple of examples.

The general idea (theme)	The clear artistic intentions	
Climate change is **threatening our world**. **We** can all do something to **help**, but it's not enough. **Governments** need to work together and **make big changes quickly**. Young people should be listened to – some of us have joined **protests** because we feel so strongly about **our future**.	Aim	To highlight climate change as a major global threat.
	Key messages	• Young people should be encouraged to protest. • Everyone should contribute. • Governments need to work together to tackle the problem urgently.
Social media sites are **useful** ways of staying in touch with friends and sharing ideas. But they can be **dangerous** because they allow **bullying** and extremism. They encourage people to **stay at home** rather than actually being with friends. There are important things to do to **stay safe online**. We want to share this with younger students.	Aim	To help Year 7 students to get the best from social media.
	Key messages	• Avoid personal details – use privacy settings. • Don't get involved in bullying or discrimination: report it instead. • Stay in touch with friends and have fun, but **be** with people too.

ASSESSMENT CHECK
These tasks will help you work together to 'make appropriate judgements during the development process.'

LOOK HERE
Pages 126–128 will help you to maintain your creative intentions during rehearsals.

DESIGN TIP
Remember that you can adapt the wording of your intentions during the rehearsal process.

FOCUS
Exploring the different forms devised theatre can take and coming to decisions about your own.

ASSESSMENT CHECK
You will be analysing and evaluating your decisions regarding how your piece communicates meaning. Considering why choices are made will help you towards AO4.

You will also show understanding of practical application and production elements.

Your choice of forms and styles will help you towards AO1.

GENRE, STRUCTURE, FORM AND STYLE

Genre
Genre could be described as the type of drama you choose for your performance. These include:

- comedy
- horror
- tragedy
- mystery
- crime.

Which genres allow you to communicate your artistic intentions in interesting ways?

A piece could be in more than one genre. Dark comedy, for example, tackles serious themes, but in amusing, thought-provoking ways.

Designers and genre
Designers play an important role in establishing genre. At the most basic level, all design elements communicate light and dark in some way. Designs for a game-show genre, for example, could include formal costumes for the presenter, bright lighting, a repeated jingle and a raised platform and podiums as part of the set.

Structure
Structure is the 'shape' of the performance, or the way it is built. Narrative structures include:

- linear
- cyclical
- episodic.

You might not be able to decide on your structure until you have spent some time exploring your piece. A structure might emerge rather than being a conscious early decision.

Designers and structure
A designer needs to think about structure as soon as it is chosen. A linear piece, for example, might need changes of costume to support the sense of time passing. In a cyclical piece, the repetition of lighting states could help the audience to recognise a return to a location or situation. Lengthy scene changes, by contrast, would disrupt a fast-moving, episodic piece.

Form
Form is the shape or style of each section or scene. Think of it as the different drama techniques you use to shape your work. There are many forms that you could include, for example:

- movement/physical theatre
- mime
- split stage
- ensemble
- duologue/monologue
- naturalistic with elements of thought-tracking and freeze-framing.

Designers and form

Set, sound and lighting can all enhance the use of split stage scenes, for example. If mime or movement sequences are involved, costumes need to allow the performers can move freely. Sound effects and music, as well as set design, are highly important for these scenes as well.

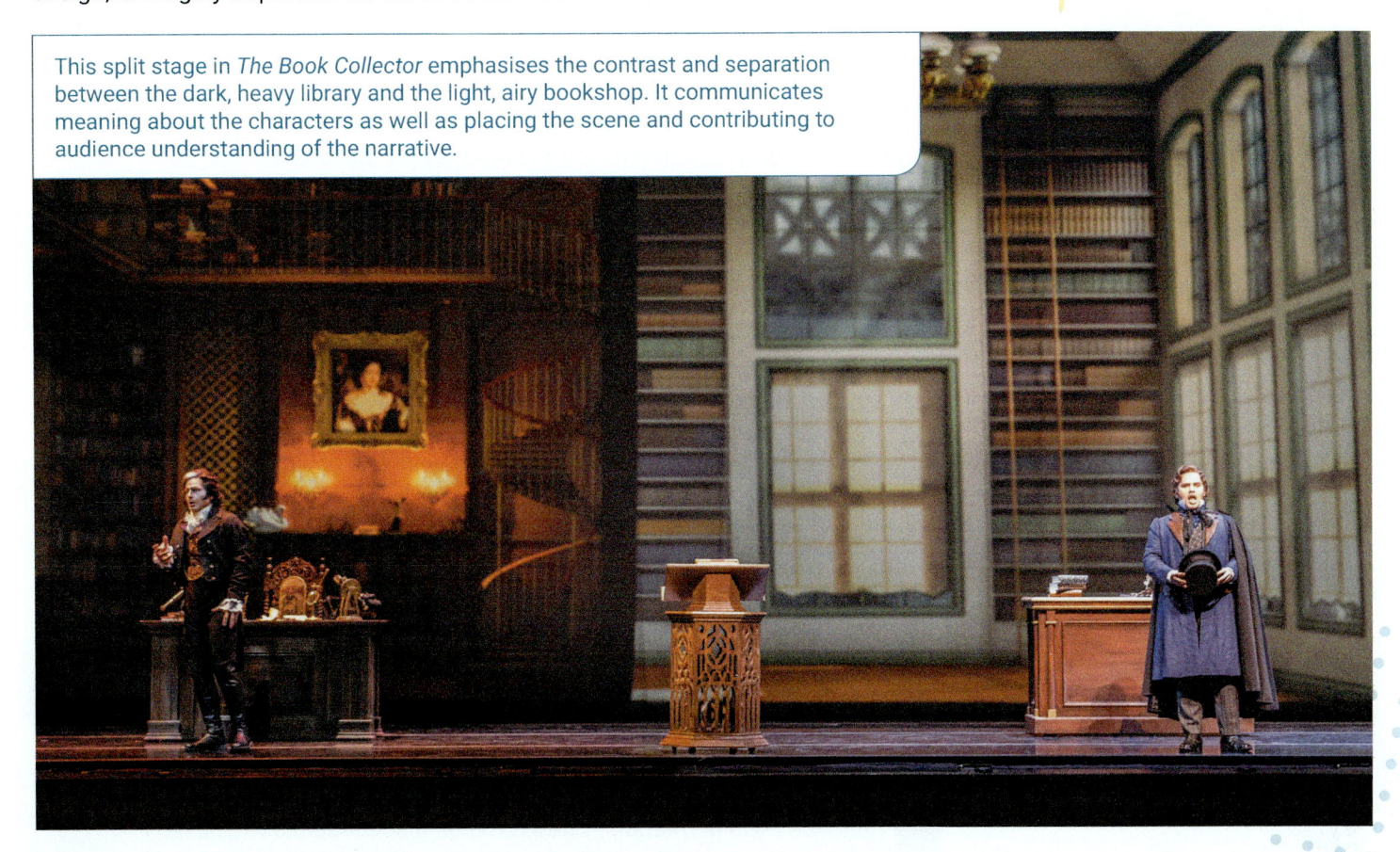

> This split stage in *The Book Collector* emphasises the contrast and separation between the dark, heavy library and the light, airy bookshop. It communicates meaning about the characters as well as placing the scene and contributing to audience understanding of the narrative.

Style

This term describes the method used to approach the performance – there might be more than one. Styles include:

- naturalistic
- non-naturalistic
- Brechtian/epic (or that specific to other practitioners, such as Boal)
- minimalist
- YPT (Young People's Theatre).

Designers and style

A naturalistic set design will seem far more real and instantly recognisable than one for a non-naturalistic piece. The same is likely to be true for naturalistic sound, costume and lighting. Silhouette and fabric choice will be important in establishing the period, for example. In this case, lighting and sound designers would be unlikely to use many non-naturalistic effects as they could clash with the main style.

Character and language

Although you might think of costume as being the most important design aspect for characterisation, it should be supported by all designers. Music can help to present a character's emotions, and lighting could sharpen our attention on a character. Set can also reflect, for example, a character's sense of freedom or restriction.

At first glance, language might not seem to have a great deal to do with design. But a character who uses formal language is likely to wear more formal clothing. Words could form part of a set design. Song lyrics should also be carefully chosen to suit the language of the piece.

CASE STUDY: CYBERBULLYING

Starting from the stimulus of a news article about increasing incidents of bullying, a group of Year 10 students set about devising a YPT docudrama on the theme of cyberbullying. They aimed for an audience of Year 7 students, whom they saw as being particularly vulnerable.

The group researched statistics, watched anti-bullying videos and shared their own experiences. They then improvised a few scenarios. They realised that it was much easier to understand the effects of cyberbullying than the reasons why young people get drawn into it. This led to further research and new improvisations.

One of the group had opted for sound design and began work on diegetic and non-diegetic sounds.

As well as the sounds of phone buttons, ringtones and notifications, the designer developed two underscores of ambient sounds. These supported characterisation by reflecting the feelings of the victim and the main perpetrator. These emerging soundtracks were used in rehearsals, where they helped to shape the devised piece.

The structure became a cyclical story of the bully. Scenes looked at her younger life and how she gradually came to understand the misery of her victim. Sound effects were an integral part of the piece.

CASE STUDY: LIES

Yevgeny Yevtushenko's poem 'Lies' was adopted as a devised performance stimulus. It begins:

Telling lies to the young is wrong.

Proving to them that lies are true is wrong.

Telling them that God's in his heaven

and all's well with the world is wrong.

The young people know what you mean.

The young are people.

Yevgeny Yevtushenko

TASK 5.7

1. Work with your group to complete a table like this to summarise advantages and disadvantages – for you – of different theatrical forms. (Examples have been included to start you off.)
2. You could complete similar tables to help you consider genre, style and structure.

Theatrical form	Strengths for our group	Challenges for our group	Notes
Physical theatre / movement scenes	<ul><li>Suits our non-naturalistic style.</li><li>Some performers feel very comfortable with this form.</li><li>Interesting for lighting – lots of scope for SFX.</li></ul>	<ul><li>Not everyone has experience of this form.</li><li>Costume design might be limited?</li><li>Is it too difficult for our audience to 'read' our artistic intentions?</li></ul>	Could mix physical theatre with docudrama.
Thought-tracking	<ul><li>Suits non-naturalistic style.</li><li>Adds depth and interest.</li></ul>		Communicates character.

CASE STUDY: BEAUTY AND THE BEAST

A small group devised a modern version of *Beauty and the Beast* as a largely physical performance. Their artistic intentions concentrated on the physical and emotional repercussions of substance abuse.

The only piece of set was a white wooden frame, the size of a doorframe. It was used to represent a door, a window, a picture frame and a cage. It was supported and moved by the performers, which made it very versatile.

Costumes were simple – mostly black – and stretchy to support the form and minimalist style.

The lighting designer made a highly significant contribution to characterisation and style. He used a range of cover washes that enhanced the atmosphere. Transitions between different lighting states were sometimes very slow, to give the impression of time passing. At other times, he used snap transitions for moments of shock or sudden change. In addition, tight white spotlights were used during monologues.

The group shared ideas about young people being lied to by adults. They worked these ideas through improvisation into a powerful episodic drama in a largely naturalistic style.

They chose to differentiate between harmless pretences, such as the tooth fairy, and lies that could be damaging. Using a range of forms, including advert and duologue, scenes focused on politicians, family and other authority figures lying to young people and the effects of this.

In end-on staging, the set created levels and 'hidden' areas with a clever arrangement of existing stage blocks. Two levels were placed upstage centre to increase the proximity of those in authority to young people. The spaces under the stage blocks created locations such as a bedroom. The set strongly supported the episodic narrative.

DESIGN TIP

Play to the strengths of your group. Remember that you can combine theatrical forms. For example, an episodic piece could include one or more scenes that are physical theatre.

FOCUS
Advice on avoiding or recovering from group-work problems.

ASSESSMENT CHECK
Together, you should 'engage with the process of collaboration, rehearsal and refinement' and 'work collaboratively within a group to realise artistic intentions.'

WORKING POSITIVELY AS A GROUP

The importance of good communication

Teachers have to consider many things when they form groups for practical work. Not everyone will be happy with the resulting make-up of their group, but the ability to work collaboratively is a valuable skill needed here, and for life.

Most importantly, good communication is essential for creating good theatre.

TASK 5.8

As a group, share thoughts of examples in life of excellent communication. Be specific and try to assess what skills are being used.

For example, a particular teacher might be really effective at communicating their subject. This could be to do with their skills in bringing the subject to life, their enthusiasm, and the way they make students feel that their ideas are listened to.

Alternatively, you might think about pedestrian crossings, where clear visual and aural cues are given to pedestrians and drivers. Bumps near the edge of the pavement also help sight-impaired pedestrians. Excellent communication in terms of design!

Building a positive group environment

Negative dynamics are a common problem in group work, with a range of causes. The chart below offers some ideas for improving your group's ability to get along socially and make practical progress.

TASK 5.9

Use the points below to evaluate a recent group session. Ask yourself:
- What are my qualities as a group member?
- How could I improve my contribution to the group?
- Am I collaborating with and supporting my group members?

KEEPING COMMUNICATION OPEN

- Have a clear objective for the session, for example to gather ideas of how the stimulus can be explored through drama.
- Highlight the positive things people say and do.
- Take turns to speak. If necessary, have an object that can be held by the speaker, and pass it on frequently.
- Listen carefully when others are speaking. Don't just wait for your turn to speak.
- Encourage everyone to talk. Go around the circle every few minutes so that everyone has a chance to contribute. Keep it positive.
- Try to be objective about difficulties. Focus on what has gone wrong rather than on an individual. Try to limit comments to those that help the objective of the meeting.
- Ask a teacher for support early on if communication is not going well.
- Always avoid blaming one person. Communication is a shared activity!

PRODUCTION MEETINGS

AGENDA PERFORMANCE PROBLEMS
CHALLENGES PROGRESS ISSUES DATES TIME
LIST COLLABORATION DESIGN DEADLINES
PLAN COSTUME PRIORITY SOURCE
TECHNICAL LIGHTING
COMMUNICATION EVALUATION SET
POSITIVITY COLLABORATE SOUND
IMPORTANT CHECK STRATEGY SOLUTION ANALYSIS

The design and performance elements of your group might often be working separately. You will need regular times to meet and check overall progress. The benefits of having regular meetings with a set agenda are:

- The agenda can be short and the meeting focused.
- All designers have a chance to give and get peer feedback.
- Deadlines and schedules can be set and checked.
- Issues can be raised and support organised.
- Notes from the meeting will help to keep your portfolio detailed and let you show progression.

As you are likely to be a small group without a director, having a representative from the performing group is a good idea. Minutes of the meeting can be shared with the rest of the group.

Agenda
- Progress report.
- Sharing of research and sketches etc (for each designer).
- Schedules and deadlines.
- Issues.
- Date of next meeting.

Highlight and make notes on your agenda of what is discussed during the meeting. Include any changes to the piece that are being made and any actions you need to take. Use these notes as a checklist.

Just me?

If you are the only designer for your devised group, you should still have brief production meetings with the performers. Deadlines need to be met and it is in everyone's interests to maintain progress towards a harmonious performance.

If you need to, ask fellow group members to support with particular design elements. For example, could one or two performers operate some basic lighting or sound equipment for you when they are not on stage?

FOCUS

Bringing the design elements together and tracking progress.

ASSESSMENT CHECK

Overcoming challenges shows 'collaborative involvement' and 'analysis and evaluation of personal contribution to the creation, development and refinement process.'

Along with rehearsals, regular meetings should help you to 'take into consideration performer/ audience relationships.'

DESIGN TIP

File old agendas to help in compiling your portfolio.

FOCUS
Working together to develop the devised piece.

ASSESSMENT CHECK
You need to demonstrate your 'engagement with the process of collaboration, rehearsal and refinement.' Keep in mind that you are working towards AO1: 'Create and develop ideas to communicate meaning for theatrical performance.'

LOOK HERE
'Your design challenge' on pages 114–115, and the appropriate practical design chapter, will support you further.

SIGNPOST
Make sure you have tried Task 5.1. Remember that it is a starting point. Your ideas will develop and change.

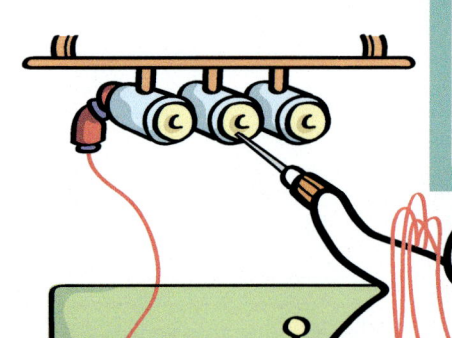

USING REHEARSALS TO DEVELOP AND REFINE YOUR DESIGNS

Focus on your design specialism

As the performers start to rehearse, you will need to turn your attention to designing.

TASK 5.10

As a way of clarifying your thoughts, begin your own version of the following journal. Add to it as you go along.

Group details: 5 performers plus Lighting, Costume, Set: Total 8

Artistic intentions	Notes on style, forms, genre, structure	Set design notes
To explore the importance of community, locally, nationally, internationally. • Gain a better awareness of what 'community' means. • Understand the value of being part of a community. • See what happens when communities are broken up or divided.	7 Oct Main style: Non-naturalistic. Forms: Ensemble, movement, duologue, freeze-frames. Genre: Social drama / YPT. Structure: Episodic.	7 Oct Use image or symbol (invented) on fabric – flag? Suggests togetherness – performers could use dramatically to connect, wrap, be a barrier? 12 Oct Circular – perform in the round? Create semi-circular shape using curved cyclorama – project onto it? 23 Oct Levels for dramatic interest? Small steps? Could show people helping others up? Sightlines? 25 Oct Colour – monochrome to allow for strong coloured lighting and give a neutral feel? Bursts of colour with the flag idea? Talk to Costume!

Remember your health and safety responsibilities, and ask for help!

Ongoing research

Your design work will progress quite rapidly as long as you 'feed' your creativity. This is continuous research, of which rehearsals are an important part. These ideas should keep you going.

- What inspiration do you find in the themes and messages of your artistic intentions?
- Keep an eye on the news. Are there topical examples of issues that relate to your artistic intentions?
- What do the form and genre suggest in terms of design? (Perhaps particular sounds or visual ideas.)
- Are there other plays related to your artistic intentions? They could be useful for design ideas. For bullying, for example, you could look at *DNA* by Dennis Kelly or *The Terrible Fate of Humpty Dumpty* by David Calcutt.
- Be in rehearsals as much as possible. An improvised scene might lead you to a new underscore or different lighting effect.

ASSESSMENT CHECK

The research and rehearsal processes will help you to:
- 'make appropriate judgements'
- 'rehearse, refine and amend work in progress'
- 'adapt designs in response to rehearsals.'

It is essential that you collaborate in order to meet AO4: 'Analyse and evaluate your own work and the work of others.'

TASK 5.11

Keep a detailed record of your research and response to rehearsals (use the table in Task 5.10) for your portfolio. Save images (or links to them). Keep in mind the 'how and why' of your design.

LOOK HERE

The case studies on pages 122–123 are examples of design developments during rehearsals.

Use the guidance on page 124 to help with offering and receiving suggestions and making changes.

Developing your design alongside performers and other designers

It is critical that you collaborate with the rest of your group. This will be a balance between presenting your ideas and responding to ideas that others bring. Together, you need to arrive at a harmonious world on the stage. Here are some ways to work collaboratively during rehearsals:

- Keep returning to your artistic intentions.
- Hold them at the front of your mind.
- Spend time in rehearsals.
- Notice what performers are doing.
- See if your design needs to be guided or adapted by a particular aspect of the performance.
- Spend a few minutes before each rehearsal with any other designers.
- Share plans supportively and check that all design elements are in harmony.
- Feed performers with your developing design ideas.
- Take in mood boards or design items as appropriate.

FOCUS
Putting together a document that communicates your group's intentions and your contribution to them.

ASSESSMENT CHECK
AO1 asks you to 'create and develop ideas that communicate meaning for theatrical performance.'

This section begins your process of 'documenting the practical creation and development of ideas, along with the analysis of this process and the devised work.'

SIGNPOST
These sections at the beginning of the chapter will be your resource for starting the portfolio:
- Your design challenge
- Responding to stimuli
- Agreeing on your artistic intentions.

LOOK HERE
See pages 122–123 for a summary of the group's ideas for this poem.

STARTING WORK ON THE PORTFOLIO

The early stages of documenting your work

Your portfolio should provide plenty of evidence that you can use specific drama language in relation to set design and to the genre, structure, form and style of the devised piece. It should, at this stage, explain how you responded to the stimuli and came to decide on your creative intentions. You are answering this key question:

What was your initial response to the stimuli and what were the intentions of the piece?

TASK 5.13
1. Look through the sections listed in the Signpost. Collect completed tasks and extra notes.
2. Write a short paragraph describing your stimulus. Include an annotated picture or copy of it.
3. Write a paragraph based on early responses to the stimulus.
4. Link your group's artistic intentions to what you as a designer want the audience to think and feel. Did your ideas change?
5. Add any set design sketches or ideas that you had at this stage.
6. Read through your paragraphs to check that they answer the question and that the word count is about right (around 300).

From 'Lies' by Yevgeny Yevtushenko
Say obstacles exist they must encounter,
sorrow happens, hardship happens.
The hell with it. Who never knew
the price of happiness will not be happy.

TASK 5.14
Read the following draft portfolio extract. What advice would you give the writer to improve it?

I contributed to my group's artistic intentions, which were to create a piece about the problems caused when young people are not told the truth. I created a specific objective around the line, 'Tell them the difficulties can't be counted', as I believe people have immense challenges to face, like climate change. I don't want to be told not to worry about it. I need to know details so that I can try to do something about my potential future.

As set designer, I began to think about how lies could be represented or symbolised. Lies involve hiding things, so I wondered if I could divide the set into hidden spaces in some way.

BUILDING IDEAS

The next section of your portfolio could cover genre, structure, character, form, style and language in relation to your devised piece. Continue to chart the devising process too, including analysis and evaluation of decisions. Judgement vocabulary will help you to evaluate. For example:

- My suggestion that... was helpful/important because...
- I thought... would be powerful because...
- My set design idea of... was effective because...

The two key questions you are answering are:
- **What work did your group do in order to explore the stimuli and start to create ideas for performance?**
- **How did you consider genre, structure, character, form, style and language throughout the process?**

TASK 5.15

1. Collect completed tasks and additional notes.
2. Write a paragraph or two about activities that your group tried in developing ideas. Recall suggestions, discussions and improvisations, writing about them with analytical and drama-specific vocabulary. Be precise and include reasons behind ideas and choices.
3. Write a further paragraph or two about your choices around genre, structure, character, form, style and language. You can always come back to this, if you need to add more. How did you decide on genre, for example?
4. How could your developing ideas be shown in your set design?
5. Read your text and keep track of the word count (about 300 to 400).

After we improvised some ideas, I suggested an episodic structure because we would be able to cover lots of different ideas. I also thought that we should find a non-naturalistic way of linking the scenes, so we explored choral speaking and mime. This was effective, but we later discovered that mime wasn't very good at communicating complex ideas. We started to use freeze-frames with thought-tracking. This was powerful as it would let the audience see the different thoughts of the adult and the child in the scene about adult illness for example. I decided to use elements of non-naturalism in my design.

The audience would be students of our age as the subject of lies felt suitable for them. The overall style became Young People's Theatre.

FOCUS
Reflecting on genre, structure, form, style and language as you develop ideas.

ASSESSMENT CHECK
You need to demonstrate understanding of different theatrical elements for AO4.

Your portfolio needs to include 'analysis and evaluation of personal contribution to the creation, development and refinement process.'

LOOK HERE
'Genre, structure, form and style' on pages 120–123 will be a good starting point. 'Two styles of set design' and 'Research for set design' on pages 18 and 19 will also be helpful as you begin to focus on design.

TASK 5.16

Read the example on the left. Which of the following has the student covered?
- Genre
- Structure
- Character
- Form
- Style
- Language

DESIGN TIP
Responding to both key questions in the same paragraph is fine!

FOCUS

Evaluating how well you are collaborating with the rest of your group.

ASSESSMENT CHECK

The 'process of collaboration' is an important part of your 'contribution to the creation, development and realisation' of your piece. You will be assessed on your 'ability to realise artistic intentions through the use of design skills to contribute to and support the performance as a whole.'

SIGNPOST

The following sections will be particularly helpful in making key decisions about your set and its development.

- Research for set design, page 19
- Understanding your resources, page 25
- How to document your set design, pages 20–24
- Working positively as a group, page 124
- Using rehearsals to develop and refine your design, pages 126–127.

CONTRIBUTING TO THE DEVELOPMENT OF THE PIECE

This section helps you to consider how productively you are working alongside your group members to create the devised piece. You will also be firming up your set design by now and writing about the process in your portfolio or taking detailed notes so that you can complete the portfolio later.

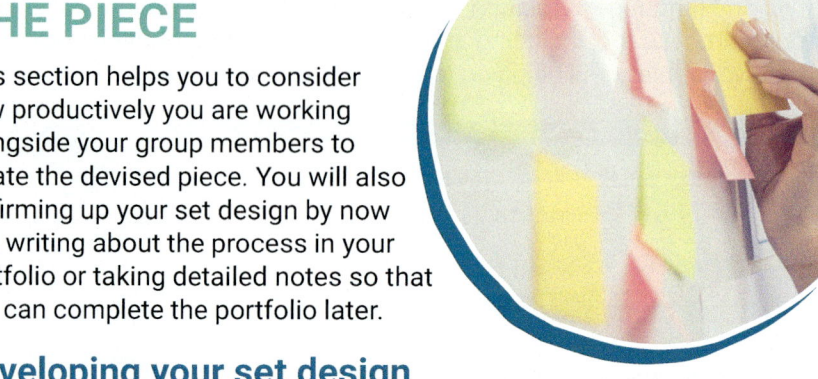

Developing your set design

Your set design should be taking shape around the time that the performers begin solid rehearsals. Use Chapter 1 of this book to guide your process. Make sure that you are completing the tasks as you come to them. As you go along, record your decisions together with the reasons for making them.

Take some time to focus on the collaboration that you are undertaking. How are you feeding and being fed by the group? What challenges are you attempting to overcome? The key question is:

What were some of the significant moments during the development process and when rehearsing and refining your work?

You should analyse the way that you worked with other people in your group. This includes overcoming difficulties as well as the times when ideas and group work flowed easily.

Note how the student-style example on the following page shows knowledge and understanding of production elements and the use of stage space and spatial relationships. The designer is also making appropriate judgements and interpreting content and style.

Students at King Edward's School in Birmingham have used a simple, rough-painted set with projections to help set the scene in their devised piece.

Chapter 5 Component 1: Devising – A Practical Guide

TASK 5.17

1. Look through the three sections from Chapter 1 in the Signpost. Keep the completed tasks and any extra notes in front of you.
2. Use them to write at least two paragraphs about how you are developing a set design that meets the group's needs. How and why are your early ideas changing? Mention your research and how you are using your resources. Include group responses to the design. Add an annotated sketch of your design.
3. Write a further paragraph or two about how your design is impacting on the rehearsal process for the performers. Ask yourself:
   - Are there any problems for the actors? How are these overcome?
   - Are there particular successes? What aspect of your design is enhancing the performance, and how?

   Also reflect upon the effect of the performers' work on your design.
4. Check your writing and keep track of the word count.

TASK 5.18

Read the portfolio extract on the left. Find at least two points that discuss collaboration.

TASK 5.19

1. Review your portfolio so far and ensure that you can pinpoint:
   - sentences that describe collaboration (working with others)
   - words that are subject-specific to set design
   - phrases that suggest significant moments in the development process.
2. What improvements can you make?

I began to think about how I could support our use of language in my design.

I found this image and thought of pasting words and quotes onto a run of flats. We knew we wanted non-naturalism in terms of style and I thought that having flats that were thematically linked, along with levels and barriers, made a meaningful and versatile set.

These are the quotes I chose to use:

'O, what a tangled web we weave, when first we practise to deceive.'
(Walter Scott, 'Marmion')

'False face must hide what the false heart doth know.'
(Macbeth)

'Integrity is the lifeblood of democracy. Deceit is a poison in its veins.'
(Edward Kennedy)

At first, I thought about writing on the flats with marker pens and spray paint. When I tested it on cardboard, however, it looked messy and wasn't easy to read. I discovered it would be better to paste large photocopies of the quotes onto three flats that we already had in school. I would paint the flats white, and use black and red lettering.

In a production meeting we decided that monochrome and red will be our colour palette. The monochrome aspects would be suitable for using coloured lights. The costume designer was keen to use red accents to suggest the danger of lies.

One day, in rehearsals, I noticed that the performers were making all their entrances and exits from the sides of the stage and that it looked clumsy. I changed my design to make large gaps between the flats to help the performers enter and exit from the back of the stage.

Chapter 5 Component 1: Devising – A Practical Guide

FOCUS
- Making sure you give enough detail.
- Checking and improving your work so far.

ASSESSMENT CHECK
Give plenty of specific examples of 'drama terminology'. Also take an 'evaluative and analytical approach' to 'creating and developing ideas to communicate meaning.'

DESIGN TIP
Remove waffle. Include brief, precise details of your design ideas.

DESIGN TIP
Look through the student-style examples for the other design elements in this chapter. They might inspire some new ideas.

DEVELOPING THE PORTFOLIO

Reviewing your portfolio

You are now approximately half way through the devising process. That means that you should also have completed around half of the portfolio or the notes that will help you to complete it at the end of the process.

TASK 5.20

Using this chapter and the key questions for each section, read through your portfolio, and check that you haven't drifted away from the questions.
- Are there sentences you can improve by using examples and evaluative language?
- Use the glossary at the end of Chapter 1. Can you include more subject-specific language?

Go through all your notes as well as re-reading what you have already written. You will improve your portfolio considerably if you do this thoroughly.

Can I write more about the devising process and the development of my set design?

With Task 5.20 completed, it is a good idea to see if you have missed anything before you move on to the final stages and evaluating your design.

TASK 5.21

Use the following questions to remind you of significant events you might not have mentioned so far.
- Were there memorable moments in rehearsals or production meetings?
- Did I hit an obstacle? What did I do?
- Has there been a moment when I felt particularly pleased or proud? What was it and what was the effect that pleased me?
- Can I say more about genre, structure, character, form and style?
- Am I using suitable technical language?
- How else did I make a contribution to the piece during rehearsals? What was the effect? (Think about performers and other designers.)
- Did I consider health and safety issues?
- Have I included sketches and draft plans?

TASK 5.22

Add around 200 to 300 words across one or more sections of your portfolio. Use your responses to the questions in Task 5.21. Aim to use more subject-specific language and add one or two detailed examples.

PRODUCING AND DOCUMENTING YOUR DESIGN

What must I produce for my final set design?

You need to present:

- drawings of the final design to be realised in the performance space and details of relevant props
- a ground plan of the performance space, including entrances and exits, audience positioning and any stage furniture
- the set used in the devised performance: this must match your final drawings.

You also need to have supervised the construction, painting, hiring or finding of the scenic elements required for your design.

Making your design

It is vital that you have considered all aspects of your group's artistic intentions and the specific points required by your course. You only need to supervise the construction elements, but you will benefit from being involved in some aspects of the build, such as painting, if appropriate.

Your finished set should be engaging and effective for the audience. It must also support the communication of your group's artistic intentions. Check that you have considered design details that enhance meaning, mood and atmosphere.

FOCUS
Documenting the completion of your set design.

ASSESSMENT CHECK
You need to show how your final design looks and the extent to which you actualised it on the stage. You should analyse and evaluate your 'personal contribution towards the creation, development and refinement process.'

LOOK HERE
Pages 20–22 will help you with technical drawings. Annotate them so that they are very clear.

TASK 5.23

Fill in your version of the following table before you construct your set.

How does my set design…		
…enhance the genre, structure, form and style of the piece?	Genre	Element of tragedy. The barriers in the set remind audience of conflict.
	Structure	Episodic. The set is easily and quickly transformed for different scenes.
	Forms	• Freeze-frames • Thought-tracking • Split stage.
	Style	Combination of naturalistic and non-naturalistic – in performance and set design – within overall YPT style.
…reflect the **artistic intentions** of my group?		• Theme of lies carried in quotes on flats. • Levels to suggest power and barriers (to truth).
…avoid **health and safety** hazards?		• Barriers light to lift. • Flats securely weighted and fire retardant. • Non-slip surfaces. • Height of levels not too great.
…enhance **mood** and **atmosphere**?		• Metal barriers suggest captivity. • Serious/harsh tone.
…show **collaboration** with performers and other designers?		• Levels and entrances between flats allow characters to eavesdrop. • Performers found practice items useful in rehearsal. • Co-ordinated choice of colour palette with lighting and costume. • Combination of costume and set is safe.
…make a substantial **impact** on the audience?		• Powerful impact because set is uncluttered. • Symbolic and practical elements like the barriers, flats and levels. • Details help to communicate meaning. • Use of colour is engaging.

Chapter 5 Component 1: Devising – A Practical Guide

DESIGN TIP

See your lighting design and your portfolio as two parts of the same whole. They must be worked on at the same time.

SIGNPOST

Chapter 2 supports your lighting design work and guides you through the entire process of designing, rigging and operating lighting. Use it here alongside the guide at the beginning of this chapter.

NOTE

This chapter assumes that you are writing your whole portfolio. If you are taking a different approach, make detailed notes, spider diagrams and so on to support your final presentation.

LOOK HERE

See page 116 for a breakdown of the portfolio contents.

LIGHTING DESIGN FOR THE DEVISED PIECE

The requirements of your lighting design

A deep blue wash is pierced by a bright white spotlight in *Bat Boy the Musical*.

Your lighting design will emerge from your role as a member of a devising group. It will be marked in terms of your ability to 'use, apply and combine design skills to support the performance as a whole'. Your lighting should create mood and atmosphere and enhance the chosen style of the piece. It must also communicate the artistic intentions of the piece effectively and have an impact on the audience.

The portfolio

The portfolio is your opportunity to explain how you have engaged fully with the process of devising from the viewpoint of group member and lighting designer. You will chart the process from beginning to end, detailing your understanding of all the skills you have used and the decisions you have made.

Your ability to work with your group to bring its artistic intentions to reality is important along with analysis and evaluation of your successes and the challenges you have faced along the way.

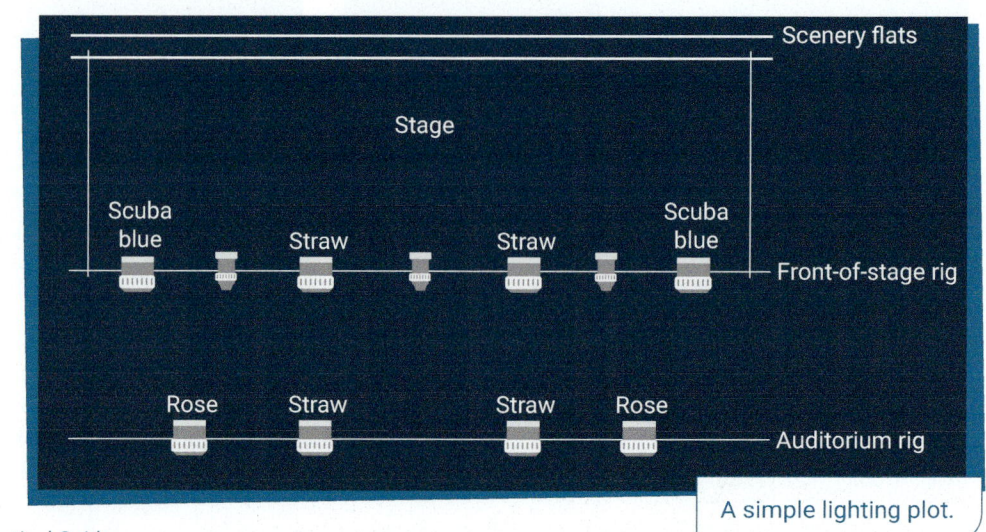

A simple lighting plot.

138   Chapter 5   Component 1: Devising – A Practical Guide

STARTING WORK ON THE PORTFOLIO

The early stages of documenting your work

Your portfolio should provide plenty of evidence that you can use specific drama language in relation to lighting design and to the genre, structure, form and style of the devised piece. It should, at this stage, explain how you responded to the stimuli and came to decide on your creative intentions. You are answering the following key question:

What was your initial response to the stimuli and what were the intentions of the piece?

TASK 5.29

1. Look through the sections listed in the Signpost. Collect completed tasks and extra notes.
2. Write a few lines describing your stimulus. Include an annotated picture or copy of it.
3. Write a further paragraph based on early responses to the stimulus.
4. Link your group's artistic intentions to what you as a designer want the audience to think and feel. Have these changed?
5. Add any plans or ideas for lighting design that you had.
6. Read through your text to check that they answer the question and that the word count is about right (around 300).

TASK 5.30

Read the draft extract below. Then select **two** of the following pieces of advice to help the writer add useful detail:

- Briefly mention whether there are other designers in your group.
- Include the song lyrics.
- Say what the song made you think when your first heard it.
- Add the names of the other people in your group and their roles.
- Describe what other members of the group felt about the song.
- Explain what the group wanted the performance to be about and why.

> I was the lighting designer for our devised performance. Our stimulus was the song 'Titanium' by David Guetta featuring Sia. It is an urban dance track and has a very energising feel. The lyrics are about being strong and resilient.
>
> Titanium is a silvery grey metal that is strong and tough and doesn't corrode easily. In terms of lighting design, I'm immediately thinking of hard-edged profile spots, high intensity and possibly gobos. I told other people in my group about the metal and it raised some excitement, so we decided to explore the idea of strength and resilience.

FOCUS

Putting together a document that communicates your group's intentions and your contribution to them.

ASSESSMENT CHECK

AO1 asks you to 'create and develop ideas that communicate meaning for theatrical performance'.

This section begins your process of 'documenting the practical creation and development of ideas, along with the analysis of this process and the devised work.'

SIGNPOST

The following sections at the beginning of this chapter will help you to start the portfolio:

- Your design challenge
- Responding to stimuli
- Agreeing on your artistic intentions.

LOOK HERE

'Introduction to lighting design' on pages 34–35 might help with Task 5.29.

Chapter 5   Component 1: Devising – A Practical Guide   139

FOCUS

Reflecting on the genre, structure, character, form, style and language of your devised piece.

ASSESSMENT CHECK

You need to demonstrate understanding of different theatrical elements for AO4.

Your portfolio needs to include 'analysis and evaluation of personal contribution to the creation, development and refinement process.'

LOOK HERE

'Genre, structure, form and style' on pages 120–123 will be a good starting point. 'Types of stage lantern', pages 36–37, and 'Understanding your lighting resources', pages 38–39, will also be helpful.

BUILDING IDEAS

The next section of your portfolio could cover genre, structure, character, form, style and language in relation to your devised piece. Continue to chart the devising process too, including analysis and evaluation of decisions. Judgement vocabulary will help you to evaluate. For example:

- I decided it would be good to... because...
- Our exploration of... was effective because...
- The choice of... as a form/structure/style... was a good decision because...

The key questions you are answering are:
- **What work did your group do in order to explore the stimuli and start to create ideas for performance?**
- **How did you consider genre, structure, character, form, style and language?**

TASK 5.31

1. Collect completed tasks and additional notes.
2. Write a paragraph or two about activities that you tried. Write about suggestions, discussions and improvisations with analytical and drama-specific vocabulary. Be precise and include reasons behind choices.
3. Write a further paragraph or two about how you arrived at your choices of genre, structure, character, forms, style and language. How did these choices affect your design ideas? If there was any conflict, how was it resolved?
4. Read your text and keep track of the word count (about 300 to 400).

TASK 5.32

Why is the following portfolio extract more effective than the one on the previous page?

The teacher set our group the task of producing some freeze-frames and physical theatre to go with the song 'Titanium'. I noticed the music had a strong, steady beat like a march. We had a character trying to break through a 'wall' of people stamping their feet. After four or five attempts, she makes it to the other side and is lifted up as a kind of hero. This suggested a design idea of a transition from dark to light.

We also made some freeze-frames of different ways that people can be titanium-like, standing up to bullying and supporting people who are struggling. We then decided that strong individuals were what we were really interested in and, in particular, young people who don't give up easily.

I carried out some research. I had the theme of strength and resilience from our stimulus, but needed to find out what was going to happen in the play. I suggested that we come back to the next lesson with examples.

My exploration of inspirational strong young people threw up some very interesting characters including:

Malala Yousafzai, the Nobel Peace prize-winner who fought for girls to go to school in Pakistan.

Greta Thunberg, the Swedish teenager who campaigns about climate change.

Jesy Nelson, the singer from Little Mix who suffered cyberbullying and made a documentary to try to help others.

The Thai football team who were trapped in an underground cave for two weeks, but stayed positive.

I knew that this would give me plenty of scope for naturalistic and non-naturalistic lighting effects.

CONTRIBUTING TO THE DEVELOPMENT OF THE PIECE

This section helps you to consider how productively you are working alongside your group members to create the devised piece. You will also be firming up your lighting design by now and writing about the process in your portfolio or taking detailed notes so that you can complete the portfolio later.

Developing your lighting design

Your lighting design should be starting to take shape around the time that the performers begin solid rehearsals. Use Chapter 2 of this book to guide your process. Make sure that you are completing the tasks as you come to them. As you go along, record your decisions together with the reasons for making them.

Take some time to focus on the collaboration that you are undertaking. How are you feeding and being fed by the group? What challenges are you attempting to overcome? The key question is:

What were some of the significant moments during the development process and when rehearsing and refining your work?

You should analyse the way that you worked with other people in your group. This includes overcoming difficulties as well as the times when ideas and group work flowed easily.

TASK 5.33

1. Look through the three sections from Chapter 2 listed in the Signpost. Keep the completed tasks and any extra notes in front of you.
2. Use them to write at least two paragraphs about how you are developing a lighting design that will meet the needs of your group's devised piece. Include the types of research you are completing and the way you are using your resources. Try to fold in the responses of your group to your design. Add a diagram of your design.
3. Write a further paragraph or two about how your design is impacting on the rehearsal process for the performers. Ask yourself:
   - Are there any problems for the actors? How are you overcoming them?
   - Are there particular successes? What aspect of your design is enhancing the performance, and how?

   Also reflect on the work of other group members on your design. Did you notice, for example, the need for a specific colour wash in a non-naturalistic scene?
4. Check over your writing and keep track of the word count.

FOCUS

Evaluating how well you are collaborating with the rest of your group.

ASSESSMENT CHECK

The 'process of collaboration' is an important part of your 'contribution to the creation, development and realisation' of your piece. You will be assessed on your 'ability to realise artistic intentions through the use of design skills to contribute to and support the performance as a whole.'

SIGNPOST

The following sections will be particularly helpful in making key decisions about your lighting and its development.
- Angles, colour and intensity, pages 40–43
- Special effects in lighting, pages 44–45
- Research for lighting, page 47
- How to document your lighting design, pages 48–50
- Working positively as a group, page 124
- Using rehearsals to develop and refine your design, pages 126–127.

DESIGN TIP

Keep your notes from group sessions. Use them to remind yourself of the research and explorations that have taken place.

TASK 5.34

Note how the following example pinpoints significant moments in the development of the lighting design. Highlight three instances of subject-specific language.

I needed to design lighting states for a range of locations, including a cave, which proved to be an interesting challenge. At first, I thought I could use a low-intensity blue wash to create atmosphere. In rehearsals, however, it looked more like an outdoor space. I tried altering the position of the fresnels and introducing some soft-edged profiles in a deeper colour (Palace Blue) to create shadows, but this did not produce the lighting state I wanted.

One of the photographs of the Thai football team showed the boys in a beam of light that must have been shone onto them by rescuers. It also showed the boys using torchlight. I came up with a new plan that would have much more impact for the audience. I asked the performers to experiment with using low-strength torches in their improvisation. Other than that, the acting area was completely dark. Suddenly, I was getting the effect that we were looking for.

When the performers saw the circle of light on the boys in the photograph, they decided to end the improvisation with the moment that the first rescuers' lights hit them. For that I used the automated moving profile in a bright, cold colour (Hampshire Frost) that they could respond to as if in shock. Movement wise, I experimented with swiping the light upwards from the floor to suddenly 'catch' the boys.

Thai Navy Seals wear head-torches during their attempts to reach the trapped football team in June 2018.

DESIGN TIP

It is helpful to include lighting details, such as the names (and numbers) of colour filters. Many of these can be found online.

TASK 5.35

1. Review your portfolio so far and ensure that you can pinpoint:
   - sentences that describe collaboration (working with others)
   - words that are subject-specific to lighting design
   - phrases that indicate significant moments in the development process of the piece and your design.
2. What improvements can you make?

Chapter 5 Component 1: Devising – A Practical Guide

DEVELOPING THE PORTFOLIO

Reviewing your portfolio

You are now approximately half way through the devising process. That means that you should also have completed around half of the portfolio or the notes that will help you to complete it at the end of the process.

TASK 5.36

1. Read through your portfolio. Use this chapter and the key questions for each section to check that you haven't drifted away from the questions.
2. Go through all your notes as well as re-reading what you have already written. You will improve your portfolio considerably if you do this task thoroughly!

TASK 5.37

Use the following questions to remind you of significant events you might not have mentioned so far.

- Have I worked with other designers? How did their work affect mine, and vice versa? (Write a short paragraph about the collaboration.)
- Have there been any discoveries during rehearsals? How were they important to my lighting design?
- Can I say more about genre, structure, character, form and style?
- What improvements have I made to my design? How and why did I make them?
- Am I using suitable technical language?

TASK 5.38

Add between 100 and 200 words across the first three sections of your portfolio. Use your responses to the questions in Task 5.37. Use more subject-specific language and add one or two detailed examples.

FOCUS
- Making sure you give enough detail.
- Checking and improving your work so far.

ASSESSMENT CHECK
You should be giving plenty of specific examples of 'drama terminology'. Also, take an 'evaluative and analytical approach' to 'creating and developing ideas to communicate meaning.'

DESIGN TIP
Remember to refer to your design ideas throughout your portfolio.

FOCUS
Documenting the completion of your lighting design.

ASSESSMENT CHECK
You need to show how your final design looks and the extent to which you actualised it on the stage. You should also analyse and evaluate your 'personal contribution towards the creation, development and refinement process.'

SIGNPOST
Chapter 2 will guide you through the completion, rigging and plotting of your design. Make sure that you have worked through it before setting your lights ready for the performance.

LOOK HERE
Pages 48–50 will help you with the technical drawings and documents that you need. These can be included in your portfolio as an appendix. (They do not contribute towards your word count.)

PRODUCING AND DOCUMENTING YOUR DESIGN

What must I produce for my final lighting design?
You need to present:
- drawings of the final design including cue sheets, rigging diagrams or plans and a lantern schedule
- a lighting plot or cue sheet showing at least four different lighting states
- the realisation of your lighting in the devised performance.

You also need to supervise the rigging, focusing, programming (if applicable) and the operating of your design if you are not doing these yourself.

Making your design
It is vital that you have considered all aspects of your group's artistic intentions and the specific points required by your course. You must also ensure that you keep a close eye on safety issues.

TASK 5.39

Fill in your own version of the following table before you finalise your design.

How does my lighting design...		
...enhance the genre, structure, form and style of the piece?	Genre	Uplifting social drama. The pace of the piece varies. This is reflected in the lighting.
	Structure	Narrative. The monologues include direct address with the use of spotlights.
	Forms	Physical/movement pieces, freeze-frames, dialogue. Lighting helps the focus of the piece and encourages audience engagement.
	Style	Mixture of naturalistic and non-naturalistic, in performance and in lighting design. The cave scene is naturalistic. 'Titanium' physical scene is non-naturalistic.
...reflect the **artistic intentions** of my group?		Theme of inner strength and resilience enhanced by use of strong, motivating lighting states.
...avoid **health and safety** hazards?		• Electric cables taped down. • Focusing avoids dazzle for audience and performers. • Safety cables in use.
...enhance **mood** and **atmosphere**?		• Coloured gels. • Pace of transitions.
...show **collaboration** with performers and other designers?		• Practical effect involving torches used by performers. • Co-ordination on timing rehearsed with sound designer. • Continuous research in rehearsals.

Chapter 5 Component 1: Devising – A Practical Guide

Bright lighting and 'industrial' sparks in Danny Boyle's production of *Frankenstein*.

Writing about bringing your lighting design to life

You need to record the actualising of your final lighting design in the portfolio.

TASK 5.40

Turn the information in Task 5.39 and your lighting design experience so far into two or three paragraphs for your portfolio (about 300 to 400 words). You could focus on the later stages in particular and address one or more of the following key questions.

- **What were some of the significant moments during the development process and when rehearsing and refining your work?**
- **How did you consider genre, structure, character, form, style and language throughout the process?**
- **How effective was your contribution to the final performance?**

TASK 5.41

What important drama skills does this student write about, in addition to lighting design?

> Before the technical rehearsal, the sound designer and myself co-ordinated many of our cues to achieve powerful effects on critical blackouts and cross-fades. This was particularly important when we were enhancing the naturalistic effects, such as the cave scene. We wanted very precise timing on the floodlight coming in with the tapping sound. We practised many times until we were confident that we could be perfectly synchronised.

TASK 5.42

Check your own writing against the AO4 specification. Can you make any improvements by adding details or removing repetition?

ASSESSMENT CHECK

Your finished set will demonstrate AO2: 'Use theatrical skills to realise artistic intentions in live performance.'

DESIGN TIP

Work closely with your human resources to ensure everything is ready in time.

Chapter 5   Component 1: Devising – A Practical Guide

FOCUS
Knowing when you have finished.

LOOK HERE
'Evaluating your lighting design', page 59, will help you with this section of your portfolio. Make sure you fill in the table in Task 2.18.

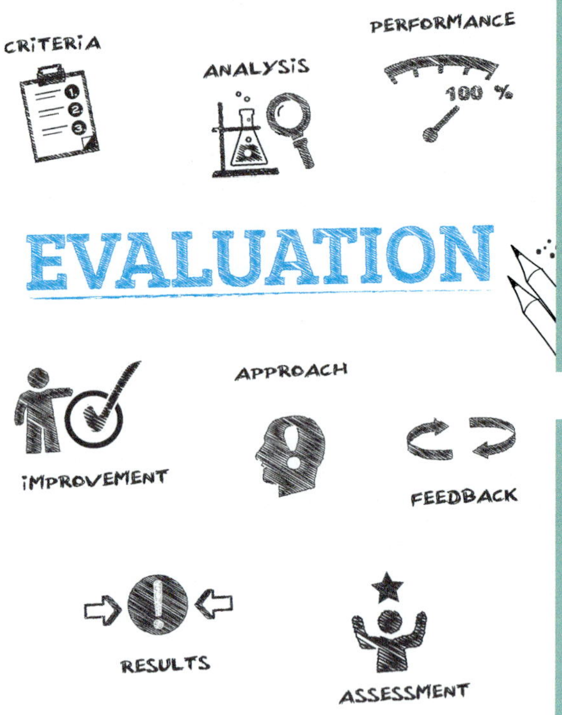

LOOK HERE
For tips on reducing or increasing your word count, see page 137.

COMPLETING YOUR PORTFOLIO

Until the performances have taken place, you won't be in a position to finish your portfolio. When you are, you need to give a detailed evaluation of the 'realisation of creative intentions within the performance, with fully balanced analysis and evaluation'. In other words, you should answer the following key questions:

- **How effective was your contribution to the final performance?**
- **Were you successful in what you set out to achieve?**

TASK 5.43

Write three or four paragraphs (around 400 words) about your lighting that are detailed and evaluative. Base your writing on the table in Task 2.18, your notes and the two questions above. You could structure it like this:

- Use evaluative language to give your design an overall judgement. Effective? Powerful? Successful?
- Give three specific examples of moments that had impact or enhanced atmosphere or helped to convey meaning. If something did not go to plan, you should analyse what happened and why.
- Refer to your artistic intentions for the piece. How did your lighting support those intentions and the production as a whole?

TASK 5.44

Note how the following example evaluates the designer's lighting work alongside the group's artistic intentions.

> I was really pleased with the way the audience thought the lighting design reflected the hopeful mood of the movement scene and made it exciting and engaging. This was very important because we wanted our piece to be an uplifting one that inspired the same strength and resilience in the audience that we were trying to show through our central characters.
>
> The pace of the lighting changes in that scene went perfectly with the music and really enhanced the atmosphere. I felt that I'd got the intensity just right and that the AMLs had been set up to catch the performers at exactly the right angles.

Editing

When you have completed your portfolio and included the diagrams that are required, proofread it and assess it against the AO1 and AO4 specifications. Have you included analysis of the devising process and evaluation of the choices made?

You must also check the word count, as you need to keep below 2000 words, including annotations.

COSTUME DESIGN FOR THE DEVISED PIECE

The requirements of your costume designs

Pastel costumes (designed by Roger Kirk) in *42nd Street* give a feeling of softness and sophistication.

Your costume designs will emerge from your role as a member of a devising group. It will be marked in terms of your ability to 'use, apply and combine design skills to support the performance as a whole.' Your costumes should help to create mood and atmosphere and enhance the chosen genre and styles of the piece. They need to communicate your group's artistic intentions effectively and have an impact on the audience.

The portfolio

The portfolio is your opportunity to explain how you have engaged fully with the process of devising from the viewpoint of group member and costume designer. You will chart the process from beginning to end, detailing your understanding of all the skills you have used and the decisions you have made.

Your ability to work with your group to bring its artistic intentions to reality is important, along with analysis and evaluation of your successes and the challenges you have faced along the way. Remember that an important element of analysis is explaining which ideas or designs you rejected and why.

DESIGN TIP
See your costume designs and your portfolio as parts of the same whole. They must be worked on at the same time.

SIGNPOST
Chapter 3 provides practical guidance for your costume design work and guides you through the entire process of designing, sourcing and creating costumes. Use it here alongside the practical guide at the beginning of this chapter.

LOOK HERE
See page 116 for a breakdown of the portfolio contents.

NOTE
This chapter assumes that you are writing your whole portfolio. If you are taking a different approach, make detailed notes, spider diagrams and so on to support your final presentation.

Chapter 5 Component 1: Devising – A Practical Guide 147

ASSESSMENT CHECK

AO1 asks you to 'create and develop ideas that communicate meaning for theatrical performance.'

This section begins your process of 'documenting the practical creation and development of ideas, along with the analysis of this process and the devised work.'

SIGNPOST

The following sections at the beginning of this chapter will be your resource for starting the portfolio:

- Your design challenge
- Responding to stimuli
- Agreeing on your artistic intentions.

TASK 5.46

What words and phrases could you add as a response to this stimulus photograph?

STARTING WORK ON THE PORTFOLIO

The early stages of documenting your work

Your portfolio should provide plenty of evidence that you can use specific drama language in relation to costume design and to the genre, structure, form and style of the devised piece. It should, at this stage, explain how you responded to the stimuli and came to decide on your creative intentions.

The guidance at the beginning of this chapter will help you respond to this key question:

What was your initial response to the stimuli and what were the intentions of the piece?

TASK 5.45

1. Look through the sections listed in the Signpost. Collect completed tasks and any extra notes.
2. Write a short paragraph describing the stimulus you used. Include an annotated picture or copy of it if you can.
3. Write a further paragraph based on early responses to the stimulus. Include spider diagrams or annotated copies of the stimuli that you created.
4. Briefly link your group's artistic intentions to what you as a designer want the audience to think and feel. How did you arrive at these decisions? Did your ideas change? How and why?
5. Add any sketches or ideas for costume design that you had at this early stage.
6. Read through your paragraphs to check that they answer the question and that the word count is about right (around 300).

A detail from a stimulus photograph that shows a range of circus performers, including acrobats and a ringmaster.

TASK 5.47

1. Would you rate the following draft example as poor, reasonable or good? Why?
2. If you think it is missing details, examples or technical vocabulary, what could you add, and where?

> At this point, each performer chose a character from the photograph and created a freeze-frame, which was thought-tracked by the rest of the group. We discovered that what they said and did was very different from what they were thinking. I know that this is something that many people do.
>
> Three of the performers in our group do dance or gymnastics which drew us towards using some of these skills in the circus setting. I knew that my design ideas would need to take the physicality into account, so I focused on the use of stretch fabric when beginning to develop my ideas.
>
> It took us quite a while to arrive at the intentions for our piece, but we finally worded it like this:
>
> Aim: To create an entertaining piece of largely physical theatre that explores contrasts in terms of onstage and backstage relationships.
>
> I think that most people have a public persona to some extent and, outside the circus setting, this idea had plenty of dramatic potential.

LOOK HERE
'Introduction to costume design' on pages 62–63 might help with Task 5.47.

DESIGN TIP
Note that the example is not a complete portfolio, so not every point in the mark scheme will be covered.

TASK 5.48

1. Check your own portfolio beginning against the AO1 specification. Can you make at least three improvements?
2. As well as checking spelling and punctuation, check that you are keeping to the point and using specific examples.

FOCUS

Reflecting on the genre, structure, character, form, style and language of your devised piece.

ASSESSMENT CHECK

You need to demonstrate understanding of different theatrical elements for AO4.

Your portfolio needs to include 'analysis and evaluation of personal contribution to the creation, development and refinement process.'

LOOK HERE

'Genre, structure, form and style' on pages 120–123 will be a good starting point. 'Introduction to costume design' on pages 62–63 will also help you to consider appropriate costumes.

BUILDING IDEAS

The next section of your portfolio could cover genre, structure, character, form, style and language in relation to the devised piece. Continue to chart the devising process too. You should include appropriate details and reflect carefully on the activities and choices you made.

How do I analyse and evaluate?

You will need to analyse the process of devising. It can be helpful to think about analysis in stages. Try using linking words and phrases such as these:

- Initially / To begin with...
- This led me to...
- Later / As we continued...
- Finally / By the end of...

Phrases containing judgement vocabulary will help you to evaluate. For example:

- My suggestion that... was helpful/important because...
- I thought... would be powerful because...
- My costume design idea of... was effective because...

You can apply these stages to different aspects of the devising process. When you reflect on, for example:

- how you overcame challenges
- how you developed the performance and your design from knowing what you wanted to achieve.

The two key questions you are answering are:

- **What work did your group do in order to explore the stimuli and start to create ideas for performance?**
- **How did you consider genre, structure, character, form, style and language?**

TASK 5.49

Read the student-style extract on the following page.

1. Use different colours to highlight:
   - phrases that show that the writer is analysing the devising process
   - sentences that describe the work done to explore the stimulus
   - sentences that explain details of form, structure, style and character.
2. Note how the writer has explained some of the group's decisions.

This led me to the idea that some dialogue would be useful to add a linear structure within a largely physical piece. I thought that naturalistic conversation would be powerful as it could lead into 'backstage' scenes that would contrast to the more physical 'onstage' theatre. This gave us structure and elements of form and style and I began to think about different on- and offstage costumes.

We decided to go for a tragi-comic genre because it gave plenty of scope for the physical side of the piece while exploring the contrast between the onstage and offstage lives of our characters. My design idea for this contrast was to introduce layering into the costumes so that changes could happen rapidly.

DESIGN TIP

Make sure that you refer to your design ideas and analyse as well as evaluate.

DESIGN TIP

Remember that at this point you are still writing about the group and the stimulus. However, you also need to comment on how the stimuli led to costume ideas.

TASK 5.50

1. Collect completed tasks from Chapter 3 and any additional notes.
2. Write a paragraph or two about some of the activities that your group tried in developing ideas from the stimulus. Recall suggestions you made and discussions you had, writing about them with evaluative and drama-specific vocabulary. Be precise and include reasons behind ideas and choices.
3. Write another paragraph or two about some of the activities that your group tried in developing ideas from the stimulus. Recall suggestions you made and discussions you had, writing about them with evaluative and drama-specific vocabulary. Be precise and include reasons behind ideas and choices. Include annotated sketches of your design ideas, copies of mood boards and so on.
4. Write a further paragraph or two about your choices around genre, structure, character, form, style and language. You can always come back to this later, so don't feel you have to cover everything here. How did you decide what genre the piece would be, for example? Was there any conflict between that and the preferred style, form or structure? If so, how was this resolved? How did these choices affect your design ideas?
5. Read through your paragraphs and keep track of the word count (probably about 300 to 400 is best). Check that you have analysed the process as well as responded to the two key questions.

Chapter 5 Component 1: Devising – A Practical Guide

FOCUS

Evaluating how well you are collaborating with the rest of your group.

ASSESSMENT CHECK

The 'process of collaboration' is a vital part of your 'contribution to the creation, development and realisation' of your piece. You will be assessed on your 'ability to realise artistic intentions through the use of design skills to contribute to and support the performance as a whole.'

SIGNPOST

The following sections will be particularly helpful in making key decisions about your costumes and their development.

- Colour and fabric for the stage, pages 68–71
- Health and safety in costume design, page 77
- Working positively as a group, page 124
- Using rehearsals to develop and refine your design, pages 126–127.

TASK 5.53

Review your portfolio so far. Can you make any improvements by adding details or removing repetition? Have you included analysis and evaluation?

CONTRIBUTING TO THE DEVELOPMENT OF THE PIECE

This section will help you to consider how productively you are working with your group members. You will also be firming up your designs by now.

Developing your costume designs

Your costume designs should be taking shape around the time that the performers begin solid rehearsals. Use Chapter 3 of this book to guide you. As you go along, record your decisions, together with the reasons for them.

Focus on your collaboration. How are you feeding and being fed by the group? What challenges are you attempting to overcome? The key question is:

What were some of the significant moments during the development process and when rehearsing and refining your work?

TASK 5.51

1. Look at the sections in the Signpost. Collect your tasks and notes.
2. Use them to write at least two paragraphs about how you are developing designs that will meet your group's needs. Mention research, resources and improvisations. Include annotated sketches and your group's responses to your designs.
3. Write a further paragraph or two about how your design is impacting on the rehearsal process for the performers. Ask yourself:
    - Are there any problems for the actors? How are these overcome?
    - Are there particular successes? What aspect of your design is enhancing the performance, and how?
    - How is the performers' work affecting your design?
4. Check your text and keep track of the word count.

TASK 5.52

Find **three** moments in the following example where a designer's supportive collaboration has been described and explained.

> I chose to design the costume for the Ring Mistress. The performer was not very comfortable with physical theatre, so we spent rehearsal time making sure that this aspect was as confident and polished as possible.
>
> I wanted to make sure that she had a well-fitting costume with a tailored effect that would boost her confidence as well as support character, style and atmosphere. It could help her get into the role. I made sure that there was plenty of scope for movement by allowing plenty of ease under the arms and across the back.
>
> The costume is an altered cherry-red jacket with black and gold embellishments. I found the jacket in a charity shop and restyled it with a friend's help. Under the jacket, the actress wore stretch black leggings and a stretch T-shirt. Her make-up and hair were bold, with back-combing adding height to her hair and helping with the air of confidence.

DEVELOPING THE PORTFOLIO

Reviewing your portfolio

You are now approximately half way through the devising process. That means that you should also have completed around half of the portfolio or the notes that will help you to complete it at the end of the process.

TASK 5.54

1. Read through your portfolio. Use this chapter and the key questions for each section to check that you haven't drifted away from the questions.
   - Are there paragraphs you can improve by including examples and evaluative language?
   - Use the glossary at the end of Chapter 3. Can you add more subject-specific language?
2. Go through all your notes as well as re-reading your portfolio so far. You could improve your portfolio considerably if you do this thoroughly.

Can I write more about the devising process and the development of my set design?

TASK 5.55

Use the following questions to remind you of significant events you might not have mentioned so far.

- Were there memorable moments in rehearsals or production meetings?
- Did I hit an obstacle? What did I do?
- Has there been a moment when I felt particularly pleased or proud? What was it and what was the effect that pleased me?
- How did I collaborate with other designers?
- Can I say more about genre, structure, character, form and style?
- Am I using suitable technical language?
- How else did I contribute in rehearsals? What was the effect?
- Have I taken health and safety issues into account?
- Do I have sketches, swatches, images of mood boards and so on?

TASK 5.56

Add 100 to 200 words across the first three sections of your portfolio. Use your responses to the questions above. Try to use more subject-specific language and add one or two detailed examples.

FOCUS
- Making sure you give enough detail.
- Checking and improving your work so far.

ASSESSMENT CHECK
You need to give plenty of specific examples of 'drama terminology'. Also, take an 'evaluative and analytical approach' to 'creating and developing ideas to communicate meaning.'

DESIGN TIP
Remove waffle! Include brief, precise detail.

DESIGN TIP
Look through the student-style examples for the other design elements in this chapter. They might inspire some new ideas.

Chapter 5 Component 1: Devising – A Practical Guide 153

FOCUS
Documenting the completion of your costume design.

ASSESSMENT CHECK
You need to show how your final design looks and is actualised on the stage. You need to analyse and evaluate your 'personal contribution towards the creation, development and refinement process'.

Acrobat / trapeze artist
- Pink hair
- Silver rhinestones?
- Purple net ruffles
- 'Natural' tights
- Snug pumps (Or bare feet?)

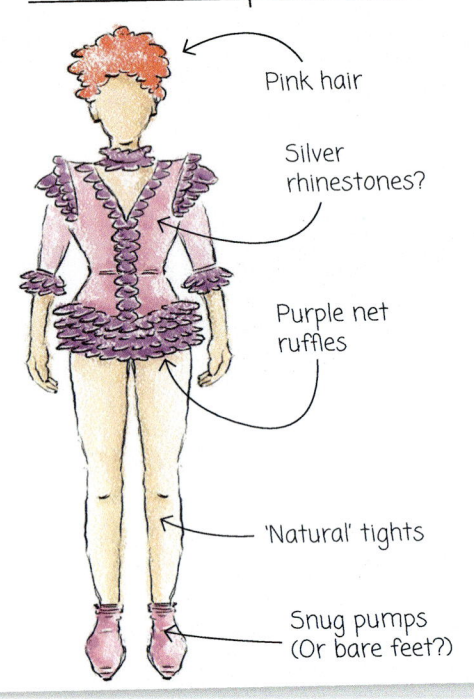

DESIGN TIP
Make sure you annotate your design drawings so that the details are very clear.

LOOK HERE
'How to document your costume design', pages 80–81, will help you with the technical drawings.

PRODUCING AND DOCUMENTING YOUR DESIGN

What must I produce for my final costume designs?

You need to present:
- final costume designs for two characters in the production, incorporating hair, make-up and mask considerations if appropriate.
- a costume plot or list of costume items and accessories worn by each performer, indicating any changes as appropriate.
- the realisation of the costume designs in the devised performance (in other words, two actual costumes used in the performance that match your final drawings).

You also need to have supervised the construction of the designed costumes if you have not made them yourself.

TASK 5.57

Fill in your version of the following table before you construct either of your final costumes.

How does my costume design...		
...enhance the genre, structure, form and style of the piece?	Genre	Tragi-comedy. Costumes are largely steam-punk/circus, with a comic element. The addition of a slouchy jumper radically affects the feel of the costume.
	Structure	Linear. Costume changes are quick.
	Forms	Physical theatre, for example. Cut and fabric enable ease of movement.
	Style	Mixture of naturalistic and non-naturalistic – in performance and in costume design.
...reflect the **artistic intentions** of my group?		Costumes transform easily on stage from backstage to onstage wear. This fits with our artistic intention of contrasting relationships.
...avoid **health and safety** hazards?		• Avoid trailing items. • Ensure freedom of movement. • Non-slippery footwear.
...enhance **mood** and **atmosphere**?		Colours and textures of circus, flamboyant styling including hair and make-up.
...show **collaboration** with performers and other designers?		• Co-ordinated use of colour palette with lighting designer. • Working together to ensure there were four costumes (for all performers), rather than just the two assessed. • Providing costume items early enough in rehearsal for plenty of practice.

Making your design

This is the moment where you finish the job of constructing and pulling together the garments, accessories, hair and make-up that are the reality of your final costume designs.

You are aiming for two costumes that:

- fit well
- include appropriate hair and make-up
- suit the style, genre and form of your devised piece
- show thorough consideration of any health and safety issues
- can be produced within the constraints of your budget
- have impact for the audience
- support the piece as a whole in terms of artistic intentions, mood and atmosphere.

I found that ballet net was quite cheap and comes in a range of colours. It was also easy to work with as it doesn't fray or need to be hemmed. Net underskirts are in many kinds of costume, so I decided to experiment with adding it to charity shop garments to produce flamboyant costume effects.

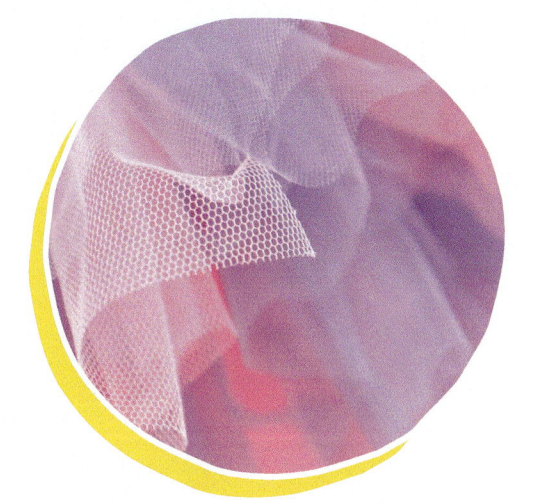

TASK 5.58

1. Use the information in Task 5.57 and the experience of making or supervising your costumes to write three or four paragraphs for your portfolio (about 300 words).
2. Check your writing against the AO4 specification. Can you make at least two improvements?

SIGNPOST
Use any sections of Chapter 3 that apply to your own design as well as notes and completed tasks.

DESIGN TIP
Remember to use your human resources, as there is no need to do the sewing yourself unless you want to.

DESIGN TIP
Check that you have included hair, make-up and mask drawings (if relevant), as well as clothing designs.

Chapter 5 · Component 1: Devising – A Practical Guide

FOCUS
Knowing when you have finished.

LOOK HERE
'Evaluating your costume design', page 87, will help you with this section.

DESIGN TIP
Remember that you are required to provide a list of costumes along with any changes which take place within the performance.

LOOK HERE
For tips on reducing or increasing your word count, see page 137.

COMPLETING YOUR PORTFOLIO

When the performances have taken place, you can finish your portfolio. Give a detailed evaluation of how well you realised your intentions, in answer to the following key questions:
- **How effective was your contribution to the final performance?**
- **Were you successful in what you set out to achieve?**

TASK 5.59

Write around 450 words about your costumes that are detailed and evaluative. Base this on the table in Task 3.16, your notes and the two questions above. The example below could help you with the structure.

TASK 5.60

Highlight and list all the words and phrases in the following example that evaluate the costume design. For example, *impact*, *emphasised*…

> I was pleased that my costume had helped the Ring Mistress really own the stage. The jacket encouraged her to keep an upright posture but allowed her to move freely so that her gestures were broad and powerful. Audience members commented on the impact of her costume and how it strengthened her character. I am very proud of that. Removing the bulky lining of the coat was successful in that the actor was able to move fluently in the physical theatre sequences. Restyling the coat to make it more fitted and with a short swallow-tail was highly effective. The tails added the required formality, and were short enough not to be trodden on.
>
> In the backstage sections of the piece, the actress swapped her coat for a broken-down red cardigan. I chose the colour for visual continuity; a reminder of her onstage role. Because the cardigan was rough, pilled acrylic with stretched cuffs and a few holes, it succeeded in supporting the character. I used a cheese grater to raise the surface and produce the holes. I stretched the cuffs by pulling them while the garment was wet. The fact that it was second hand made it easier to produce this look.
>
> The actress changed her posture when she wore the cardigan by rounding her shoulders and slouching a little, which emphasised the difference between her on- and offstage personalities. Her hairstyle could be flattened for the backstage scenes. Again, this powerfully reinforced the differences in her personality.

Editing

When you have completed your portfolio and included the drawings required, proofread it and assess it against the AO1 and AO4 objectives.

Check the word count is under 2000 words, including annotations.

SOUND DESIGN FOR THE DEVISED PIECE

The requirements of your sound design

Your sound design will emerge from your role as a member of a devising group. It will be marked in terms of your ability to 'use, apply and combine design skills to support the performance as a whole'. Your sound should create mood and atmosphere and enhance the chosen genre and styles. It needs to communicate your group's artistic intentions effectively and have an impact on the audience.

The portfolio

The portfolio is your opportunity to explain how you have engaged fully with the process of devising from the viewpoint of group member and set designer. You will chart the design process from beginning to end, detailing your understanding of all the skills you have used and the decisions you have made.

Your ability to work with your group to bring its artistic intentions to reality is important, along with analysis and evaluation of your successes and the challenges you have faced along the way. You should refer to your design ideas throughout your portfolio.

DESIGN TIP
See your set design and your portfolio as two parts of the same whole. They must be worked on at the same time. This could involve taking detailed notes or writing the portfolio as you go along and reviewing it at the end of the process.

SIGNPOST
Chapter 4 provides practical guidance for your sound design work and guides you through the entire process of designing, mixing, plotting and operating sound effects.

LOOK HERE
See page 116 for a breakdown of the portfolio contents.

NOTE
This chapter assumes that you are writing your whole portfolio. If you are taking a different approach, make detailed notes, spider diagrams and so on to support your final presentation.

FOCUS
Putting together a document that communicates your group's intentions and your contribution to them.

ASSESSMENT CHECK
AO1 asks you to 'create and develop ideas that communicate meaning for theatrical performance.'

This section begins your process of 'documenting the practical creation and development of ideas, along with the analysis of this process and the devised work.'

SIGNPOST
The following sections at the beginning of this chapter will help you to start the portfolio:
- Your design challenge
- Responding to stimuli
- Agreeing on your artistic intentions.

TASK 5.63
Check your own portfolio so far. Can you make at least two improvements? As well as spelling and punctuation, check that you are keeping to the point and using specific examples.

My first response was that it is a very weird picture, but interesting. It seemed to have a mixture of nature and man in it. The title is interesting too because memory is about time, which links to the clocks. Persistence is about keeping going. I suppose some memories do persist, but what about the things we forget?

As sound designer, I started to think about a clock ticking and the possibility of slowing it down or speeding it up to suggest time passing at different rates.

STARTING WORK ON THE PORTFOLIO

The early stages of documenting your work

Your portfolio should provide plenty of evidence that you can use specific drama language in relation to sound design and to the genre, structure, form and style of the devised piece. It should, at this stage, explain how you responded to the stimuli and came to decide on your creative intentions. You are answering the key question:

What was your initial response to the stimuli and what were the intentions of the piece?

TASK 5.61
1. Look through the sections listed in the Signpost. Collect completed tasks and extra notes.
2. Write a short paragraph describing the stimulus you chose or were given. Include a copy of it if you can.
3. Write a further paragraph based on early responses to the stimulus material. You could include spider diagrams or an annotated copy of the stimulus.
4. Link your group's artistic intentions to what you as a designer want the audience to think and feel. Have your ideas changed?
5. Add any ideas for sound design that you had at this stage.
6. Read through your paragraphs to check that they answer the question and that the word count is about right (around 300 words).

TASK 5.62
Annotate the painting below.
- What do you see?
- What does the painting make you think and feel?
- What ideas for sound does it suggest?

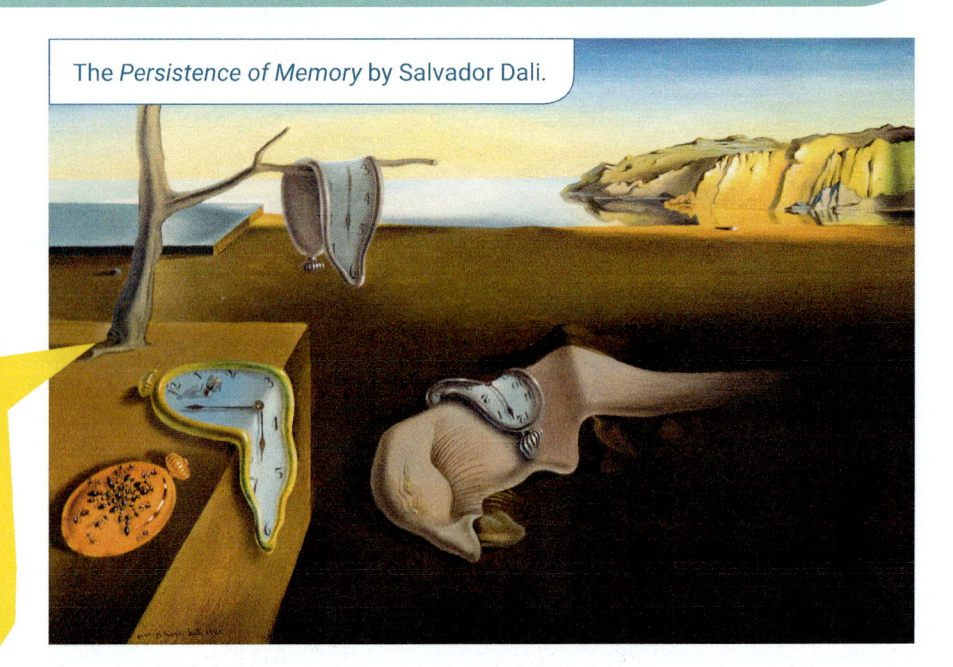

The *Persistence of Memory* by Salvador Dali.

BUILDING IDEAS

The next section of your portfolio could cover your understanding of genre, structure, character, form, style and language in relation to your devised piece. Continue to chart the devising process, including analysis and evaluation of the decisions made.

The two key questions you are answering are:
- **What work did your group do in order to explore the stimuli and start to create ideas for performance?**
- **How did you consider genre, structure, character, form, style and language?**

TASK 5.64

1. Collect completed tasks from Chapter 4 and any additional notes.
2. Write a paragraph or two about activities that your group tried in developing ideas. Recall suggestions, discussions and improvisations, writing about them with analytical and drama-specific vocabulary. Be precise and include reasons behind ideas and choices.
3. Write a further paragraph or two about your choices around genre, structure, character, form, style and language. (You can come back to this later.) How did you decide on a genre, for example? How did those choices affect your design ideas?
4. Read your text and keep track of the word count (about 300 to 400).

TASK 5.65

In this draft example, highlight and comment on the analysis of how the work grew from the stimulus.

> An interesting idea grew in response to the painting, as one of us has a grandparent with dementia. He talked about how difficult it was for him and for his gran (Joyce) because her memory loss was pretty bad. This was a circumstance where memory is not persistent at all.
>
> When I looked at the stimulus and thought about dementia, the sliding clock faces really made sense. For Joyce, time and memories have mainly slipped away from her. The ants on the watch are dementia eating away at her memories. I thought this was a moving story which could be excellent for our devised piece and give us lots of opportunity to be creative.
>
> One of my design ideas was to reflect Joyce's anxiety and confusion through the use of discordant sounds. I also thought of the sound effect of a ticking clock sometimes getting louder and softer and quicker and slower in a random, out-of-control way. These developed well and ended up in the final piece.

FOCUS
Reflecting on genre, structure, form, style and language as you develop ideas.

ASSESSMENT CHECK
You need to understand theatrical elements for AO4.

Your portfolio needs to include 'analysis and evaluation of personal contribution to the creation, development and refinement process.'

LOOK HERE
'Genre, structure, form and style' on pages 120–123 will be a good starting point.

'Research for sound design', pages 94–95, will also be helpful.

Pages 131 and 140 have some useful evaluation sentence starters.

DESIGN TIP
An important element of analysis is explaining which ideas or designs you rejected and why.

Chapter 5   Component 1: Devising – A Practical Guide   159

FOCUS

Evaluating how well you are collaborating with the rest of your group.

ASSESSMENT CHECK

The 'process of collaboration' is part of your 'contribution to the creation, development and realisation' of your piece. You should be able to 'realise artistic intentions through the use of design skills to contribute to and support the performance as a whole.'

SIGNPOST

The following sections will be particularly helpful in making key decisions about your sound design and its development.

- Sourcing, creating and mixing sounds, pages 96–98
- Special sound effects, pages 100–101
- How to document your sound design, pages 102–103
- Working positively as a group, page 124
- Using rehearsals to develop and refine your design, pages 126–127.

CONTRIBUTING TO THE DEVELOPMENT OF THE PIECE

This section will help you to consider how productively you are working alongside your group members. You will also be firming up your sound design by now.

Developing your sound design

Your sound design should be taking shape around the time that the performers begin solid rehearsals. Use Chapter 4 of this book to guide your process. As you go along, record your decisions, together with the reasons for making them.

Focus on your collaboration. How are you feeding and being fed by the group? What challenges are you attempting to overcome? The key question is:

What were some of the significant moments during the development process and when rehearsing and refining your work?

TASK 5.66

1. Collect completed tasks and notes from the sections in the Signpost.
2. Use them to write at least two paragraphs about how you are developing a sound design that will meet your group's needs. Mention research, resources and improvisations. Include annotated plans and cues and your group's responses to your design.
3. Write a further paragraph or two about how your design is impacting on the rehearsal process. Ask yourself:
   - Are there any problems for the actors? How are these overcome?
   - Are there particular successes? What aspect of your design is enhancing the performance, and how?

   Reflect on the effect of the performers' work on your design. Is there a speech, for example, during which you need to fade up an underscore?
4. Check your text and keep track of the word count.

TASK 5.67

What moments of your process might it be useful to make a recording of?

> Quite early in the process, the lighting designer and I sat down to share our ideas. We were very keen to make sound and lighting complement each other, which meant working together. This worked particularly well when we started to consider moments that could be enhanced by fast-paced sound and lights.
>
> I had already been thinking about the sound of a ticking clock, so I got a metronome from the music department and set it at a slow speed. We discovered that the rhythmic sound helped the actors to time their movements as well as adding to the surrealism of the scene. The lighting designer enhanced the effect by experimenting with colours and transition speeds. We recorded a short video so that we could re-create the scene another time.

DEVELOPING THE PORTFOLIO

Reviewing your portfolio

You are now approximately half way through the devising process. That means that you should also have completed around half of the portfolio or the notes that will help you to complete it at the end of the process.

> **TASK 5.68**
>
> 1. Using this chapter and the key questions for each section, read through your portfolio, and check that you have not drifted away from the questions. Remove waffle. Include brief, precise detail.
>   - Are there sentences you can improve by using examples and evaluative language?
>   - Use the glossary at the end of Chapter 4. Can you include more subject-specific language?
> 2. Go through all your notes as well as re-reading your portfolio so far. You will improve your portfolio considerably if you do this thoroughly.

Can I write more about the devising process and the development of my sound design?

With Task 5.68 completed, it is a good idea to see if there are more things you could add about the process before you move onto the final stages and evaluating your design.

> **TASK 5.69**
>
> Use the following questions to remind you of significant events you might not have mentioned so far.
> - Were there memorable moments in rehearsals or production meetings?
> - How and why did my ideas change?
> - How did I use different styles and types of sound?
> - What did I produce that contributed significantly to mood and atmosphere?
> - Did I experiment with live sound? How and why?
> - Have I considered health and safety issues?
> - Did I experiment with mixing sound? What were the results?

> **TASK 5.70**
>
> Add 100 to 200 words across the first three sections of your portfolio. Use your responses to the questions above. Aim to use more subject-specific language and add one or two detailed examples.

FOCUS
- Making sure you give enough detail.
- Checking and improving your work so far.

ASSESSMENT CHECK
Your teachers want to give you as many marks as possible for your portfolio. You can help them by giving plenty of specific examples of 'drama terminology'. They also want you to have an 'evaluative and analytical approach' to 'creating and developing ideas to communicate meaning.'

DESIGN TIP
Look through the student-style examples for the other design elements in this chapter. They might inspire some new ideas.

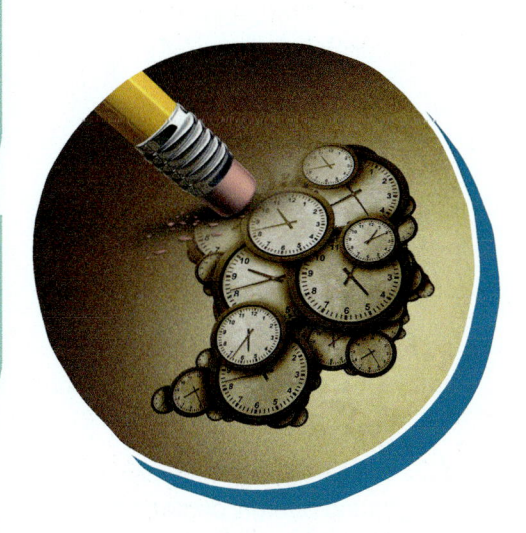

FOCUS

Documenting the completion of your sound design.

ASSESSMENT CHECK

For AO2, your teachers need to know about your final design and how it sounds as part of the final performance. You should analyse and evaluate your 'personal contribution towards the creation, development and refinement process.'

SIGNPOST

Chapter 4 will guide you through all aspects of creating your design.

LOOK HERE

'How to document your sound design' on pages 102–103, will help you with the evidence needed.

PRODUCING AND DOCUMENTING YOUR DESIGN

What must I produce for my final sound design?

You need to present:

- a source sheet showing at least two sound cues: original, live or found sounds
- a cue sheet that includes the source, order, length and output level of each sound used
- the realisation of the sound design in the performance.

You also need to supervise the operation of the sound design in performance and the creation and recording of live and/or sampled material (if not doing these yourself).

A cue sheet created in Macs Cue software.

Making your design

Your finished sounds should be engaging and effective for the audience. They must also support the communication of your group's artistic intentions. Check that you have considered design details that enhance meaning, mood and atmosphere.

TASK 5.71

Fill in your own version of this table before you finalise your design:

How does my sound design…		
…enhance the genre, structure, form and style of the piece?	Genre	Dark comedy. Soundscapes and carefully chosen music.
	Structure	Episodic. Transition sound effect brings sense of unity.
	Forms	Naturalistic dialogue and movement scenes. Sound is engaging for an audience of our peers.
	Style	Mixture of naturalistic and non-naturalistic – in performance and in sound design, both diegetic and non-diegetic.
…reflect the **artistic intentions** of my group?		• Theme of persistence of memory. • The clock effects enhance the theme. • Music evokes particular periods. • Soundscape helps to raise questions around memory.
…avoid **health and safety** hazards?		• Sound levels checked. • Cables taped down.
…enhance **mood** and **atmosphere**?		Atmospheric effects and music enhance performance.
…show **collaboration** with performers and other designers?		• Close work with performers improved the piece. • Used sound effects during rehearsals. • Worked closely with lighting designer.

Writing about bringing your sound design to life

You need to record the actualising of your final sound design in the portfolio. Remember that you are allowed to supervise the programming of your sound design as well as the operating.

In general, your task is to come up with a minimum of two sound effects (including music) that will be played during the performance. It is worth saying that you will need to make your sound design reasonably complex to attain high marks. Ideally, you will go beyond the minimum requirements and:

- mix sounds to create a soundscape
- experiment with both live and recorded sound
- consider using special effects such as echo and reverb, even if you decide not to use them in the end
- remember the power of silence – don't use sound just for the sake of it
- select music carefully
- pay attention to pre-set and post-show music, as well as scene transitions.

DESIGN TIP

Remember that your sound sources and effects should take into consideration performer/audience relationships and health and safety issues.

TASK 5.72

Turn Task 5.71 and the experience of compiling your sound into two or three paragraphs for your portfolio. Focus on these key questions:

- **What were some of the significant moments during the development process and when rehearsing and refining your work?**
- **How did you consider genre, structure, character, form, style and language throughout the process?**
- **How effective was your contribution to the final performance?**

TASK 5.73

Highlight at least four examples of sound design vocabulary here.

> I included several non-diegetic soundscapes and effects to enhance atmosphere and to support our artistic intentions. A good example was the scene where the lady with dementia was with her grandson. I researched effects of dementia and put together a soundscape which included both naturalistic and non-naturalistic sounds. I used the sound of children playing (from her distant memories) and added a slow metronome effect and a distorted drone sound to create some of the confusion she was experiencing.
>
> For this complex mix, I created the three sound effects individually and ensured they had the qualities I wanted. The metronome was recorded live; the other two were from the internet. I varied the volume of the playground sound so that it faded in and out from very quiet to about 40%. I also added reverb to the drone effect to add atmosphere. Then, I experimented with mixing them. I played with the balance in terms of volume and was reasonably pleased in the end. I tried adding a piece of 1940s swing music, but there was too much going on, so I used it to transition into the scene instead.
>
> This is one way in which I refined my work. The final soundscape enhanced our artistic intention of exploring the persistence of memory and supported the scene effectively. The research of trialling the effect in rehearsals benefited the scene considerably.

TASK 5.74

Check your own writing so far. Can you improve it by adding details or removing repetition? Have you included analysis and evaluation?

FOCUS
Knowing when you have finished.

LOOK HERE
'Evaluating your sound design', page 111, will help you here. Make sure you fill in the table in Task 4.21, as the information will form the basis of the final part of your portfolio.

DESIGN TIP
A large percentage of the marks for this component will be carried by how well you analyse and evaluate. Make sure this final part of your portfolio is the best it can be!

LOOK HERE
If you are struggling to make your portfolio fit the desired word count, try the tips on page 137.

COMPLETING YOUR PORTFOLIO

Until the performances have taken place, you will not be in a position to finish your portfolio. When you are, you need to give a detailed evaluation of the 'realisation of creative intentions within the performance, with fully balanced analysis and evaluation'. In other words, you should answer the following key questions:

- **How effective was your contribution to the final performance?**
- **Were you successful in what you set out to achieve?**

TASK 5.75

Annotate the following portfolio example. Where has the writer used audience feedback as a basis for their own evaluation?

> The other scene that was commented on in relation to sound was about a young child that got lost on a ship. It came from an early memory of one group member, and I aimed to show how time can feel that it is moving very quickly. For this scene, it was important to suggest location and I used some diegetic sea and boat effects mixed with the metronome set to a fast speed. This scene also worked successfully with the lighting, which was mainly blue and cold. I was told that the scene actually raised the heart-rate of some of the audience and I was very proud of that achievement, as we had wanted to convey fear.
>
> I learned a great deal from designing the sound for our devised piece, particularly linked to mixing sound to create soundscapes.
>
> Although I think I could have improved the volume of the sound in one or two places, I think my design was very successful overall.

TASK 5.76

Write three or four paragraphs (around 450 words) about your sound design that are detailed and evaluative. Base them on the table in Task 4.21, your notes and the two key questions above.

Final checks

When you are confident that your portfolio:

- is the best it can be
- is between 1800 and 2000 words long or hits the upper end of the recorded audio-visual piece
- contains the source and sound cue sheets
- meets the requirements of the AO1 and AO4 specifications, you have finished!

COMPONENT 2: DESIGNING FOR THE PERFORMANCE FROM TEXT

Chapter 6

How your design skills will be assessed	166

Six Steps to Set Design for the Scripted Performance — 168

1 Working on your own with the script	168
2 The design brief meeting and rehearsals	170
3 Revisiting the script	171
4 Confirming your set designs	172
5 The final design meeting	173
6 The completed set design	174
The written explanation for set design	175

Six Steps to Lighting Design for the Scripted Performance — 176

1 Working on your own with the script	176
2 The design brief meeting and rehearsals	178
3 Revisiting the script	179
4 Confirming your lighting designs	180
5 The final design meeting	181
6 The completed lighting design	182
The written explanation for lighting design	183

Six Steps to Costume Design for the Scripted Performance — 184

1 Working on your own with the script	184
2 The design brief meeting and rehearsals	186
3 Revisiting the script	187
4 Confirming your costume designs	188
5 The final design meeting	189
6 The completed costume design	190
The written explanation for costume design	191

Six Steps to Sound Design for the Scripted Performance — 192

1 Working on your own with the script	192
2 The design brief meeting and rehearsals	194
3 Revisiting the script	195
4 Confirming your sound designs	196
5 The final design meeting	197
6 The completed sound design	198
The written explanation for sound design	199

FOCUS
- Advice on what examiners expect to see on their visits to schools.
- Details of the assessment criteria and how to meet them.

DESIGN TIP
You can choose different options for each extract. You could perform in the first extract, for example, and design for the second.

LOOK HERE
Explanation and guidance for the central concept of artistic intentions are given on pages 114–119.

There is specific guidance on the written explanation for each role following each set of six steps.

DESIGN TIP
You do not need to finish your written explanation until just before the examiner comes into your school, but you should prepare notes for it and collect your work-in-progress as your design develops.

HOW YOUR DESIGN SKILLS WILL BE ASSESSED

Component 2 is assessed by a visiting examiner. For the scripted extracts, the examiner will look for two types of evidence of your design skills:
- your written explanation, which discusses your artistic intentions
- the two designs you produce – one for each extract from the chosen text.

The written explanation
Your explanation is a guide to what you intend for your design in performance. It contributes to the examiner's understanding of your design and the process you have been through, so is very important.

You need to produce between 100 and 200 words for each extract, detailing:
- your design (or performance) role
- the central concept in your design
- how your design interprets the extract
- what you want your design to communicate to the audience.

You must also include:

SET
- At least one drawing of the final design, including props
- A ground plan that includes stage furniture, entrances, exits and audience seating (with consideration of sightlines and safety).

LIGHTING
- The final lighting design, which includes plans and a lantern schedule for at least two different lighting states and thoughts of:
  - health and safety implications
  - ways in which lighting can enhance performer/audience relationships)
- A lighting plot or cue sheet showing a minimum of four lighting cues.

COSTUME
- Drawings for the final design that take into account:
  - how detailed the costume needs to be, given the performance space and stage configuration
  - health and safety implications and the suitability of the costume
- A list of costumes and accessories worn by your chosen character(s)
- Details of when and how they make costume changes, if any (for example: *Page 14: Hansel puts on his coat*).

SOUND
- A source sheet showing at least two sound cues for original, live or found sounds. Your design should consider:
  - performer/audience relationships
  - health and safety implications
  - performer usage (showing that you have thought about how mics will be used and that sound levels are appropriate).
- A cue sheet with sources, order, lengths and output levels.

The designs in performance

AO2 is the objective for the finished designs: 'Apply theatrical skills to realise artistic intentions in live performance.' In Component 2, it carries 20 per cent of the total GCSE. Your designs should therefore demonstrate the application of your knowledge about how to develop and create finished designs for the extracts.

The examiner will be looking very carefully for the way design is used during the performance of both extracts. As the extracts are assessed separately, you might want to create a noticeably different design for each extract. The examiner will be assessing your ability to:

INTERPRET
the text creatively and believably, making your design a significant and harmonious part of the production.
Aim to create designs that inform the audience about the play and the character/s. These designs should be in keeping with the work of other designers and enhance the artistic intentions of the piece.

PRODUCE
creative and engaging designs that match your written explanations.
Check that your written explanation accurately reflects the process that led to the finished designs. These designs should make a significant impact on the audience.

USE DESIGN
to amplify the mood, atmosphere, genre and style of the performance as a whole.
Think about being accurate to the period and fitting the style of the text, for example whether it is naturalistic or non-naturalistic. How does your design match the feel of the piece?

SIGNPOST
You will get the most out of this chapter if you refer closely to the guidance and tasks in the relevant Practical Guide to Design chapter at the beginning of this book.

DESIGN TIP
Make sure that you are in touch with what is going on in rehearsals throughout the process. It is sure to influence the way your design develops.

MAKE THE BEST USE
of the resources and time available.
Plan your time. Take up offers of help. Avoid putting anything that looks unfinished onto the stage.

UNDERSTAND AND APPLY
the technical aspects of your design.
Aim for the most professional-looking designs possible.

The performers in their muted period costumes are dominated by the back projection in this scene from *1984* at Nottingham Playhouse.

Chapter 6 Component 2: Designing for the Performance from Text

FOCUS
- The process of set design from page to stage.
- How to interpret, analyse and evaluate as you experiment with different designs, select those that are most successful and then realise your designs.

ASSESSMENT CHECK
Your design work will demonstrate your ability to 'develop interpretations independently and collaboratively' as you 'respond and adapt your designs in response to rehearsal work.'

SIGNPOST
Chapter 1 is designed to help you with every aspect of your practical work.

DESIGN TIP
Use a notebook or a secure folder. Loose bits of paper get lost or become disorganised!

LOOK HERE
Pages 20–24 have guidance on making and using model sets. However, being ready to talk through your ideas with a couple of sketches is fine for now.

SIX STEPS TO SET DESIGN FOR THE SCRIPTED PERFORMANCE

STEP 1
Working on your own with the script

As soon as you know that you are designing the set, start your independent work. This is likely to be at the same time as rehearsals begin.

A non-naturalistic set design for Uchenna Dance's Hansel and Gretel. It is a very modern style that uses bold, primary colours, geometric shapes and click-together panels that recall children's building toys. This also makes the set versatile, as items can be put together differently to represent, for example, both the forest and the cottage.

You will need to look at the script through the eyes of a set designer. This means thinking about the genre, style, context and locations you will need to enhance. Your teacher should tell you what the stage configuration will be.

1. Read the whole play (or a detailed summary). As you go through, use a table like the one below to note details that could influence your set design choices. (An example has been suggested.)

Play: Alice by Lorna Wade
Genre: Black comedy

Staging configuration	Location/s	Historical, social and cultural contexts	Themes/ messages	Style, moods and atmosphere
Proscenium arch.	• Wonderland • Alice's living room • Alice's attic.	Contemporary (modern day).	• Family • Growing up • Dealing with grief.	• Fantasy and realism • Mixture of naturalism and non-naturalism • Comic moments.

2. Carefully read each extract. Highlight and mark brief annotations on:
   - locations – specific (such as an attic) and more general (Wonderland, for example)
   - key events and moments of action where an item of set is important
   - the economic and social situation of characters
   - special settings, including levels (these might be given in the script)
   - any questions that crop up.

3. Ask your teacher what style of production is most likely. You might be dealing with a highly naturalistic style, for example. From that information, what images pop into your head as you read? Draw some sketches to capture your ideas.

    If you have time, make white-card models of your favourite designs.

4. Make more detailed notes from your table, above. These include the page and line number from the script, or a quotation. For example:

> **DESIGN TIP**
> Remember that there must be a separate design for each extract, if you are the set designer for both.

SET DESIGN

Keep these?
Scenery

Style: → Abstract? → Naturalistic?

p13: Are there beds in the cottage?

'Hansel and Gretel' has the structure of a nightmare. A few domestic objects – buckets, a knife, a blanket, a plate, a jug, an axe – create both the house and the forest and appear in the Witch's house. The Mother also reappears, grotesque, as the Witch. A chorus of three is always present, and active. [...] The story is one of starvation, terror and catharsis. The rhythms of speech are taut and violent, containing the fearful tensions and, finally, joyous release of the drama.

Location: in house   *Silhouette?*

Father It was no more than once upon a time when a poor woodcutter lived in a small house at the edge of a huge, dark forest. Now, the woodcutter lived with his wife and his two young children – a boy called Hansel and a little girl called Gretel. [...] Night after hungry night, he lay in bed next to his thin wife, and he worried so much that he tossed and he turned and he sighed and he mumbled and moaned and he just couldn't sleep at all. [...]

Bed? Boxes?

Where? Bedroom?

And as he fretted and sweated in the darkness, back came the bony voice of his wife; a voice as fierce as famine. [...]

Levels?

Hansel Now, Hansel and Gretel had been so hungry that night that they hadn't been able to sleep either, and they'd heard every cruel word of their mother's terrible plan.

Gretel Gretel cried bitter salt tears, and said to Hansel: 'Now we're finished.'

Hansel 'Don't cry, Gretel. Don't be sad. I'll think of a way to save us.'

And when their father and mother had finally gone to sleep, Hansel got up, put on his coat, opened the back door, and crept out into the midnight hour.

Level?

Location Outside. Bright light.

There was bright, sparkling moonlight outside and the white pebbles on the ground shone like silver coins and precious jewels. Hansel bent down and filled his empty pockets with as many pebbles as he could carry. [...]

Literal?

Along the path. Hansel keeps stopping and turning back. [...]

Spaced-out pebbles he collects?

The family go deeper into the dark heart of the forest.

Gretel The forest was immense and gloomy. [...]

Hansel Hansel and Gretel collected a big pile of firewood and when it was set alight and the flames were like burning tongues, their mother said:

Props?
Scattered?

Mother 'Now lie down by the fire and rest.'

How do we create:
- forest
- house
- interior/exterior?

Revolving flats?
Composite?

Forest could be: imaginary
- hung fabric
- brooms/twigs
- flats
- scenery
- actors?

Flooring:
- Wooden, neutral – house and forest?
- Rush mats?
- Vinyl?

Chapter 6 Component 2: Designing for the Performance from Text 169

DESIGN TIP

In professional theatre, a white-card meeting might be held once the set designer has constructed a simple 3D version of the set in paper or card. Alternatively, there might be 2D sketches of the set and possibly some costume sketches.

STEP 2
The design brief meeting and rehearsals

Now that you have an understanding of the script and have some set design ideas, arrange a meeting with your group. Take your script and notebook and any sketches and models you have. If you have a costume, sound or lighting designer, they should be there too. Other designers (particularly lighting) won't get far with their work until they have some clarity about the set.

You will not be able to finalise your designs until you know the style of the production. This will tell you whether you are aiming for a representative set, or a naturalistic one that seeks to fully create the illusion of reality.

This design of the cottage for Glyndebourne Opera is more naturalistic, but note the use of soft cardboard more suitable for temporary boxes.

- Is it set in a particular time period?
- If there is to be a forest, for example, will there be literal representations of trees or something much simpler, such as strips of fabric hanging from the rigging? Or will trees be depicted by actors or simply imagined by the actors and audience?
- Will there be a composite set or will the stage be divided into different locations?
- Will buildings and rooms be physically on stage in some form? Will there be stage furniture? What form might it take?

During the meeting

1. Share your thoughts so far about set design. Show any sketches or models and invite feedback. Try to deal with any criticism positively: very few designers are likely to get it all right first time.
2. Listen carefully to others and give similar sensitive feedback.
3. Make sure you discuss the following questions:
   - Do we have issues from Step 1 that can be answered in this meeting? If not, how and when can they be addressed?
   - Are we beginning to move towards a shared artistic vision for the performance? What do we imagine it looks like?
   - How will we communicate our ideas to each other? Can we create a shared resource bank for notes and images as we work independently? (This could be a folder on your school's intranet or a service such as Dropbox, which many professional theatres use.)
   - What shall we work on before we next meet? What do we want to achieve and by when?
4. Make detailed and well-organised notes of the discussions and any decisions made. You could put them under the heading 'Design Brief Meeting' in your notebook.
5. Agree on a date for the next design meeting.

LOOK HERE

'Two styles of set design' on page 18 and 'Understanding your resources' on page 25 will be helpful at this point.

Chapter 6 Component 2: Designing for the Performance from Text

STEP 3
Revisiting the script

This step is another stage you can complete independently. You should, however, be continuously checking in on rehearsals, as developments might influence your design. Similarly, other designers and the performers will benefit from your updates.

1. Add details to your script annotations and ideas table, based on what you learned at the design brief meeting.
2. Make any alterations to your draft designs as required. For example, does your colour palette need to change to fit in with the overall mood, or costume or lighting designs?

> You might have ideas for a modern, highly stylised *Hansel and Gretel*. Tall, thin trees could be made from long cardboard tubes or by hanging long strips of dark green and brown fabric, for example.

Are there special considerations that need to be planned for, such as interaction with furniture? An outdoor fire, for example, is required in Carol Ann Duffy and Tim Supple's version of *Hansel and Gretel*. You would need to work closely with the lighting designer to achieve something workable.

3. Carefully consider space. Your design needs to use the available space to its best potential. This includes leaving plenty of space for the actors to perform in, checking audience sightlines and making the set work well in terms of interesting spatial interactions through the use of levels, for example.
4. Continue to note down any questions that emerge.
5. Explore what materials you will need and where you might find them.

ASSESSMENT CHECK
During this review of the script, you will be working on AO2, 'developing your ability to apply theatrical skills to realise artistic intentions.'

DESIGN TIP
Be clear on how your set design could enhance your shared artistic intentions (the central concept). Make sure your design is clearly influenced by these intentions.

LOOK HERE
'Research for set design' on page 19 and 'Understanding your resources' on page 25 will be helpful here.

Chapter 6   Component 2: Designing for the Performance from Text

ASSESSMENT CHECK

In reviewing and selecting your designs, you are developing good habits for AO4: 'Analyse and evaluate your own work.' You are also 'making appropriate judgements during the development process.'

DESIGN TIP

AO4 is tested in the written exam, but this step will give you excellent practice in the key skills of analysis and evaluation.

LOOK HERE

'How to document your set design' on pages 20–24 provides detailed guidance on how to make plans, drawings and model boxes.

'Sourcing materials for the set', page 26, and 'Creating your design for the stage', page 28, will support you with staying within budget and constructing your sets.

STEP 4
Confirming your set designs

For your designs to be agreed at the final design meeting, they need to be at the final design stage themselves.

Rehearsals will be well underway now. You should take your final design ideas into the rehearsal room and check if there are any new developments that affect you. For example, a character might need somewhere to hide on stage. Can you include this in your design?

1. Complete ground plans and sketches for each extract. While you do not have to make model boxes, you might find that they help you to examine how workable your set designs are. Whoever constructs your sets will also find them invaluable.

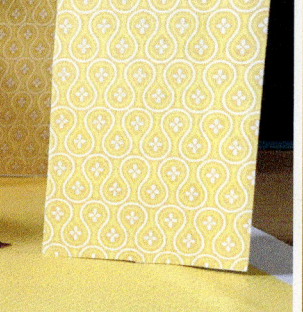

2. Check with the other designers that the artistic intentions are being met and that lighting and costume, in particular, will work safely and effectively with your set. Complete the checklist below.

Extract:					
Period, mood, style and genre?	Practicalities including furniture and health and safety?	Supports artistic intentions?	Good use of space?	Compatible with other design elements?	Approximate costings
Y/N	Y/N	Y/N	Y/N	Y/N	

3. Check with your human resources that your designs are achievable in terms of construction and sourcing. For example, is there time to build the platform you want to put into your design?

172   Chapter 6   Component 2: Designing for the Performance from Text

STEP 5
The final design meeting

Hold a last design meeting. In professional theatre, the stage manager, production manager and other specialists would also be present.

This is the meeting where everything is agreed, including budgets. As a designer, you should not buy or make anything final until the designs have been signed off.

1. Bring the finished plans of your designs to be signed off. The documentation could include the ground plan, marked with entrances and exits, your annotated script plus any notes and models you have made. Through discussion, confirm the final designs.

   In terms of collaboration, this is the final chance to check that your designs harmonise with the other designers' work. Lighting and costume in particular have to complement your designs.

2. Remember that it is essential that the actors can move freely around the stage and set. This is a health and safety issue. You are also creating a world where the characters can live and breathe. The actors cannot inhabit a theatrical world if they are unable to function properly or maintain their characters fully.

3. Don't be afraid to ask questions and raise concerns. It is vital that you leave this meeting ready to realise your designs.

4. Complete a table like this one during or straight after the meeting. (An example has been started for you.)

Extract:		
Agreed set design (including changes)	**Agreed budget**	**Notes**
• As sketch and model boxes. • Change colour palette.	£50	Replace blue tones with amber ones.

Chapter 6 Component 2: Designing for the Performance from Text

SIGNPOST

Task 1.11 in 'Sourcing materials for the set' (page 26) will be very useful now if you haven't completed it already. Also look at 'Creating your design for the stage' (page 28).

STEP 6

The completed set design

Finally, you can construct your set ready for the performance.

Preparation and construction

You will need to work very closely with the people building your set and helping you with materials, tools and equipment. Supervising the construction might involve basic assistance while things are being made or more actively helping to paint flats and so on.

Answer the questions below to help you produce your sets successfully and in good time.

- Are other items (including furniture and props) that need to be borrowed or bought being sorted in good time?
- When will the set be put into the performance area?
- What is the date of the technical rehearsal?
- Are there any issues with items that need to be built, such as the late arrival of materials ordered for a platform? If so, chase them up.
- Have I taken health and safety issues into account, including actors' entrances and exits?
- Are there additional stage dressings such as table cloths or cushions to be sourced?

LOOK HERE

Follow the guidance on page 27 for health and safety procedures.

DESIGN TIP

Refreshments are nearly always appreciated during builds!

Chapter 6 Component 2: Designing for the Performance from Text

THE WRITTEN EXPLANATION FOR SET DESIGN

Your finished set will be seen in the performance. In addition, you are required to provide information about how your set design fits the artistic intentions of the scripted piece. This written explanation allows the examiner to match your intentions to your set designs. It should be between 100 and 200 words for each extract.

Including the information so briefly can be tricky, but you need to explain how your design interprets the extract. Remember to cover these points:

- What is your central set design idea in the key extract?
- How have you interpreted this key extract through your set design?
- What are you hoping to communicate to the audience?

You could also include a sketch or plan within your explanation, as below. Your final sketches and plans are required too.

> My central idea as set designer was to create a non-naturalistic, fairly minimalist set that would powerfully convey the frightening and gloomy atmosphere. This was key to the artistic intentions of the piece.

I used the colour red to communicate the danger that the children faced and contrasted this with white to suggest their innocence. I used blocks to create levels that worked for the trees and for levels in the woodcutter's cottage. The actors moved the blocks while in character. This added to the sense of hard work which even the children had to endure. I wanted the audience to understand that they live in quite deprived circumstances, suggested when the mother says 'Get up, you lazy scraps, we're going into the forest to cut wood'. She also only gives them a 'miserable mouthful of bread'.

As part of my set design, I made heart shapes out of twigs and scattered white pebbles within them. Hansel picks up the pebbles at the start of the extract and the children pick up the twigs that form the heart shapes when they gather firewood later. This symbolised the breaking of their hearts when they are abandoned.

FOCUS
How to approach the explanation of your set design.

ASSESSMENT CHECK
Your supporting documents should show that you have developed skills in:

- 'interpreting content, narrative, style and form'
- 'communicating intention to an audience'

and can 'apply theatrical skills to realise artistic intentions in live performance' (AO2).

DESIGN TIP
The written explanation should show how your designs match the artistic intentions you set out with. Check this carefully.

LOOK HERE
See pages 166–167 for a reminder of what you need to produce for the examiner.

FOCUS
- The lighting design process from page to stage.
- How to interpret, analyse and evaluate as you experiment with different designs, select those that are most successful and realise your designs.

ASSESSMENT CHECK
Your design work will demonstrate your ability to 'develop interpretations independently and collaboratively' as you 'respond and adapt your designs in response to rehearsal work.'

SIGNPOST
Chapter 2 will help you with every aspect of your practical lighting work.

DESIGN TIP
Use a notebook or secure folder. Loose bits of paper get lost or become disorganised.

SIX STEPS TO LIGHTING DESIGN FOR THE SCRIPTED PERFORMANCE

STEP 1
Working on your own with the script

As soon as you know that you are designing the lighting, start your independent work. This is likely to be at the same time as rehearsals begin.

You will need to look at the script with the eyes of a lighting designer. Think about the genre, style, context and locations you will need to enhance. Your teacher should be able to tell you what the stage configuration will be.

1. Read the whole play (or a detailed summary). As you go through, use a table like the one below to note details that could influence your choices.

Play: *Sparkleshark* by Philip Ridley				
Genre: Social drama				
Staging configuration	Location/s	Historical, social and cultural contexts	Themes/ messages	Style, moods and atmosphere
In the round.	Rooftop of block of flats.	• Contemporary (modern day) • Youth culture.	• Friendship • Bullying.	• Mixture of naturalism and non-naturalism • Comedy • Fantasy.

2. Carefully read each extract. Highlight, and mark brief annotations on:
    - locations – specific (such as a rooftop) and more general (city, for example), and whether they are interior or exterior
    - weather/season and time of day
    - shifts in mood and atmosphere
    - the need for a special lighting state, such as colours for a fantasy scene
    - any questions that crop up.

    See the example on the following page.

3. Make more detailed notes from your table, above. Use your annotations to begin a chart like the following.

Locations	Interior/exterior	Time of day (or night)	Weather/season
• Street • Kitchen.	Forest (p27).		

Shifts in mood or atmosphere	Special lighting state	Direct address or other non-naturalistic feature	Questions/ideas
	Opening fridge (p5, l11).		

LIGHTING

'Hansel and Gretel' has the structure of a <u>nightmare</u>. A few domestic objects – buckets, a knife, a blanket, a plate, a jug, an axe – create both the <u>house</u> and the <u>forest</u> and appear in the <u>Witch's house</u>. The Mother also reappears, grotesque, as the Witch. A chorus of three is always present, and active. [...] The story is one of starvation, terror and catharsis. The rhythms of speech are taut and violent, containing the fearful tensions and, finally, joyous release of the drama.

House interior (1a)

Q Build up father

Is this a special, eg spot? Or is there other action here?

Father It was no more than once upon a time when a poor woodcutter lived in a <u>small house</u> at the <u>edge of a huge, dark forest</u>. Now, the woodcutter lived with his wife and his two young children – a boy called Hansel and a little girl called Gretel. [...] <u>Night after hungry night</u>, he lay in bed next to his thin wife, and he worried so much that he tossed and he turned and he sighed and he mumbled and moaned and he just couldn't sleep at all. [...]   *Q Build*

And as he fretted and sweated <u>in the darkness</u>, back came the bony voice of his wife; a voice as fierce as famine. [...]

   Outside. Bright light.   *Location 1b*

There was <u>bright, sparkling moonlight</u> outside and the <u>white pebbles</u> on the ground <u>shone like silver coins and precious jewels</u>. Hansel bent down and filled his empty pockets with as many pebbles as he could carry. [...]

   Inside.   *Location 1a returning*

'Don't worry, Gretel, you can go to sleep now. We'll be fine, I promise.' And he <u>got back into bed</u>.

Q Sunrise state

Mother At <u>dawn, before the sun had properly risen</u>, their mother came and woke the two children. [...]   *Q Location 2 - Forest*

Father Then the whole family <u>set off along the path to the forest</u>. [...]

Mother 'You stupid boy, that's not your kitten. It's just <u>the light of the morning sun glinting</u> on the chimney. Now come on.' [...]

   The family go <u>deeper into the dark heart of the forest</u>.   *Time passing*

Gretel The forest was <u>immense and gloomy</u>. [...]   *Darkening*

Hansel Hansel and Gretel collected a big pile of firewood and when it was <u>set alight</u> and the <u>flames were like burning tongues</u>, their mother said: *SFX*

Mother 'Now lie down by the fire and rest.'

Locations:

1) <u>House</u>   (a) <u>interior</u> – 2 spaces?
2) <u>Forest</u>   (b) <u>exterior</u> – night, bright moonlight dawn
3) <u>Witch's house</u>

(SFX) – <u>Fire</u> – They light it: Practical
        – Battery and bulb?
        <u>OR</u> Staging – Footlights? Unit within set?

Chapter 6   Component 2: Designing for the Performance from Text

STEP 2

The design brief meeting and rehearsals

Now that you have an understanding of the script and have some lighting design ideas, arrange a meeting with your group. Take your script and notebook and any lighting ideas you might already have. If you have a set, sound or costume designer, they should be there too.

You will not be able to finalise your lighting designs until there is agreement on:

- the staging configuration (Is it in the round, traverse, end on?)
- a rough idea of the set design
- the style and setting of the performance (Is it naturalistic or stylised? Do you need a practical special such as a table lamp, for example? If so, what period does it need to suit?)

DESIGN TIP
Details on making a mood board for lighting can be found on page 227.

During the meeting

1. Share your thoughts so far about lighting. Show any sketches or mood boards and invite feedback. Try to deal with any criticism positively: very few designers are likely to get it all right first time.
2. Listen carefully to others and give similar sensitive feedback.
3. Make sure you discuss the following questions.
   - Do we have issues from Step 1 that can be answered in this meeting? If not, how and when can they be addressed?
   - Are we beginning to move towards a shared artistic vision for the performance? What do we imagine it looks like?
   - How will we communicate our ideas to each other? Can we create a shared resource bank for notes and images as we work independently? (This could be a folder on your school's intranet or a service such as Dropbox, which many professional theatres use.)
   - What shall we work on before we next meet? What do we want to achieve by when?
4. Make detailed and well-organised notes of the discussions and any decisions made. You could put them under the heading 'Design Brief Meeting' in your notebook.
5. Agree on a date for the next design meeting.

STEP 3
Revisiting the script

This step is another stage you can complete independently. You should, however, be continuously checking in on rehearsals, as developments might influence your design. Similarly, other designers and the performers will benefit from your updates.

1. Add details to your script annotations and ideas tables, based on what you learned at the design brief meeting. Your new knowledge of the staging and possible set design, for example, might allow you to think more clearly about locations, lighting states and use of colour. Similarly, a shared sense of artistic intention for the performance might prompt you to consider moods that you would like to enhance at particular moments.

   Be clear on how your designs could enhance your shared artistic intentions (the central concept). Make sure your lighting designs are clearly influenced by those intentions.

2. Sketch the acting area and mark areas with the positions for different locations that you might want to light separately. Collaborate with the set designer to ensure that you have covered all the areas that need to be lit. These might include specific 'rooms', outdoor sites or a space on the stage that is used for monologues, for example.

   Once you have identified the areas, you can use them in different ways. For example, you could subtly highlight one area by increasing intensity. This will lead the audience's focus to, for example, the children who are listening on the other side of the door. Or, you could light just one area of the stage and leave the rest in darkness.

3. Are there special effects that need to be planned for? How could you use lights to create moonlight, for example, or fire or bright sunlight? Do you need to plan for a spotlight for a narrator or for a monologue?

4. Create a key to use on your script that links to notes or sketches in your notebook. These could be asterisks, numbers or a letter Q, for example, to indicate a lighting change (see Step 1). An arrow down the side of a script extract could show where you intend to build or decrease the intensity of a lighting state.

5. Carefully consider space, using it to its best potential. This includes lighting the stage in a way that encourages interesting spatial interactions. For example, you could light an area in the auditorium to use for a monologue.

6. Continue to note down any questions that emerge.

ASSESSMENT CHECK

During this review of the script, you will be working on AO2, 'developing your ability to apply theatrical skills to realise artistic intentions.'

LOOK HERE

See page 50 for a lighting plan for *Hansel and Gretel*.

'Understanding your lighting resources', pages 38–39, and 'Research for lighting', page 47, will be helpful here.

ASSESSMENT CHECK

In reviewing and selecting your designs, you are developing good habits for AO4: 'Analyse and evaluate your own work.' You are also 'making appropriate judgements during the development process.'

SIGNPOST

Chapter 2 provides important information on creating lighting designs.

DESIGN TIP

AO4 is tested in the written exam, but this step will give you excellent practice in the key skills of analysis and evaluation.

STEP 4

Confirming your lighting designs

For your lighting designs to be agreed at the final design meeting, they need to be at the final design stage themselves.

Rehearsals will be well underway now. You should take your final design ideas into the rehearsal room and check if there are any new developments that affect you. An extra lighting state might be needed if the performers have introduced a flashback, for example. Do you still have time to fold this into your design?

1. Revisit the tasks on pages 38–39 before you finalise your lighting designs on paper. Now is also the time to look back at 'Research for lighting', page 47. What additional items, such as colour gels or gobos, are included in your design?

2. If you are thinking of using special effects, experiment with the equipment to create them. Test their practicality and impact before committing them to the final design.

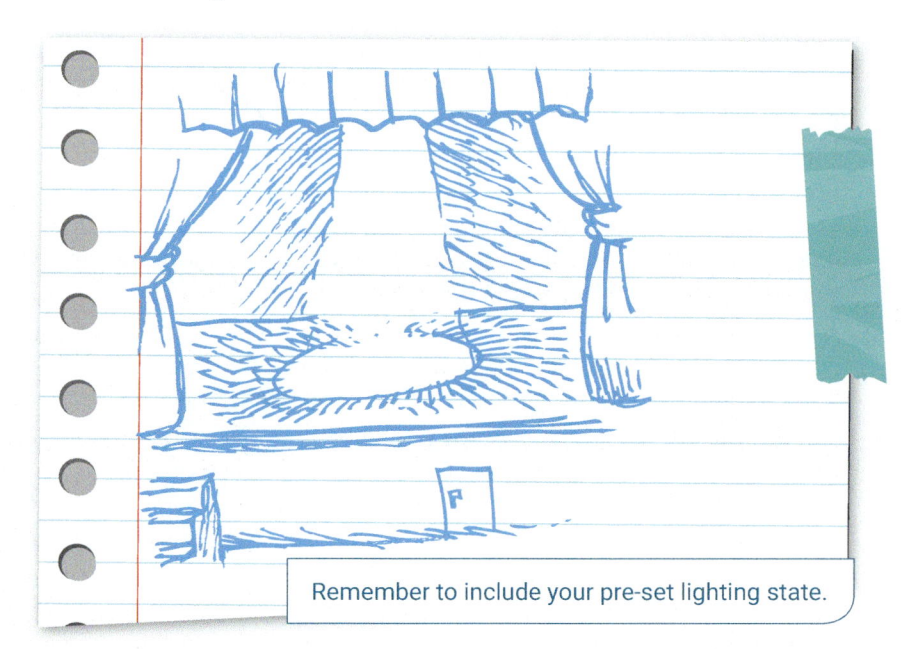

Remember to include your pre-set lighting state.

3. Check with the other designers that all the designs are compatible, both artistically and in terms of keeping performers and audience safe. Complete the checklist below.

Extract:					
Period, mood, style and genre?	Supports artistic intentions?	Compatible with set design?	Compatible with costume?	Any notes on use of space and health and safety	Notes on special effects, colour, types of lantern, etc.
Y/N	Y/N	Y/N	Y/N		

Chapter 6 Component 2: Designing for the Performance from Text

STEP 5
The final design meeting

Hold a last design meeting. In professional theatre, the stage manager, production manager and other specialists would also be present.

This is the meeting where everything is agreed, including budgets. As a designer, you should not buy or make anything final, or start putting special effects together, until the designs have been signed off.

1. Bring the finished plans of your designs to be signed off. The documentation could include a rigging diagram, sketch of acting area(s) with lighting locations marked, your annotated script, plus any notes. Through discussion, confirm the final designs.

    In terms of collaboration, this is the final chance to check that your designs harmonise with the other designers' work. Set and costume in particular have to complement your designs.

2. Don't be afraid to ask questions and raise concerns. It is vital that you leave this meeting ready to realise your designs.

DESIGN TIP

Help your group to envision the world of the stage. Make sure that you bring with you enough detail about your designs, including, for example, gobos that you want to use.

3. Complete a table like this one during or straight after the meeting. (An example has been started for you.)

Extract:		
Agreed lighting design (including changes)	**Agreed budget**	**Notes**
All fine, but add an extra special effect for the monologue.		

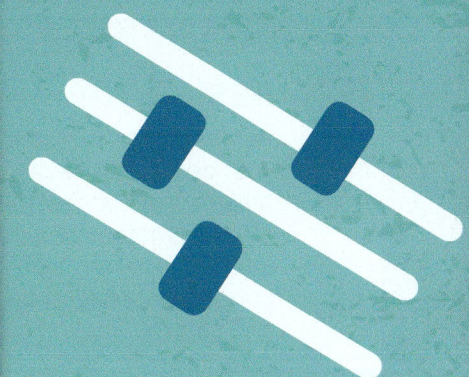

Chapter 6 — Component 2: Designing for the Performance from Text

STEP 6
The completed lighting design

Clever use of lighting creates an oversized shadow and a sinister atmosphere in this scene from The Woman in Black.

Finally, you can set up your lighting ready for the performance.

You will supervise the rigging and focusing, so be sure to arrange suitable times for these tasks with your human resources.

Preparation

The last thing you want is to get to the day of rigging and focusing only to discover that something is missing. This checklist should help.

- Rigging diagrams – checked and accurate.
- If some lanterns are already rigged, do I know which ones are to be moved and where to?
- Lanterns clean and ready to be rigged.
- Sufficient cables in place or ready to be attached.
- Safety equipment ready (eg, heat-resistant gloves and security cables).
- Performance space booked/reserved for rigging.
- Ladders or scaffolding tower located and booked in.
- Lighting desk/board ready for focusing process.

Actualising

1. Make sure you know the date of the technical rehearsal. Have your lighting designs operable and tested in good time.
2. Check that all lanterns are rigged and focused in good time and that your plan and cue sheet are finished and clear.
3. Once your lighting is rigged and focused, allow plenty of time for the operation of your lighting cues to be practised.

LOOK HERE
Refer to Chapter 2 for guidance on rigging, plotting and operating.

DESIGN TIP
Remember to evaluate your designs at each stage. How successfully are they matching your intentions in terms of concept, interpretation and communication of meaning?

THE WRITTEN EXPLANATION FOR LIGHTING

Your lighting will be seen in the performances. In addition, you are required to provide information about how your lighting design fits the artistic intentions of the scripted piece. This written explanation allows the examiner to match your intentions to your lighting designs. It should be between 100 and 200 words for each extract.

Including the information so briefly can be tricky, but you need to explain how your design interprets the extract. One way of doing this could be to look back at the final task from Step 1 and include a version of it in your explanation. Add notes to show how you interpreted the extract through lighting.

For example:

Extract 1: interpretation		
Interior location: Small house at the edge of forest (p13). A lighting state that includes a straw-coloured spotlight positioned to suggest light coming through the window.	**Exterior location**: Forest (p15). Dappled-leaf-effect gobo on 2 profile spotlights.	**Atmosphere**: Moonlit night (p14). A cobalt blue filter on 3 of the fresnels.
Passing time: The forest gradually darkens (p15). Changing the intensity of the lighting state from 50% to 20% over about 50 seconds.	**Special lighting state**: Fire (p15). A battery and a red bulb activated by a performer.	

A further list or paragraph should explain what your lighting design should communicate to an audience, as in the example below.

Your cue sheets, annotated scripts and rigging diagrams are required too.

> The main atmosphere that I want to enhance for the audience is the fear that the children feel when they are alone in the forest. The gobo of the dappled light along with the use of dim light (30% intensity) is an effective example of this.

FOCUS
How to approach the explanation of your lighting design.

ASSESSMENT CHECK
Your supporting documents should show that you have developed skills in:
- 'interpreting content, narrative, style and form'
- 'communicating intention to an audience'

and can 'apply theatrical skills to realise artistic intentions in live performance' (AO2).

DESIGN TIP
The written explanation should show how your designs match the artistic intentions you set out with. Check this carefully.

In this scene, a bright, non-naturalistic, pink wash gives an alien, eerie and somewhat sickly effect, especially in combination with the lights of the gingerbread men's eyes and house biscuits. (Lighting designed by Oliver Fenwick for Regent's Park Open Air Theatre.)

FOCUS
- The process of costume design from page to stage.
- How to interpret, analyse and evaluate as you experiment with different designs, select those that are most successful and realise your designs as a completed costume for each extract.

ASSESSMENT CHECK
Your design work for Component 2 will demonstrate your ability to 'Develop interpretations independently and collaboratively' as you 'respond and adapt your designs in response to rehearsal work.'

SIGNPOST
Chapter 3 is designed to help you with every aspect of your practical costume work.

DESIGN TIP
Use a notebook or a secure folder. Loose bits of paper get lost or become disorganised!

SIX STEPS TO COSTUME DESIGN FOR THE SCRIPTED PERFORMANCE

STEP 1
Working on your own with the script

As soon as you know that you are designing a costume for an extract, start your independent work. This is likely to be at the same time as the performers begin rehearsals.

You will need to look at the script through the eyes of a costume designer. This means thinking about genre, styles and contexts. Your teacher should be able to tell you what the stage configuration will be.

1. Read the whole play (or a detailed summary). As you go through, use a table like the one below to note details that could influence your costume choices. (An example has been suggested.)

Play: *Dracula* by Bram Stoker/David Calcutt Genre: Horror					
Main characters	**Location/s**	**Historical, social and cultural contexts**	**Themes/ messages**	**Style, moods and atmosphere**
- Dracula - Jonathan - Mina - Lucy - Van Helsing - Renfield.	- Whitby - Dracula's castle.	- End of 19th century - Vampire stories.	- Fear - Love - The supernatural.	- Mainly naturalistic - Suspense - Horror.

2. Carefully read each extract. Highlight and mark brief annotations on:
   - locations – specific (such as the living room in a wealthy Victorian home) and more general (north-east coast of England, for example)
   - weather and time of year and time of day, as this will influence what a character would wear
   - the economic and social situations of characters
   - personality aspects that might affect characters' choice of clothing
   - a stated requirement for a special feature (pocket, bag, hat and so on)
   - any questions that crop up.

   See the example on the following page.

3. Make more detailed notes from your table. These should take the form of the page and line number or quotation from the script and then your note. For example:

> p14: 'Hansel got up, put on his coat... filled his empty pockets with as many pebbles as he could carry...' Does he have nightwear, or is he in everyday clothes? Coat with big pockets could be a handed-down jacket from his father?

COSTUME

Style? – Germanic?
Period? – Victorian? Modern?
Times of famine, hunger, starvation
Freedom of movement

'Hansel and Gretel' has the structure of a nightmare. A few domestic objects – buckets, a knife, a blanket, a plate, a jug, an axe – create both the house and the forest and appear in the Witch's house. The Mother also reappears, grotesque, as the Witch. A chorus of three is always present, and active. [...] The story is one of starvation, terror and catharsis. The rhythms of speech are taut and violent, containing the fearful tensions and, finally, joyous release of the drama.

Woodcutter: Poor; works outdoors – manual
Outer clothes: Boots? Waistcoat? Belt? Pouch?
Nightwear?
Wife: Thin; angular silhouette – a hard woman
Hansel: 8? Coat: Threadbare – with pockets – size?
Gretel: 6 or 7? Apron with pocket – size?

Father It was no more than once upon a time when a poor woodcutter lived in a small house at the edge of a huge, dark forest. Now, the woodcutter lived with his wife and his two young children – a boy called Hansel and a little girl called Gretel. It was hard enough for him to feed them all at the best of times – but these were the worst of times; times of famine and hunger and starvation. [...]

Night after hungry night, he lay in bed next to his thin wife, and he worried so much that he tossed and he turned and he sighed and he mumbled and moaned and he just couldn't sleep at all. [...]

Hansel Now, Hansel and Gretel had been so hungry that night that they hadn't been able to sleep either, and they'd heard every cruel word of their mother's terrible plan. [...]

And when their father and mother had finally gone to sleep, Hansel got up, put on his coat, opened the back door, and crept out into the midnight hour. [...]

Hansel bent down and filled his empty pockets with as many pebbles as he could carry. [...]

Mother Then she gave each of them a miserable mouthful of bread: 'There's your lunch; think yourselves lucky, and don't eat it all at once, because there's nothing else.'

Gretel Gretel put the bread in her apron pocket, because Hansel's pockets were crammed with pebbles.

Father Then the whole family set off along the path to the forest.

Where does the bread come from?

DESIGN TIP
Think which character(s) you would like to design a costume for.

DESIGN TIP

In professional theatre, a white-card meeting might be held once the set designer has constructed a simple 3D version of the set in paper or card. Alternatively, there might be 2D sketches of the set and possibly some costume sketches.

STEP 2

The design brief meeting and rehearsals

Now that you have an understanding of the script and have some costume ideas, arrange a meeting with your group. Take your script and notebook and any costume sketches you have. If you have a set, sound or lighting designer, they should be there too. A costume designer needs to consider potential movement restrictions of the set, for example.

You will not be able to properly develop your costume designs until you know:

- the style and setting of the performance (Is it naturalistic or stylised? Is it set in a particular time period? Do you need to create a typical Victorian gown, or are you setting the play in modern times?)
- which character(s) you will design for.

Your choice should give you plenty of scope for creativity and impact. It should allow you to contribute to characterisation and meaning. It must also set you a sufficient challenge. If you design costumes for both extracts, you might want to make the two designs quite different from each other.

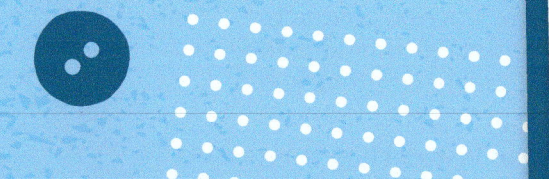

Rough sketches for a contemporary costume design for *Hansel and Gretel*.

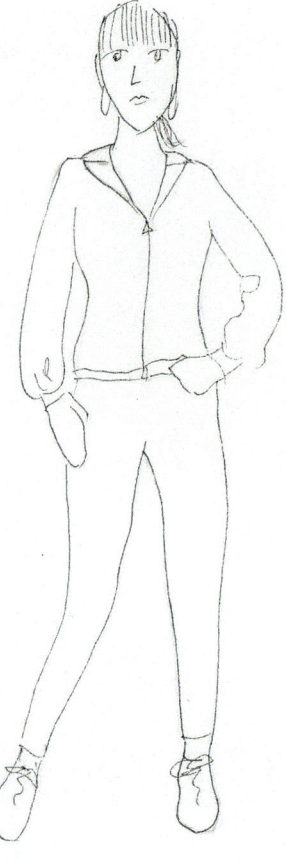

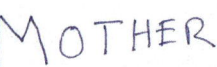

During the meeting

1. Share your thoughts so far about costumes. Show any sketches or mood boards and invite feedback. Try to deal with any criticism positively: very few designers are likely to get it all right first time.
2. Listen carefully to others and give similar sensitive feedback.
3. Make sure you discuss the following questions.
   - Do I have questions from Step 1 that can be answered in this meeting? If not, how and when can they be addressed?
   - Are we beginning to move towards a shared artistic vision for the performance? What do we imagine it looks like?
   - How will we communicate our ideas to each other? Can we create a shared resource bank that we can put notes and images in as we work independently? (This could be a shared folder on your centre's intranet or a service such as Dropbox, which many professional theatres use.)
   - What shall we work on before we next meet? What do we want to achieve by when?
4. Make detailed and well-organised notes of the discussions and any decisions made. You could put them under the heading 'Design Brief Meeting' in your notebook.
5. Agree on a date for the next design meeting.

STEP 3
Revisiting the script

This step is another stage you can complete independently. You should, however, be continuously checking in on rehearsals, as developments might influence your design. Similarly, other designers and the performers will benefit from your updates.

1. Add details to your script annotations and ideas table, based on what you learned at the design brief meeting. Your new knowledge of the agreed style and historical period, for example, will allow you to develop your costume ideas.

   Similarly, a shared sense of artistic intention for the performance might prompt you to consider enhancing atmosphere with a particular aspect of costume design. This could come from colour, shape and fabric choices.

   Be clear on how your design could enhance your shared artistic intentions (the central concept). Make sure your costume design is clearly influenced by these intentions.

More traditional versions of the Witch and the Mother.

2. Sketch a number of versions for your initial costume designs.
3. Are there special considerations, such as pockets, masks or wigs, that need to be planned for? For pockets, for example, you will need to know what they will hold so that you can make them the correct size. Make sure details like this are included in your preliminary sketches, along with footwear, headgear, accessories, make-up and masks as appropriate.
4. Carefully check the script for points where costumes might need to be changed. (These are often signposted in stage directions.)
5. Carefully consider space. This could mean shortening hemlines at the front to make steps easier. Alternatively, it could mean adding lots of detail to the back of a dress if the audience will see it frequently.

   It is essential that the actors can move freely around the stage and set. This is a safety issue. You are also creating a world where the characters can live and breathe. The actors cannot inhabit a theatrical world if they are unable to function properly or maintain their characters fully.
6. Continue to note down any questions that emerge.
7. Explore additional fabrics or accessories that might be needed and where they could come from.

ASSESSMENT CHECK

During this review of the script, you will be working on AO2, 'developing your ability to apply theatrical skills to realise artistic intentions.'

ASSESSMENT CHECK

In reviewing and selecting your designs, you are working towards AO4: 'Analyse and evaluate your own work.'

DESIGN TIP

AO4 is tested in the written exam, but this step will give you excellent practice in the key skills of analysis and evaluation.

LOOK HERE

Pages 72–81 will help you to create and document your costume design.

STEP 4

Confirming your costume designs

For your designs to be agreed at the final design meeting, they need to be at final design stage themselves.

This means that you need to produce quality designs that are your best work. You don't need to be a great artist, but you do need to take time and care.

Rehearsals will be well underway now. You should take your final design ideas into the rehearsal room and check if there are any new developments that affect you. For example, a character might need an additional garment such as a cloak to hide something under. Can you include this in your design?

1. If you have a number of designs that you like, try to bring it down to two. Just one is ideal. Completing the table below should help you to decide which costume is the most effective. Remember that your design needs to contribute to meeting the artistic intentions of the whole group.

   Check with the other designers that colour palettes work together and that the costumes will suit the proposed set and lighting.

Extract:					
Period, mood, style and genre?	Compatible with other design elements?	Suits social and economic background?	Suits personality/ character?	Suitable for the space and actor's comfort and safety?	Approximate costings, including accessories and make-up
Y/N	Y/N	Y/N	Y/N	Y/N	

2. Annotate your chosen sketch to help explain colour, fabric texture and finish.
3. Even if you will not be making your garment from scratch, it is useful to apply swatches to the design. These will help your fellow group members to see the 'look' you are aiming for.

THE WITCH

- RED CONTACT LENSES TO BE WORN.
- OFF CENTRE FASTENING ON COAT
- KEY FOR LOCKING UP CHILDREN
- SAME WOOL SKIRT AS MOTHER

MOTHER

- FLORAL FABRIC FOR THE HEAD SCARF
- LEG OF MUTTON SLEEVES
- OVERALL LOOK OF CLOTHES TO BE WELL WORN
- Wool Skirt

STEP 5

The final design meeting

Hold a last design meeting. In professional theatre, the stage manager, production manager and other specialists would also be present.

This is the meeting where everything is agreed, including budgets. As a designer, you should not buy or make anything until the designs have been signed off.

1. Bring your finished designs to be signed off. If you still have alternatives to be decided on, bring them for your colleagues to consider. Through discussion, confirm the final designs.

    In terms of collaboration, this is the final chance to check that your designs harmonise with the other designers' work. Set and lighting in particular have to complement your designs.

2. Check that there have been no changes to the set or the amount of physical movement used by the actor, as this could mean having to change aspects of your costume design.

3. Don't be afraid to ask questions and raise concerns. It is vital that you leave this meeting ready to realise your designs.

4. Complete a table like this one during or straight after the meeting. (An example has been given for you.)

Extract:		
Agreed costume design (including changes)	Agreed budget	Notes
As final drawings – design approved.	£20	Need to find cheaper fabric for cape.

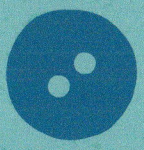

DESIGN TIP

Help your group members to envision the world of the stage by making sure that you show the detail of your designs. As well as your designs, bring notes, fabric swatches and images of garments, styles and make-up.

DESIGN TIP

Gather everything you need in one place and know where it all is! Add to your selection as you go along, including tools, accessories and make-up materials.

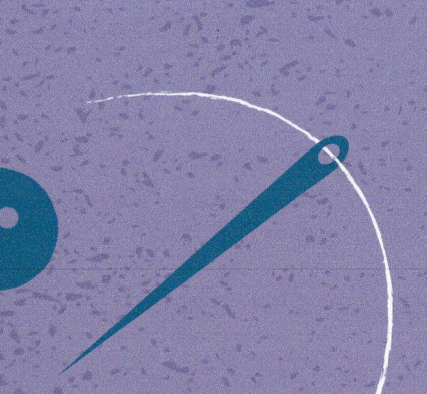

STEP 6
The completed costume design

Finally, you can make your costumes for the performance.

Preparation

Use your designs and budget to complete the following tables. (Some examples have been included to guide you.)

Extract:			
Character:			
Actor:			
Costume item	**Source**	**Estimated cost**	**Completed**
Skirt	Alter existing one	none	
Apron	Charity shop?	£3	
Shoes	Actor's own	none	✓
Belt – with keys	Make	£2	
Make-up	Actor's and mine	none	✓

DESIGN TIP

Remember to evaluate your designs at each stage. How successful are they in contributing to characterisation, meaning and atmosphere?

LOOK HERE

The guidance on page 86 will help you with using rehearsals.

Actualising

1. Refer to Chapter 3 for help with sourcing, making, adapting and fitting. Remember that you need to supervise any making and alterations if you are not doing these yourself. Try to allow time for the actor to wear the costume in rehearsal to check that it works well for them in practice.
2. As you complete items of costume, add to or amend the table above.
3. Make sure you know the date of the technical rehearsal. You will need to have your costumes made and fitted in good time.

Chapter 6 Component 2: Designing for the Performance from Text

THE WRITTEN EXPLANATION FOR COSTUME

Your finished costume will be seen in the performance. In addition, you are required to provide information about how your costume design fits the artistic intentions of the scripted piece. This written explanation allows the examiner to match your intentions to your costume designs. It should be between 100 and 200 words for each extract.

Including the information so briefly is often tricky, so an annotated sketch of your design ideas could be useful. You could add notes to the sketch to explain how your design interprets the extract or add a list of bullet points. For example (for seven-year-old Edward in *Blood Brothers*):

> The smart white shirt, shiny shoes and bow-tie indicate that Edward is not dressed for playing outdoors.

> The shoes, button-up shirt and bow-tie contrast strongly with Mickey's rather tatty clothes.

A further list or paragraph should explain what your costume should communicate to an audience. For example:

> The main point that I want the audience to understand is that Edward comes from a well-off family who are concerned with appearances. The way that Edward's hair has been so carefully neatened should help the audience to imagine the type of mother he has. Similarly, the choice of garments and accessories suggests a clean and well-ordered household. The red bow-tie adds a touch of class and suggests academic aspirations.

Along with your 200-word explanation, submit a list of costumes and accessories worn by your chosen character(s). This should include details of when and how they make any costume changes during each extract (for example, 'Edward takes off his tie').

FOCUS
How to approach the explanation of your costume design.

ASSESSMENT CHECK
Your supporting documents should show that you have developed skills in:
- 'interpreting content, narrative, style and form'
- 'communicating intention to an audience'

and can 'apply theatrical skills to realise artistic intentions in live performance' (AO2).

DESIGN TIP
The written explanation should show how your designs match the artistic intentions you set out with. Check this carefully.

FOCUS

- The sound design process from page to stage.
- How to interpret the script, analyse and evaluate as you experiment with different designs, select those that are most successful and realise your designs as sounds in performance.

ASSESSMENT CHECK

Your design work for Component 2 will demonstrate your ability to 'develop interpretations independently and collaboratively' as you 'respond and adapt your designs in response to rehearsal work.'

SIGNPOST

If you are new to sound design, dive into Chapter 4. The tasks are designed to help you with every aspect of your sound design work.

DESIGN TIP

Use a notebook or secure folder. Loose bits of paper get lost or become disorganised.

SIX STEPS TO SOUND DESIGN FOR THE SCRIPTED PERFORMANCE

STEP 1

Working on your own with the script

As soon as you know that you are designing sound, start your independent work. This is likely to be at the same time as rehearsals begin.

You will need to look at the script through the eyes of a sound designer. This means thinking about the genre, style, context and locations you will need to enhance. Your teacher should tell you what the stage configuration will be.

1. Read the whole play (or a detailed summary). As you go through, use a table like the one below to note details that could influence your sound design choices. (An example has been suggested.)

Play: *Romeo and Juliet* by William Shakespeare
Genre: Tragedy

Staging configuration	Location/s	Historical, social and cultural contexts	Themes/ messages	Style, moods and atmosphere
End on.	• Grand house: bedroom, balcony • Street.	• Modern-day setting. • Race: Capulets are white; Montagues black.	• Love • Romance • Grief/sorrow • Racial tension.	• Naturalistic • Romance • Violence • Tragedy.

2. Carefully read each extract. Highlight and mark brief annotations on:
   - locations, and whether they are interior or exterior
   - key moments where music or a sound effect is important
   - weather/season and time of day
   - shifts in mood and atmosphere
   - a specified requirement for a sound cue
   - any questions that crop up.

3. Make more detailed notes from your initial table, above. Use your annotations to begin a chart like the following. (Some examples for *Hansel and Gretel* have been given for guidance.)

Locations	Interior/exterior	Time of day (or night)	Weather/season
House in the woods.	Forest (p27).	Moonlight.	Gloomy.

Shifts in mood or atmosphere	Sound effect	Direct address or other non-naturalistic feature	Questions/ideas
The flames were like burning tongues.	Owl.	Father narrates at the start of the extract.	Is a soundscape appropriate? Lots of scope for non-diegetic sound.

SOUND

Period? Victorian? *Style?*

'Hansel and Gretel' has the structure of a nightmare. A few domestic objects – buckets, a knife, a blanket, a plate, a jug, an axe – create both the house and the forest and appear in the Witch's house. The Mother also reappears, grotesque, as the Witch. A chorus of three is always present, and active. [...] The story is one of starvation, terror and catharsis. The rhythms of speech are taut and violent, containing the fearful tensions and, finally, joyous release of the drama.

Reflect in sound design
Diegetic: Forest – Owl
- Wind in trees
- Creaking
- Creatures – birds?
- Dripping brook?
- Blazing fire
- 'Wild beasts'

Non-diegetic:
Discordant music in minor key – wind instruments – falling.
Soundscape:
- Hunger, despair
- Creaking – samples

Soundscape before lights up

Creaking

Owl

Father It was no more than once upon a time when a poor woodcutter lived in a small house at the edge of a huge, dark forest. Now, the woodcutter lived with his wife and his two young children – a boy called Hansel and a little girl called Gretel. [...] Night after hungry night, he lay in bed next to his thin wife, and he worried so much that he tossed and he turned and he sighed and he mumbled and moaned and he just couldn't sleep at all. [...]

And as he fretted and sweated in the darkness, back came the bony voice of his wife; a voice as fierce as famine. [...]   *Soundscape*

Father 'No, no, wife, I can't do that. How could I have the heart to leave young Hansel and Gretel in the forest? The wild beasts would soon sniff them out and eat them alive.' [...]

And when their father and mother had finally gone to sleep, Hansel got up, put on his coat, opened the back door, and crept out into the midnight hour.

Outside. Bright light.   *Location*

There was bright, sparkling moonlight outside and the white pebbles on the ground shone like silver coins and precious jewels. Hansel bent down and filled his empty pockets with as many pebbles as he could carry.

Inside. [...]

Mother At dawn, before the sun had properly risen, their mother came and woke the two children. [...]

The family go deeper into the dark heart of the forest.   *Volume*

Gretel The forest was immense and gloomy. [...]

Hansel Hansel and Gretel collected a big pile of firewood and when it was set alight and the flames were like burning tongues, their mother said: *Fire SFX*

Mother 'Now lie down by the fire and rest.'

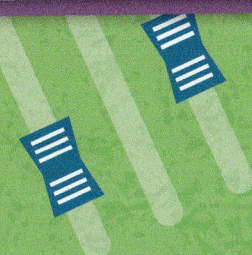

DESIGN TIP

In professional theatre, a white-card meeting might be held once the set designer has constructed a simple 3D version of the set in paper or card. Alternatively, there might be 2D sketches of the set and possibly some costume sketches.

STEP 2
The design brief meeting and rehearsals

Now that you have an understanding of the script and have some set design ideas, arrange a meeting with your group. Take your script and notebook and any ideas for sound that you might already have. If you have a set, lighting or costume designer, they should be there too.

You will not be able to proceed much further with your sound designs until there is agreement on:

- the staging configuration (Is it in the round, traverse, end on?)
- the style and setting of the performance (Is it naturalistic or stylised?)
- whether it is set in a particular time period that music should reflect (Music you choose for a modern interpretation of *Romeo and Juliet* would be very different from a 16th-century version, for example.)

During the meeting

1. Share your thoughts so far about sound design. Play any effects or music extracts you have found, and invite feedback. Try to deal with any criticism positively: very few designers are likely to get it all right first time.
2. Listen carefully to others and give similar sensitive feedback.
3. Make sure you discuss the following questions.
   - Do we have questions from Step 1 that can be answered in this meeting? If not, how and when can they be addressed?
   - Are we beginning to move towards a shared artistic vision for the performance? What do we imagine it looks like?
   - How will we communicate our ideas to each other? Can we create a shared resource bank for notes and images as we work independently? (This could be a folder on your school's intranet or a service such as Dropbox, which many professional theatres use.)
   - What shall we work on before we next meet? What do we want to achieve by when?
4. Make detailed and well-organised notes of the discussions and any decisions made. You could put them under the heading 'Design Brief Meeting' in your notebook.
5. Agree on a date for the next design meeting.

STEP 3
Revisiting the script

This step is another stage you can complete independently. You should, however, be continuously checking in on rehearsals, as developments might influence your design. Similarly, other designers and the performers will benefit from your updates.

1. Add details to your script annotations and ideas tables, based on what you learned at the design brief meeting. Your new knowledge of the style of the production might allow you to think more clearly about, for example, non-naturalistic soundscapes. Similarly, a shared sense of artistic intention for the performance might prompt you to consider moods that you would like to enhance at particular moments.
2. Are there special effects that need to be planned for? How could you use sound to create the sense of night-time in a forest, for example?
3. Create a key to use on your script that links to notes or sketches in your notebook. These could be asterisks or numbers or a letter Q, for example, to indicate a change in sound. An arrow down the side of a script extract could show where you intend to build or decrease the volume of an effect.
4. Think carefully about the space and where, for example, to best place your speakers to create the best sound quality for the audience.
5. Continue to note down any questions that emerge.

ASSESSMENT CHECK

During this review of the script, you will be working on AO2, 'developing your ability to apply theatrical skills to realise artistic intentions.'

DESIGN TIP

Be clear on how your designs could enhance your shared artistic intentions. Make sure your sound designs are clearly influenced by those intentions.

LOOK HERE

Chapter 4 provides important information on creating sound designs.

Chapter 6   Component 2: Designing for the Performance from Text   195

ASSESSMENT CHECK

In reviewing and selecting your designs, you are developing good habits for AO4: 'Analyse and evaluate your own work.' You are also 'making appropriate judgements during the development process.'

STEP 4

Confirming your sound designs

For your sound designs to be agreed at the final design meeting, they need to be at the final design stage themselves.

Rehearsals will be well underway now. You should take your final design ideas into the rehearsal room and check if there are any new developments that affect you. For example, you might need an additional piece of underscoring to enhance a moment of tension. Can you include this in your design?

1. Revisit the tasks in 'Sourcing, creating and mixing sounds', pages 96–99, before you finalise the sound designs on paper. Now would also be a good time to check that you have all the resources you need. Have you made your music choices, for instance? Do you know what will play as the audience come in and leave the performance space?

2. If you are thinking of using special effects, such as reverb or echo, use 'Special sound effects' on pages 100–101 to guide you. Experiment with building the effects that you want. Test their practicality, suitability and impact before committing them to the final design.

3. Check with the other designers that all the designs are compatible, both artistically and in terms of keeping performers and audience safe. Complete the checklist below.

Extract:			
Period, mood, style and genre?	Compatible with other design elements?	Contributes to artistic intentions?	Safety notes and use of space, speaker positions
Y/N	Y/N	Y/N	
Y/N	Y/N	Y/N	

DESIGN TIP

AO4 is tested in the written exam, but this step will give you excellent practice in the key skills of analysis and evaluation.

Chapter 6 Component 2: Designing for the Performance from Text

STEP 5
The final design meeting

Hold a last design meeting. In professional theatre, the stage manager, production manager and other specialists would also be present.

This is the meeting where everything is agreed, including budgets. As a designer, you should not buy or make anything final, or start putting special effects together, until the designs have been signed off.

1. Bring the finished plans of your designs to be signed off. The documentation could include a rough cue sheet, sketch of acting area(s) with locations of speakers marked, your annotated script, plus any notes. Through discussion, confirm the final designs.

In terms of collaboration, this is the final chance to check that your designs harmonise with the other designers' work. Lighting in particular needs to complement your designs.

2. Don't be afraid to ask questions and raise concerns. It is vital that you leave this meeting ready to realise your designs.
3. Complete a table like this one during or straight after the meeting.

Extract:		
Agreed design (including changes)	**Agreed budget**	**Notes**

LOOK HERE
You might find these sections useful at this point:
- How to document your sound design, pages 102–103
- Research for sound design, pages 94–95
- Positioning sound equipment, pages 104–105.

DESIGN TIP
Help your group to understand the style of your effects and music by having some available to play.

LOOK HERE
Chapter 4 offers plenty of support and guidance in terms of creating and finding sound effects and music, taking care of health and safety and so on.

SIGNPOST
Work through 'Plotting the sound design' (pages 106–107) first.

DESIGN TIP
Remember that you will need one for each script extract if you design sound for both.

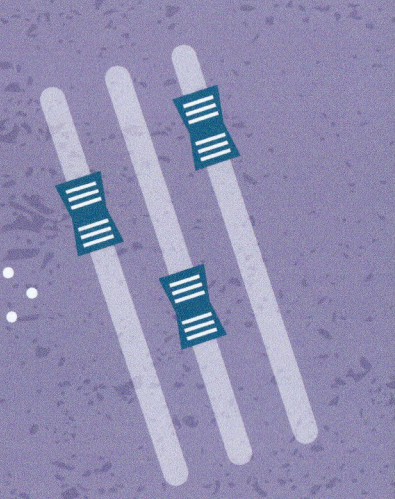

DESIGN TIP
Remember to evaluate your designs at each stage. How successfully are they matching your intentions in terms of concept, interpretation and communication of meaning?

LOOK HERE
The notes on page 110 will help you to make use of rehearsals.

STEP 6
The completed sound design

Finally, you can finish setting up and mixing your sounds ready for the performance.

Preparation
Once you have all your effects and music saved in a folder on a laptop or organised for other playback devices, you need to plot them.

Plotting
Plotting is the crucial stage where you get your cues in order and create the cue sheet.

An example cue sheet is given on page 200. The cue sheet is an essential guide for whoever operates the sound for your production, whether or not you do this yourself. It gives the source, order, length and volume of each sound.

Make sure that you know the date of the technical rehearsal. Have your sound designs plotted and practised in good time.

Once your sounds are set, allow plenty of time for your sound operator to practise your sound cues.

THE WRITTEN EXPLANATION FOR SOUND

Your finished sounds will be heard in the performances. In addition, you are required to provide information about how your sound design fits the artistic intentions of the scripted piece. This written explanation allows the examiner to match your intentions to your sound designs. It should be between 100 and 200 words for each extract.

FOCUS
How to approach the written explanation for your sound design.

ASSESSMENT CHECK
Your supporting documents should show that you have developed skills in:
- 'interpreting content, narrative, style and form'
- 'communicating intention to an audience'

and can 'apply theatrical skills to realise artistic intentions in live performance' (AO2).

DESIGN TIP
The written explanation should show how your designs match the artistic intentions you set out with. Check this carefully.

Chapter 6 Component 2: Designing for the Performance from Text

Including the information so briefly can be tricky, but your cue sheets will help. For example:

Extract 1

Sound cue sheet: Hansel and Gretel

Cue no and page no	Cue signal	Sound	Playback device (if more than one)	Level (dB)	Transition	Notes and timings
1 Pre-set	House open	Play music	CD player	-10		Pre-set from time house is open. Visual cue
2 p1	Visual: actors walk on	Music off		All out	Fade out	Over 10 seconds (in time with lighting)
3 p3	'Come over here!'	Soundscape 1	Laptop	+6	Fade up	Over 5 seconds gradual fade

You do need to cover these points:
- What is your central design idea in the extract?
- How have you interpreted this extract through your design?
- What are you hoping to communicate to the audience?

The example below is for an extract based on *Hansel and Gretel*.

I am the sound designer for our production. My central idea is to create a mixture of naturalistic and non-naturalistic sounds that will help the audience to understand the location, mood and atmosphere.

My interpretation of the first extract is to satisfy the need to signpost the location of the forest through diegetic sound effects such as the owl and the crackling fire. However, I also want to create non-diegetic soundscapes so that the audience can experience the tensions between the mother and the children as well as their alarm at being left alone in the forest. To get the richness of sound that I think is necessary for the soundscapes, I have mixed a number of effects and added reverb to make an eerie sound.

I want the audience to get a powerful sense of atmosphere and for them to empathise with the children.

Gretel and Hansel at Manitoba Theatre for Young People. With a stark, simple, non-naturalistic set design such as this one, sound could be especially important for creating atmosphere and meaning.

Chapter 7

COMPONENT 3: THEATRE MAKERS IN PRACTICE

Introduction to design in the written exam	202
Preparing for the exam	206
Section A: Set design from a director's viewpoint	208
Section A: Set design from a designer's viewpoint	212
Section B: Evaluating a set design in live theatre	218
Section A: Lighting design from a director's viewpoint	222
Section A: Lighting design from a designer's viewpoint	226
Section B: Evaluating a lighting design in live theatre	230
Section A: Costume design from a director's viewpoint	234
Section A: Costume design from a designer's viewpoint	238
Section B: Evaluating a costume design in live theatre	241
Section A: Sound design from a director's viewpoint	244
Section A: Sound design from a designer's viewpoint	248
Section B: Evaluating a sound design in live theatre	253

FOCUS

- Preparing for the written exam.
- Understanding what the examiner is looking for.

INTRODUCTION TO DESIGN IN THE WRITTEN EXAM

The written exam requires every student to have a detailed understanding of **all** aspects of theatre included in the GCSE Drama course. Note that Edexcel says, 'This component focuses on the work of theatre makers and the **theatrical choices** that are made by crucial members of the **creative and production team** in order to **communicate ideas to an audience**.'

These team members are the director, designers and performers who collaborate to realise their artistic intentions and create a harmonious world on the stage. They want their audience to be entertained and inspired and to have an unforgettable experience.

Masks help to characterise the Moon and the Sun in this movement performance.

Studying and analysing drama

How should I think about my writing in the exam?

For Section A, it would be useful to imagine that you are a team member (sound designer for one question perhaps, and director for another) giving an explanation for your set text.

Imagine that you are staging a performance as part of a real team that works creatively to make the best choices to communicate ideas to the audience. This should help your written response have detail and depth.

Similarly, you watch the work of the creative team in the live performance you watch for Section B, and analyse and evaluate the impact of their work. Again, it helps to remember that these are people who made lots of choices throughout the process of getting the production on the stage. Did they make good decisions? How did these impact on you as a member of the audience?

What must I be able to do?

You need to have and demonstrate:

- a thorough and extensive knowledge of the set text you are studying and of the live performance you have seen
- knowledge of all the creative aspects of staging a theatre production, including the various roles of the people who put together a performance
- knowledge and experience of creating a piece of theatre, which will help to make your writing clear
- the ability to comment meaningfully and confidently about how the extract **could** be staged and about how the performance you saw **was** staged.

DESIGN TIP

Remember that a harmonious world is skilfully and collectively created by every person involved in a production. Understanding this is the key to success in Component 3.

LOOK HERE

The Practical Guide to Design chapters at the beginning of this book will give you valuable experience in how different theatrical elements can create impact and convey meaning.

Using your practical experience, knowledge and understanding

To succeed in the written exam, it is essential to prepare for it throughout your course.

Different roles and elements in drama

The four main theatre elements for production and design are set, lighting, costume and sound, but you might be asked more specifically about, for example, props and stage furniture or staging. These might overlap with other design elements, for example:

- Staging might include the use of set on a specific type of stage.
- Props and stage furniture might form part of a set design.
- Personal props, such as a phone, pen or spectacles, might form part of the costume design for certain characters.

A Curious Incident of the Dog in the Night-Time at the Gielgud Theatre.

- Do more than simply take part in drama lessons. Step back and really think about what is happening. Keep a project notebook to record your thoughts. You could have separate sections for performance and the different design elements.
- Use the knowledge and experience that you have gained to examine all elements of drama.
- Take an interest in all the elements of drama. For example, talk to the performers if you are the costume or lighting designer, and so on.
- Keep a glossary of technical terms you come across and try to use them in lessons and in your writing so that they become really familiar.
- Carry out as many tasks as you can from the Practical Guide to Design chapters at the beginning of this book.

TASK 7.1

Start a drama journal or scrapbook and add to it every week. Use the ideas above and include sketches, images and mood boards to keep yourself interested. (Search on Pinterest for some useful examples.)

Take inspiration from the fact that your journal will be invaluable when it comes to revising for your exam and the mock exams you take during your course.

Your experience from the whole course will help you

It would be a mistake to think of the exam as a big new element that takes place at the end of your course. Instead, try to think of it as an opportunity to show what you have learned over the years you have studied and been interested in drama.

Director Gerry Mulgrew of Communicado Theatre, on the set of *The Government Inspector* at Aberystwyth Arts Centre.

Chapter 7 Component 3: Theatre Makers in Practice 203

Local Hero at Edinburgh Lyceum.

Recognising artistic intentions and practical processes

Professional theatre makers are skilled in their fields. Similarly, you have developed your own knowledge and skills in a range of disciplines during your Drama course. You might have focused on acting and have learned a great deal about voice, movement and characterisation. Alternatively, you might have developed your skills as a designer, or studied both design and performance.

Either way, the devised and scripted performances you work on involve all of your group aiming to communicate a common artistic intention. If you work practically on lighting, sound, costume or set, you will have an opportunity to use those skills and knowledge very productively in the written exam. If not, you can develop your knowledge of the design elements by doing some design work as part of your exam preparation.

The portfolio is a major piece of written work for your devised theatre piece for Component 1. For Component 3, you are again writing from a very practical viewpoint:

- How would I perform or design an extract from my set play?
- How would I create impact for my audience within this crafted world?
- How do the performers and designers of live performances I have seen use their skills to create impact?

Sharing your skills and knowledge of design in the written exam

You will not know the exact questions or the extract you will be given in the written exam. You will, however, know the **kind** of questions to expect. The examiners are not trying to catch you out.

You simply need to use and develop the skills and knowledge you have already achieved and prepare carefully for these written tasks.

You have developed your own knowledge and skills in a range of disciplines, such as costume and set design, during the course. If you have worked practically on lighting, sound, costume or set, you will be able to use those skills and knowledge very productively in the written exam. You will need to prepare thoroughly, however, in order to apply them to the set text.

Even if you have not opted for design in Components 1 and 2, you will have appreciated the use of costume, lights, set and sound. This might have been in performances you have been part of as well as ones you have seen.

You are unlikely to be an expert at every performance and design discipline. You should, however, have sufficient knowledge and specialist vocabulary to make insightful comments about techniques and designs and how they enhance the artistic intentions of a scene or moment.

You will be asked to explain, interpret, analyse and evaluate design from the perspective of an audience member, a designer and as a director.

LOOK HERE

The Component 3 mark schemes are available at https://qualifications.pearson.com/en/qualifications/edexcel-gcses/drama-2016.coursematerials.html#filterQuery=Pearson-UK:Category%2FExam-materials.

TASK 7.2

Ask yourself how confident you are in your drama skills and knowledge. Complete your own version of this table.

Drama skill	Good / OK / Not so good	Strengths and weaknesses
Costume design	🙂	✓ Helped to create my own costume for devised piece. + Need to know more technical terms to analyse costume for live production seen.
Set design	🙂	✓ Designed set for scripted piece and can make a model box and ground plan. + Need to create design for set text and analyse set for live production seen.
Lighting design	😠	✓ Know how effective lighting can be. + Need to understand different types of lantern and technical terms. + Explore lighting design for set text and live production seen.
Sound design	🙂	✓ Have explored sound design for set text and analysed sound for live production seen. + Make notes for live production and consider how director would think about sound for set text.
Performance	🙂	✓ Acted in some pieces and understand about voice and movement. + I've focused on lighting recently and need to remind myself of the technical terms linked to performing.

DESIGN TIP

Revisit and update the table in Task 7.2 at regular intervals.

This design by Kirk Bookman for *An Inspector Calls* separates certain characters and areas of the stage, bathing the Birling family in an eerie blue light. (Maltz Jupiter Theatre.)

Chapter 7 Component 3: Theatre Makers in Practice

PREPARING FOR THE EXAM

When revising for the design questions in the exam:

- use the specialist language glossaries in this book when you are writing – including notes and annotations – or reviewing your writing
- study your set play in detail and annotate it with design ideas that spring to mind or that you notice in the stage directions
- consider how you would use design to stage your set play
- make notes using specialist language about all the design options for the live performance you are writing about
- develop your ability to **interpret**, **analyse** and **evaluate**.
- make use of any design experience you have gained outside your course, such as in amateur theatre or further reading.

Designers and performers work together harmoniously to convey meaning and create atmosphere in *The Crucible* at Pacific Conservatory Theatre.

Section A: Bringing texts to life: The study of one performance text

The idea of 'bringing a text to life' implies that you can imagine it on the stage. You will be assessed on the extent of your **knowledge** of the extract and the play as a whole and how that interacts with your **understanding** of how it could be staged in terms of performance and design skills. These critical judgements will also be used in Section B when you write about a live performance.

You will be working with the guidance of your teacher on a particular text for this section of the exam, where you will be given an extract of the play along with a series of questions about how you would perform and stage it.

This involves the key skills of interpretation and analysis. The two concepts are closely linked as it is your close study and knowledge (**analysis**) that will lead you to put forward choices (**interpretation**) of aspects of the play.

ASSESSMENT CHECK

This question in the exam assesses AO3: 'Demonstrate knowledge and understanding of how theatre is developed and performed.'

TASK 7.3

1. Choose a design option that you are less familiar with.
2. Pick an extract from your set play that has plenty of scope for that design role.
3.
   - For **set** or **costume**, draw some sketches to interpret the extract in an exciting way.
   - For **lighting** or **sound**, think about the locations, period and atmosphere you could create.
   - For **lighting**, put together a mood board using the guidance in Chapter 2.
   - For **sound**, jot down some diegetic and non-diegetic sound effects that you would like to hear, perhaps with some music choices.

Chapter 7   Component 3: Theatre Makers in Practice

Section B: Live theatre evaluation

In this section of the written exam, you will answer two questions about a show you have seen. (This cannot be a performance of your set play.)

- The six-mark question will ask you to analyse an aspect of the performance.
- The nine-mark question will ask you to evaluate a different aspect of the same production.

One question will deal with acting and the other with an element of design. There are no choices of questions.

> **ASSESSMENT CHECK**
> This question tests your ability to 'analyse and evaluate the work of others' for AO4.

> If you were fortunate enough to see a show anything like this *Twelfth Night* (at Hartford Stage in Connecticut), you would have plenty of scope for writing about set, costume and lighting designs.

You will be able to take an A4 sheet of paper into the exam with 500 words of **notes** on it. It can also include sketches and diagrams, so use all the available space to ensure you have reminders of design elements as well as acting. Simple, annotated sketches can easily sum up set and costume design, for example, so be sure to include some.

Blue Stockings costume.

DNA set design.

> **TASK 7.4**
>
> 1. Work in your group to re-create, roughly, how the stage looked for a scene you all remember clearly or that your teacher suggests. Use levels, objects and pieces of furniture to stand in for pieces of set.
> 2. On your 'stage', create a freeze-frame for a key moment in the scene.
> 3. Take it in turns to 'come out' of the freeze-frame and describe the costumes, sound and lighting for that moment.
> 4. If possible, photograph the freeze-frame you created. Include it in your journal with annotations about set, sound, costume and lighting. (Bear in mind, however, that photographs cannot form part of your 500-word notes.)

Chapter 7   Component 3: Theatre Makers in Practice

FOCUS

How to write as if you are a director.

ASSESSMENT CHECK

In exploring a director's role and how they create impact and meaning, you are demonstrating 'knowledge and understanding of how theatre is developed and performed' (AO3). These notes will help you to 'offer possible interpretations from the perspective of a director.'

SECTION A: SET DESIGN FROM A DIRECTOR'S VIEWPOINT

To succeed with this question, which asks you to consider a design element from a director's viewpoint, rather than a designer's, you should show your understanding that the two roles are different. In the exam, you will need to give examples that are 'well developed and supported by reasons that fully connect the response to the extract and the chosen design element.'

Thinking as a director for your set text

A director will always consider set design with a focus on the overall piece. They will be most interested in the way that set helps to communicate meaning and themes and enhance style and atmosphere, and less concerned with the technical aspects of the set itself.

In this set design by Ruth Neeman for An Inspector Calls, *the furnishings reflect the family's wealth. They are solid, high quality and well designed, but perhaps show signs of wear. What meaning is suggested by the crooked window?*

DESIGN TIP

Try to identify and keep in mind the main difference between being a designer and a director.

You will need to comment on the context of the play and its performance in the exam.

TASK 7.5

Consider the period in which your set text was created and the performance context of the play.

1. Find out about:
    - the playwright's intentions
    - the design of the first performance.
2. Explore how these link to:
    - the period the play is set in
    - its relevance to a modern audience.

Revising set design in your set text

> **TASK 7.6**
>
> 1. Research and make notes on the social, historic, political and economic contexts of the set text you have studied.
>
>   *An Inspector Calls*, for example, was written at the end of the Second World War. Britain was about to hold a general election which could, if Labour were elected, lead to major developments for the working class. JB Priestley was in favour of the social responsibility that the NHS and other reforms could bring about. His play was written with this in mind.
>
> 2. Use your research to complete your own version of the table below. (Examples have been given using *An Inspector Calls*.)
>
> | | How set design could communicate meaning, theme, context and atmosphere |
> |---|---|
> | **Setting** (time and location): The dining room of a wealthy family, one evening in 1912. | • Furniture and flooring/walls should suggest the period. Priestley says, 'the general effect is substantial and heavily comfortable, but not cosy and homelike.'
• As items are there for show, the set should be furnished with stiff fabrics rather than ones that flow and drape.
• Angular shapes to reflect family's stiffness? |
> | **Theme**: Class inequality and the need for greater social responsibility. | • Contrast between the wealth of the Birling family and the poverty of ordinary people should be made obvious. A sense of the outside world should be present in the set design.
• A different area where Eva Smith can be seen? A **gauze** that could be backlit to show what's going on outside?
• The dining room should somehow feel like a fortress to be defended from invaders. Perhaps there are bars on the window?
• A raised level in the room would give opportunities for power to be emphasised at particular moments. |
> | **Context** | • The fact that Birling is a businessman could be reflected in large photographs or paintings of his factories.
• Although the play is set in 1912, the context of 1946 needs to be indicated. Perhaps rubble in the outside world could suggest destruction?
• Is the Birling house at risk of falling somehow, to suggest the context that the wealthy might be about to tumble from their heights? |
> | **Mood/ atmosphere** | • Mood shifts dramatically after the entrance of Inspector Goole.
• The part of the set that shows the working-class world of 1945 could be lit more clearly so that more of it is seen. |

LOOK HERE

'Introduction to design in the written exam', pages 202–205, has several tasks and plenty of advice. Read it carefully and complete Task 7.2 in particular.

What symbolic meaning is conveyed by the collapse of the Victorian part of the set in this scene from the end of *An Inspector Calls*? How does this link to the destruction in the wartime section? (Original design by Ian MacNeil.)

Exam practice

You need to practise how you will respond in the written exam itself. If you have prepared well, it should not be too daunting.

A potential risk in any exam is running out of time. You need to be ready to write confidently and fairly rapidly as soon as you have understood the question and decided which design option to write about. Completing the tasks above will put you in the best possible position.

Working with an example answer

The student-style answer on the facing page is about *An Inspector Calls* (Act 3, from 'Eric: Because you're not the kind of father...' to 'Inspector: But each of you helped to kill her. Remember that. Never forget it.').

As a director, discuss how you would use **one** of the **production elements below** to bring this extract to life for your audience. You should make reference to the context in which the text was created and performed. Choose **one** of the following:

- Costume
- Sound
- Set.

[9 marks]

Chapter 7 Component 3: Theatre Makers in Practice

The original performance style was naturalistic, whereas I would include non-naturalistic features in my set design. As with the original production, I would use Edwardian details, such as a period telephone and heavy, dark wooden furniture.

The set would be for an end-on configuration and would have a very strong echo of 1945, despite being set in 1912. This would be achieved by showing more than the Birlings' dining room. I would have a gauze curtain hanging from the front edge of the dining room continuing to DSR. It would be painted with a scene of war devastation. Lighting would highlight the necessary parts of the set including the area behind the gauze as needed. This is one way in which I would keep the context of the play alive for the audience.

At the start of the extract, the gauze curtain would show the painted image. This would focus the audience onto the dining room area, where the set design uses stiff, dark, expensive-looking wall and floor coverings with plenty of gilt and glass in the furnishings. I would want the audience to be very aware of the contrast between wealth and poverty.

At the point where the Inspector says, 'She went to your mother's committee for help... Your mother refused to help', an image would be seen through the gauze. This would depict a visibly pregnant young woman, dressed in a poor 1940s outfit, and other women whose gestures show that they need support. Also in the image, the audience would see a woman, whose clothes and bearing suggest Mrs Birling, on a raised platform with her head turned away from the other women. I would use set in this way to highlight the plight of Eva and all those in need after the war.

The emotions of the Birling family have reached great heights by the moment the Inspector starts his speech beginning 'Stop!' If possible, I would use hydraulics to 'shake' the dining room part of the set slightly. This would make real for the audience the possibility that the wealthy of 1945 were in danger of losing their stability. This would last for only 4 seconds, then fade. It is at precisely this moment, while the family 'are suddenly quiet, staring at him' that the Inspector would step onto the platform in the dining room and slowly turn to face them, building tension.

At the very end of the extract, as the Inspector orders the family to 'Remember that. Never forget it', he would still be standing on the platform. The gauze would gradually reveal a cluster of poor people, some of whom are carrying shabby suitcases. As a director, I would guide the thoughts and emotions of the audience; reminding them of the context and what is at stake.

DESIGN TIP

Remember to focus on how set design reflects themes and artistic intentions as a whole. You **must** refer to context.

TASK 7.7

1. Label the example answer with:

    F – Focus on the question

    Ex – Example to support argument or point

    T – Appropriate technical language

    U – Understanding and knowledge of the design skill in relation to directing the performance

    C – The 1945 context.

2. Use the AO3 mark scheme to decide on a band and then a mark out of 9.

TASK 7.8

Test yourself.

Answer the same question yourself, using an extract from your own set text.

FOCUS
How to write as if you are a designer.

ASSESSMENT CHECK
Section A assesses AO3: 'Demonstrate knowledge and understanding of how theatre is developed and performed.' These notes will help you to study your set text in order to 'offer possible interpretations from the perspective of a designer.'

DESIGN TIP
Using specialist design language is one of the most important things you can learn to do.

LOOK HERE
'Introduction to design in the written exam', pages 202–205, has several tasks and plenty of advice to help here.

SECTION A: SET DESIGN FROM A DESIGNER'S VIEWPOINT

The final question in Section A carries 14 marks, which is the highest number of marks for any single question in the paper. What might this mean in terms of how much time you should spend preparing for it?

If you have only worked practically as a performer, the design questions might seem rather daunting. This book is here to support you and increase your knowledge and confidence.

You will have a choice of three design elements to write about for this question. Writing as a set designer might not be an option on the big day, so make sure you have studied and revised the other design skills in relation to your set text.

Ian MacNeil's original set for the 1992 production of *An Inspector Calls* at the National Theatre. It used a bold, non-naturalistic style, with a false proscenium arch recalling the theatres that were a popular diversion from the hardships of the Second World War.

Thinking as a set designer for the set text

You will not know in advance what extract you will be given, but you will know which play it will be from.

To start you off, can you think of three ways you could explore the text? Anything that helps you to become familiar with the text on the page and in performance is worth spending time on. The best way to revise, however, is to create set designs yourself.

What do you think the set should look like?

Once you are familiar with the whole play, begin to imagine how the set might look.

It is often useful to study the original designs for the play. The designer will have had an excellent understanding of the playwright and director's artistic intentions and the circumstances of its production. *DNA* is a good example of a very particular design that used projections to suggest the various locations. You will want to put your own creativity to the test, however. How could you suggest a variety of locations in a different way?

Creating a mood board

Mood boards help a designer to think about style and atmosphere and artistic intentions in terms of impact and meaning. It could be digital or produced on paper or card.

TASK 7.9

1. To begin your own mood board, quickly think of ten adjectives for your set text. Words for *DNA* might include *sharp*, *tangled*, *cold*, *grey*.
2. Gather images that match your adjectives in some way.
3. Move on to think about suitable nouns, such as *street*, *wood*, *teenager*, and gather images for them with the same 'feel' as those for your adjectives.
4. Now think about how to organise these images onto the page. They could overlap or be grouped in ways that inspire you.
5. You could also add pictures or actual items showing colours and textures, such as rope or wire.

DESIGN TIP

There is an interesting conversation with designer Simon Daw at http://simondaw.com/interview-with-simon-daw/. You can see his video mood boards and model boxes for the original production of *DNA* in the same Resources section of his website.

A set design mood board for *DNA*.

Planning your set design

TASK 7.10

1. After you have read the whole play, begin your own version of this table with factual, stylistic and atmospheric clues that could influence set design choices.

Stage configuration:			
Historical period	Locations/s	Genre and style	Atmosphere/s

2. Taking your mood board and the table above as a guide, make some decisions about your design (as much as you can so far).
   - What will the stage configuration be? Where will the audience sit?
   - Will the set be permanent, changed for different scenes, or composite (all locations on stage at the same time)?
   - How will locations be suggested?
   - Will your set be naturalistic or abstract?
   - What colour palette would you use?
   - What textures and materials would work well (for instance, smooth and shiny metal or rough and earthy untreated wood)?
   - What should be on the floor of the acting area?

This recent version of *DNA* at Queen's Theatre, Hornchurch, takes a simple, stark approach to set design, for a thrust stage.

DESIGN TIP

Deciding on your stage configuration (end on, in the round, and so on) is a vital early step.

LOOK HERE

There is an example of a set design sketch on page 20.

DESIGN TIP

If you do create a ground plan, you could base it on these approximate sizes:
- end on: 5 x 3 metres
- in the round: 4 x 4 metres
- traverse: 3 or 4 metres wide.

DESIGN TIP

You don't need to build your set design, but you could construct a simple one if you are rehearsing sections of the text in lessons.

Documenting your set design

Why is it useful to document a set design that is unlikely to be constructed?

- Ground plans and sketches in your answer will show your skills and present an extremely clear idea of your design. These are often quicker to produce than a detailed description.
- You can annotate your drawing, which will also be quicker than writing in prose.
- A model box that you might make during revision would allow you to explore how practical your design is. You can move things around and see how it would look.
- Working with your design practically will make it memorable when it comes to the written exam.
- If you are new to set design, you will gain practical knowledge and subject-specific language that could be useful in the exam and in real life.
- It is also fun!

This labelled sketch of a set for *Blood Brothers* provides a lot of information in a few words!

Labels on sketch:
- 'BLOOD BROTHERS' written on back wall in graffiti
- zig-zag 'crack' down centre
- Johnstone side reds and browns
- Lyons side creams and blues
- streetlamp
- shrub
- overflowing rubbish bin
- platform for narrator
- audience

TASK 7.11

1. Draw some rough sketches of possible designs for your set text and decide which works best. You could work in pencil or add colour and annotations, if you wish.
2. When you have a sketch that you are happy with, follow the instructions on page 21 to create a ground plan.
3. It is useful to create a 3D model, using the guidance on pages 22–24.

LOOK HERE

You will find plenty of information about staging configurations on pages 12–14.

Considering a key element of set design: levels

When writing about your own set design or one that you have seen, the use of levels is an important consideration. As well as adding interest, raising areas of the acting area offers potential for:

- creating more than one location
- enhancing a split focus (with the aid of lighting)
- suggesting power relationships.

How to include levels

Professional productions might use expensive methods to create levels, but they can be created without spending much at all. For example:

- Purpose-made staging blocks might be available in your school. Some versions are stackable. Alternatively, you might be able to borrow blocks from another learning setting, or your local theatre or hall. If not, it is possible to hire stage blocks reasonably cheaply.
- If there is a fixed stage (in the hall, for example), you could design a set with some action taking place on the floor and some on the stage.
- A technical department might be able to build some simple levels.
- Actors could sit or stand on low benches, chairs or stools.

Writing about levels in set design

You should explain the significance of levels in the set design you are writing about. Ask yourself questions similar to those below.

Professional set designers often include more than one level in their designs. This one by Tony Ferrieri for *The Morini Strad* takes place in a stringed-instrument repair shop. The platform is in the shape of a violin. The polished wood tones also match the material of a violin.

DESIGN TIP
Take care to ensure that seats, steps or platforms are sturdily built and safe to use.

DESIGN TIP
Think carefully about where levels are used in the acting area. Performance should still be versatile, and sightlines considered.

* How have the levels been positioned in this set for *The Crucible*? Draw a quick sketch.

* What shape are the raised sections? Why? (Straight edges might suit the severity of the court setting.)

* How high are the levels? Why? (There might be a variety of heights to add interest and meaning.)

* How are levels used by performers? Be specific here. (A character or location might be associated with a level. Characters might use a level to show that they have power at a certain moment.)

Chapter 7 Component 3: Theatre Makers in Practice 215

SECTION B: EVALUATING A SET DESIGN IN LIVE THEATRE

In this part of the exam, you need to give a detailed evaluation of the set design in a performance you have seen. You should justify your opinions with examples that 'are well developed and fully support evaluation and conclusions'. You are also aiming to use technical language.

Preparation for a set design question

Look in the show programme, theatre marketing material and online for information about the set designer to add to your exam notes. Major productions and tours often have images, information and reviews online. Photographs in particular will help to remind you of details in the set and how they complemented other elements of the performance, although these cannot be included in your notes.

Remember that you were a member of the audience. The exam will ask you to comment on the impact design had on the audience. Share your different responses with your classmates, but aim to write about your own viewpoints in the exam. You are expected to make a critical evaluation.

Marti Pellow in *Blood Brothers*. The 'broken' aspect of the set and the cool detachment of the Narrator's character is enhanced by the cold blue lighting.

TASK 7.14

1 Study any notes about the set that you made after seeing the performance.
2 Make some simple sketches based on your notes and images you find.
3 Annotate them with details of the set that created impact or otherwise contributed to meaning and mood. What do you remember about the set, and why?
4 Discuss the set with your classmates. Pooling your memories is valid and the discussion will help you to recall the experience of seeing the production.

ASSESSMENT CHECK

Section B assesses AO4: 'Analyse and evaluate your own work and the work of others.' The tasks on these pages help you to:

- 'understand how the meaning of a text can be interpreted and communicated to an audience'
- 'form critical judgements about live theatre based on your understanding of drama and theatre'
- 'analyse and evaluate the ways in which different production elements are brought together to create theatre.'

DESIGN TIP

A programme from the performance is likely to be a useful source of information.

DESIGN TIP

There is an interview with set and production designer Andy Walmsley at https://thefrontrowcenter.com/2017/01/interview-andy-walmsley-production-designer/. Visit his own website, andywalmsley.com/show.php?project_id=100, for images of his iconic *Blood Brothers* set.

LOOK HERE

Look over Chapter 1 to help you with technical language and the period accuracy of your sketches.

Evaluation as a skill

TASK 7.15

1. Read 'Evaluating your set design' carefully and complete Task 1.12.
2. Complete Task 1.13 with examples from the live performance. Remember that you are evaluating someone else's set design, not your own.

Set design evaluation

The exam question will ask you about a design element of the production as a whole: it will not specify which moments to write about. So, evaluate moments that stood out as examples of how the set was used to good effect.

TASK 7.16

1. If you can, find a copy of the script for the live performance you are writing about. Browse through it until you find a section where you remember the set having an impact on you.
2. Try to remember what the set looked like at key points in this section. These could be as short as a single moment or as long as a whole scene or more.
3. Write at least two paragraphs of critical judgement, which include:
   - subject-specific language, such as *flats*, *gauze*, *trucks* and so on
   - how lighting changed the look of the set and the effect of that
   - the way the set was used by the actors and the effect of that
   - atmosphere or meaning that was enhanced for the audience
   - evaluations supported by detailed examples, such as, 'The use of... was powerful because...' and 'I was impressed by... because it ...'
4. Swap your writing with someone else's for feedback. You could use the bullet points above as a checklist.

SIGNPOST

'Evaluating your set design' on pages 30–31 gives guidance on evaluative writing about sets.

DESIGN TIP

Consider including one or two of your sketches in your notes for the exam.

Lianne Harris and Fraser Macrae make use of levels in Strange Town's production of *Dr Korczak's Example*. The stage furniture is naturalistic while the other set dressings are simple, plain and severe.

Chapter 7   Component 3: Theatre Makers in Practice

Working with an example answer

The mark scheme is a valuable tool when you are preparing for the written exam. The following task will allow you to assess a sample answer and then practise one of your own.

> **TASK 7.17**
>
> 1. Highlight the key words in the following example question:
>
>   > Evaluate how the set designer of the performance used levels and/or colour to create impact for the audience. **[9 marks]**
>
> 2. Now check your understanding of these key words, using a glossary if necessary.
> 3. Annotate the answer below, about *Blood Brothers*, with:
>
>   **F** – Focus on the question
>
>   **Ex** – Example to support argument or point
>
>   **T** – Appropriate technical language
>
>   **U** – Understanding and knowledge of set design in relation to the performance
>
>   **E** – Evaluation in terms of how successful the set was.
> 4. Use the AO4 mark scheme to decide on a band and then a mark out of 9.

DESIGN TIP

Try as many exam-type questions as you can. Your teacher should be able to set you suitable questions. When you feel ready to practise under exam conditions, keep only your 500 words of notes with you. Give yourself a maximum of 20 minutes to complete your answer.

The designer, Andy Walmsley, created a set for an end-on stage configuration that strongly conveyed the brothers' environment. Levels, in particular, added versatility, and were used to change location and atmosphere.

The high-level backdrop made an impression on me at the moment the play began. It showed the city, with the council houses on the lower level and tall buildings, such as the Liver Building, above. Blue LEDs illuminated the image. We were immediately in the world of 1960s Liverpool.

One effective detail of the set was how the high metal platform, or bridge, covered part of the backcloth. It was positioned in front of a trough housing the footlights for the backdrop. We looked through the bridge to the city. This made the city look more distant, and made me feel that the characters were dwarfed by the big city.

Cleverly, the focus moved away from the backdrop for much of the play due to the interaction between lighting and set. For example, the window panes were made of transparent material rather than being painted on. The set and lighting collaboration also created the effects of the windows on the upper floors of the houses, throwing shadows across the floor of the stage.

Levels were important to the set design, right down to the Johnstones' front step, which offered an intimate space for Mrs Johnstone to cradle Mickey. Something as seemingly unimportant as the front step of a house also added realism to the whole set at moments such as when the creditors take items from the house. It was details such as these that made the largely naturalistic set so powerful.

The 2019 cast of *Blood Brothers* at the Birmingham Hippodrome.

At the other end of the scale, the high walkway (about 4 metres) towered over the stage and gave the Narrator an area where his authority was made clear. It distanced him from the action and made us feel that he was an onlooker, like us. The walkway also added interest to various scenes, such as the wedding, where the guests could gather for a multi-level photograph. *Blood Brothers* has a large cast, so levels are useful in providing different areas, particularly when the action moves rapidly from one location to the next.

Balconies outside the first-floor windows provided other spaces where characters could overlook the action. A powerful example of this is when Mrs Johnstone is calling Mickey. She appears above the boys, who are playing in the street below. I could see the shock on her face when she recognises Edward.

TASK 7.18

Test yourself.

1 Based on the live performance you have chosen:

> Evaluate how set was used to enhance mood and atmosphere.
> **[9 marks]**

Use the AO4 mark scheme and other tasks to guide you.

You might find it helpful to ask yourself:
- Did the set include colours and textures to enhance mood and atmosphere?
- How did the use of levels and scenery contribute?
- Was there anything about the way the set was divided (or not) that made a contribution?

2 If possible, ask another student or your teacher to mark your answer. Make improvements based on their comments.

FOCUS

How to write as if you are a director.

ASSESSMENT CHECK

In exploring a director's role and how they create impact and meaning, you are demonstrating 'knowledge and understanding of how theatre is developed and performed' (AO3). These notes will help you to study your set text in order to 'offer possible interpretations from the perspective of a director.'

SECTION A: LIGHTING DESIGN FROM A DIRECTOR'S VIEWPOINT

To succeed with this question, which asks you to consider a design element from a director's viewpoint, rather than a designer's, you should show your understanding that the two roles are different. In the exam, you will need to give examples that are 'well developed and supported by reasons that fully connect the response to the extract and the chosen design element.'

Thinking as a director for your set text

A director will always consider lighting design with a focus on the overall piece. They will be most interested in the way that lighting helps to communicate meaning and themes and enhance style and atmosphere, and less concerned with the technical aspects of lighting.

You will need to comment on the context of the play and its performance in the exam. Consider the period in which the play was written as well as the period it is set in and its relevance to a modern audience.

Lighting revision for the set text

It is important to try to immerse yourself in the idea of being a director making use of lighting, rather than a performer.

A student production of *DNA* at the Technical University of Berlin. The warm colour and high intensity of the spotlight on Adam suggests sunlight. This contrasts starkly with the very low intensity and cold colours on the rest of the gang, indicating the darkness of their behaviour.

DESIGN TIP

Try to identify and keep in mind the main difference between being a designer and a director.

TASK 7.19

1. Research and make notes on the social, historic, political and economic contexts of the set text you have studied.

   DNA, for example, was written in 2008 and first staged by the National Theatre using a minimal set with complex lighting and projection. The play is said (by Dennis Kelly) to have been inspired by current feelings at the time in Britain, specifically, fear of terrorism and the sense that young people were becoming wild and dangerous. It was an era when young people were demonised by the press and various laws were passed in an attempt to 'control' them.

   By showing such an extreme example of youth violence in *DNA*, Kelly could be saying that people's fears are getting out of control. He is also asking the question 'Is it ever right to sacrifice the individual for the good of the group?'

2. Use your research to complete your own version of the table below. (An example has been given using *DNA*.)

	How lighting could communicate meaning, theme, context and atmosphere
Settings: • Street • Field • Wood	• Lighting and projection will be important in the creation of location, time of day. • Gobos could create the leafy effect of the wood.
Themes: • Violence • Bullying • Power • Morality	• Red gels could enhance themes like violence and bullying. • **Uplighting** could create menacing shadows and suggest power.
Context: Britain in the 2000s	• LEDs could be used on stage for a modern look. • Tungsten street lights?
Mood/atmosphere: • Dark • Moments of humour • Fear	• Shadows could be created to add dark drama. • Brighter, warmer lighting would help the atmosphere during moments of humour. • Torches as practical effects could be very atmospheric.

DESIGN TIP

There is a useful interview with designer Simon Daw and clips from his video ideas boards on his website http://simondaw.com/resources/.

A real location that you know or see could inspire your lighting design.

LOOK HERE

'Introduction to design in the written exam' on pages 202–205 has several tasks and plenty of advice. Read it carefully and complete Task 7.2 in particular. You could focus just on lighting at this stage.

Exam practice

You need to practise how you will respond in the written exam itself. If you have prepared well, it should not be too daunting.

A potential risk in any exam is running out of time. You need to be ready to write confidently and fairly rapidly as soon as you have understood the question and decided which design option to write about. Completing the tasks above will put you in the best possible position.

Working with an example answer

The following student-style answer is about *DNA* (Section Three, from 'Brian: She loves violence now' to 'Adam: The light was… this').

As a director, discuss how you would use **one** of the **production elements below** to bring this extract to life for your audience. You should make reference to the context in which the text was created and performed. Choose **one** of the following:

- Costume
- Sound
- Lighting.

[9 marks]

The lighting for DNA is very important in terms of bringing locations to life, as well as in creating atmosphere and representing the context of teenage alienation. For example, the street scenes throughout the play would be lit with quite dim, cool colours.

I would use stylised lighting at points in the extract to enhance the disoriented mood of the scene. In Adam's long speech about his experience after the fall, I would match the text to lighting effects to take the audience with Adam on his journey.

When Adam says 'I was in a dark…', the stage lighting would snap off and the rest of the gang would shine their phone torches onto his face. This is a reminder of the modern context and the way some young people misuse their technology. It should remind the audience that the gang are responsible for his terrible experience.

These lights could also add to the illusion that Adam is moving through tunnels. As he says 'crawling in the dark', the actors would swirl their phone torches over his face.

At the moment where Adam wakes up 'with liquid on his head', a red light should fade up directly above Adam. Because there would be no front or low-level lighting, Adam's features would be shadowy. This stylised lighting should help bring his suffering to life for the audience. The red gel would also symbolise the violence done to Adam.

When Adam says 'I remember leaves…', a single white fresnel for daylight would fade in above DSL (not directly above the actor). It would be very low intensity and the audience would only become aware of it as Adam says 'maybe a light high, high, high, high…'. This adds more naturalism to the lighting scheme.

Naturalism is also an important aspect of lighting in terms of helping to create the setting of the wood. I would use a gobo with an abstract, leafy effect to suggest the trees. Pale green and yellow lights would wash across the stage.

Laura Fontana's lighting design for *DNA* at the Southwark Playhouse. The ribbons of light reference DNA strings and the woodland setting and show Adam as trapped. The red colour suggests the physical violence done to Adam and his mental difficulties.

Helen Murray / ArenaPAL

At the start of the extract, Brian asks if the others can feel the day licking their skin. Close to nature, Brian's guilt for what the gang have done is starting to surface in a kind of madness. I would involve the audience by using slightly brighter and warmer lighting to suggest the sunshine that Brian claims to feel. It would quickly snap to a cooler colour, however, as Cathy slaps him. This would help the audience understand that the warmth might only be in Brian's mind. It would also emphasise the violence of Cathy's action.

At the very end of the extract, when Adam says 'the light was... this', he is confused, remembering that the light wasn't him approaching death, but the world outside the tunnel. To bring this to life for the audience, I would use a followspot from the wings to make quick sweeps across the stage and over the audience. (The light would be fairly low intensity so as not to blind the audience.) This should remind the audience that they are part of the same world as Adam and, indeed, the gang.

TASK 7.20

1. Label the example answer with:

    F – Focus on the question

    Ex – Example to support argument or point

    T – Appropriate technical language

    U – Understanding and knowledge of the design skill in relation to directing the performance

    C – The 2008 context of the play.

2. Use the AO3 mark scheme to decide on a band and a mark out of 9.

TASK 7.21

Test yourself.

Answer the same question using an extract from your own set play.

DESIGN TIP

Remember to focus on how lighting design reflects themes and artistic intentions as a whole. You **must** refer to context.

> **FOCUS**
> How to write as if you are a designer.

> **ASSESSMENT CHECK**
> Section A assesses AO3: 'Demonstrate knowledge and understanding of how theatre is developed and performed.' These notes will help you to study your set text in order to 'offer possible interpretations from the perspective of a designer.'

SECTION A: LIGHTING DESIGN FROM A DESIGNER'S VIEWPOINT

The final question in Section A carries 14 marks, which is the highest number of marks for any single question in the paper. What might this mean in terms of how much time you should spend preparing for it?

If you have only worked practically as a performer, the design questions might seem rather daunting. This book is here to support you and increase your knowledge and confidence.

You will have a choice of three design elements to write about for this question. Writing as a lighting designer might not be an option on the big day, so make sure you have studied and revised the other design skills in relation to your set text.

Thinking as a lighting designer for your set text

> **Do you watch television and films? Have you been to a music concert?**
>
> If yes, you will be able to harness your subconscious knowledge of how lighting can be used creatively.
>
> Next time you go to a gig or watch a film, notice where the designer has gone beyond the use naturalistic lighting. Try to concentrate on the mood or meaning being enhanced. This might mean watching out for the use of colour, angle and pace of lighting transitions. Alternatively, it might simply mean noticing how bright or dim the lighting is, or how dramatic shadows are being produced.

You will not know in advance what extract you will be given, but you will know which play it will be from.

To start you off, can you think of three ways you could explore the text? Anything that helps you to become familiar with the text on the page and in performance is worth spending time on. The best way to revise, however, is to create lighting designs yourself.

Revising lighting design

- Working with your design practically will make it memorable when it comes to the written exam.
- If you are new to lighting, you will gain practical knowledge and technical language that could be useful in the exam and in real life.
- It is also fun!

> **LOOK HERE**
> 'Introduction to lighting design' on pages 34–35 will develop your thinking.

> **DESIGN TIP**
> Using specialist design language is one of the most important things you can learn to do.

What early decisions about lighting need to be made?

Once you are familiar with the whole play, ask yourself:

- Will non-naturalistic lighting work with the production style?
- What do I want to communicate to the audience?
- Are special effects needed?
- How else can I enhance the artistic intentions and mood and atmosphere? Gobos? Colour?

Why is it useful to create a lighting design for the set text?

LOOK HERE

'Introduction to design in the written exam', pages 202–205, has several tasks and lots of advice. Read it carefully and complete Task 7.2 in particular, relating it to lighting design.

Creating a mood board

Mood boards help a designer to think about style, atmosphere, colour and artistic intentions in terms of impact and meaning. It could be digital or produced on paper or card.

A lighting mood board for *An Inspector Calls*.

TASK 7.22

With a partner, discuss what lighting effects the creator of this mood board might produce.

TASK 7.23

1. To begin your own mood board, quickly think of ten adjectives for your text. Words for *An Inspector Calls* might include: *moonlit, pink, cold, intimate, brighter* (these are in the stage directions).
2. Gather images that match your adjectives in some way.
3. Move on to think about suitable nouns, such as *responsibility, destruction, bleach, Titanic*, and gather images for them with the same 'feel' as those for your adjectives.
4. Now think about how to organise these images onto the page. They could overlap or be grouped in ways that inspire you.
5. You could also add pictures or actual items showing colours and textures, such as metal and wood.
6. With a partner, discuss lighting effects suggested by your mood board.

Chapter 7 Component 3: Theatre Makers in Practice

Careful lighting that considers colour, intensity and use of shadow creates atmosphere. Here, this is enhanced with a smoke effect.

Planning your lighting design

TASK 7.24

1. After reading the play, begin a version of this table with factual, stylistic and atmospheric clues that could influence lighting choices.

Stage configuration:			
Location/s	Historical setting	Style, genre and atmosphere	Time of day, season, weather

2. Taking your mood board and the table above as a guide, begin to make some decisions about your design (as much as you can so far).
   - What will the stage configuration be? Where will the audience sit? (This has a crucial effect on where you position the lights.)
   - How will locations be suggested?
   - What are the main moods and atmospheres?
   - How might you fit in with the colour palette of set and costume?

Exam practice

You need to practise how you will respond in the written exam itself. If you have prepared well, it should not be too daunting.

A potential risk in any exam is running out of time. You need to be ready to write confidently and fairly rapidly as soon as you have understood the question and decided which design option to write about. Completing the tasks in this section will put you in the best possible position.

Working with an example answer

TASK 7.26

1. Highlight and check your understanding of the key words in this question:

> Discuss how you would use **one** design element to enhance the production of this extract for the audience. Choose **one** of the following:
> - Lighting
> - Set
> - Sound.
>
> [14 marks]

TASK 7.25

1. Select a section of your set text that offers plenty of opportunities for interesting lighting and transitions.
2. Make a list of the lighting effects that you want to create.
3. Read sections in Chapter 3 to help you make notes about how you could create those effects.

2. Label the example answer on the following page with:

   F – Focus on the question

   Ex – Supporting example

   T – Appropriate technical language

   U – Understanding and knowledge of lighting in the performance.

3. Use the mark scheme to decide on a band and then a mark out of 14.

LOOK HERE

'Angles, colour and intensity', pages 40–43, and 'Research for lighting', page 47, provide inspiration and advice on achieving lighting effects.

'Types of stage lantern', pages 36–37, will help you with technical language.

This response is about *An Inspector Calls* (Act One, from 'Edna: Please, Sir, an inspector's called' to 'Birling: You've had enough of that port, Eric!').

I would use lighting here to signal the importance of Inspector Goole's arrival. I imagine it on a proscenium stage in a large auditorium.

At the start of the extract, a low-intensity light (around 30%), is focused on a small area of the stage. This creates an enclosed feeling, suggesting the Birlings' inward-looking approach to life. As the family are sitting around a table, I would position fresnels on all four sides to ensure they are equally visible. I would also use colour to create a warm feeling in the room. Medium Amber (Lee 020) would give the effect of candlelight. LED candles in candlesticks on the table give a natural effect without a safety risk.

I would use Birling's line 'Show him in here. Give us some more light' as the cue to start a transition. The well-off Birling family are likely to have had electric lights. I would have Edna move to a small table DSR and switch on an ornate table lamp. The cable would be taped down discreetly (matching the flooring). I would also take her action as a visual cue to rapidly fade in three cold blue profile spots for a bright, hard light (as called for in the script). The intensity will be 40%. I wouldn't snap them in because in Edwardian times switching on electric lights wouldn't be as instant as today.

When the Inspector enters, he would immediately move to the bright DSR area so that he is lit more coldly and brightly than the family. I would increase the lighting in this area to 50%. This would symbolise his role in the play as representing clear sightedness and truth. The audience should be aware of his importance even though they should not be conscious that the light has changed.

Before Edna leaves, she should switch on a ceiling light above the dining table, to come on as Birling says 'Sit down, Inspector.' This lighting cue would be a profile spotlight fitted with a whiter blue (Lee 500) positioned on the rigging above the stage. This dramatic **downlight** would whiten the faces of the Birling family. However, I would keep this to quite a low intensity (around 20%) so that their faces would still be fully visible.

Later, when the Inspector shows the photograph to Birling, I want the audience to be aware of Eva. To create this, I would use a silhouette behind the window of a girl in Edwardian factory-style clothing. The gauze window panes would be backlit to enable the ghostly figure to be seen...

DESIGN TIP

You might find it helpful to memorise a few filter colours that would be suitable for your set text.

Lee Filters colour temperature set of gels.

TASK 7.27

Test yourself.

1. Choose an extract from your set text of around 80 lines.
2. Have a go at the question in Task 7.26 under exam conditions. Allow yourself no more than 35 minutes.

DESIGN TIP

You are expected to include technical detail because you are writing from the viewpoint of someone with a lot of subject knowledge. Try to use appropriate technical terms.

ASSESSMENT CHECK

Section B assesses AO4: 'Analyse and evaluate your own work and the work of others.' The tasks on these pages help you to:

- 'understand how the meaning of a text can be interpreted and communicated to an audience'
- 'form critical judgements about live theatre based on your understanding of drama and theatre'
- 'analyse and evaluate the ways in which different production elements are brought together to create theatre.'

DESIGN TIP

A show programme is likely to be a useful source of information.

DESIGN TIP

The way lighting worked with sound and set or contributed to atmosphere and context would be valuable information to include in your written exam.

SECTION B: EVALUATING A LIGHTING DESIGN IN LIVE THEATRE

In this part of the exam, you need to give a detailed evaluation of the lighting design in a performance you have seen. You should justify your opinions with examples that 'are well developed and fully support evaluation and conclusions'. You are also aiming to use technical language.

Preparation for a lighting design question

Look in the show programme, theatre marketing material and online for information about the lighting designer to add to your exam notes. Major productions and tours often have images, information and reviews online. Photographs in particular will help to remind you of details of the lighting and how they complemented other elements of the performance, although these cannot be included in your notes.

Remember that you were a member of the audience. The exam will ask you to comment on the impact lighting had on the audience. Share your different responses with your classmates, but aim to write about your own viewpoints in the exam. You are expected to make a critical evaluation.

Made in Dagenham at the Adelphi Theatre.

TASK 7.28

1. Study any notes about the lighting that you made after seeing the performance.
2. Draw a quick sketch of the set, with lighting special effects added.
3. Annotate it with details of the lighting that created impact or otherwise contributed to meaning and mood. What do you remember about the lighting, and why?
4. Discuss the lighting with other people in your class. Pooling your memories is valid and the discussion will help you to recall the experience of seeing the production.

Evaluation as a skill

TASK 7.29
Read 'Evaluating your lighting design' carefully and complete Task 2.18, using examples from the live performance. Remember that you are evaluating someone else's lighting design, rather than your own.

Evaluating lighting
The exam question will ask you about a design element of the production as a whole: it will not specify which moments to write about. So, evaluate the moments that stood out for you as examples of effective lighting.

TASK 7.30
1. If you can, find a copy of the script for the live performance you are writing about. Browse through it until you find a section where you remember lighting having an impact on you.
2. Try to remember the lighting at key points in this section. These could be as short as a single moment or as long as a whole scene or more. Consider transitions between lighting states.
3. Write at least two paragraphs of critical judgement, which include:
   - subject-specific language, such as *intensity, transitions, colour gels, automated lights*, and so on
   - how lighting enhanced style and helped to create settings
   - how the use of lighting changed the look of the set and the effect that had on atmosphere and meaning
   - evaluation supported by detailed examples, such as, 'The use of… was powerful because…' and 'I was impressed by… because it made me feel/think…'
4. Swap your writing with someone else's for feedback. You could use the bullet points above as a checklist.

SIGNPOST
'Evaluating your lighting design' on page 59 gives guidance on evaluative writing about lighting.

DESIGN TIP
Try as many exam-type questions as you can. Your teacher should be able to set you suitable questions. When you feel ready to practise under exam conditions, keep only your 500 words of notes with you. Give yourself a maximum of 20 minutes to complete your answer.

Note the effective use of lighting in *Anything Goes* (at the Ahmanson Theatre, Los Angeles). What is the effect of putting lights behind the portholes? The couple downstage are lit from the front. How does their appearance differ from the couples on the platforms?

Working with an example answer

The mark scheme is a valuable tool when you are preparing for the written exam. The following task will allow you to assess a sample answer and then practise one of your own.

TASK 7.31

1. Highlight the key words in the following example question:

   > Evaluate how the lighting designer supported the themes of the performance to create impact for the audience. **[9 marks]**

2. Now check your understanding of these key words, using a glossary if necessary.

3. Annotate the example answer on the facing page (about *A Curious Incident of the Dog in the Night-Time*). Look for:

   F – Focus on the question

   Ex – Example to support argument or point

   T – Appropriate technical language

   U – Understanding and knowledge of lighting design in relation to the performance

   E – Evaluation in terms of how successful the lighting was.

4. Use the AO4 mark scheme to decide on a band and a mark out of 9.

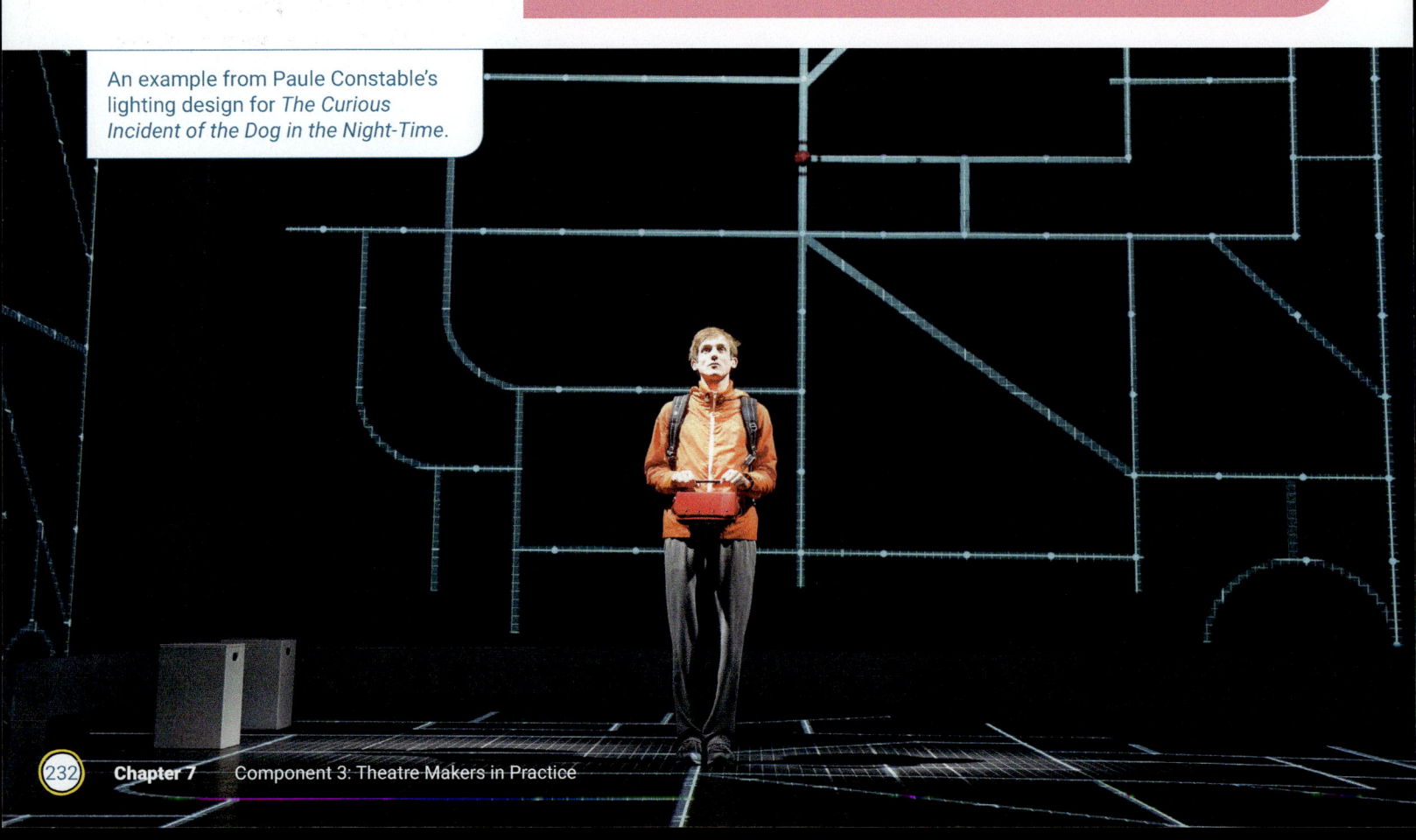

An example from Paule Constable's lighting design for *The Curious Incident of the Dog in the Night-Time*.

The designer, Paule Constable, has developed a magical lighting design from the original staging in the round at the National Theatre to the proscenium staging I saw at the Lowry.

The lighting can only be described in relation to the set, which is basically a box. It represents Christopher's brain. How Christopher's brain works is a main theme of the play.

The floor and the three sides of the box are made of something that can be pixelated, so lighting happens alongside the images that appear on all of the surfaces. Moving projections add to the overall effect of looking into a box full of moving images and light.

One of the simplest special lighting effects was the use of small par cans within the moveable white cubes, which were used as seats, for example. These threw white light onto the faces of nearby actors at moments such as when Christopher found the letters from his mother. Their relationship is another central theme. This cold and stark uplighting cast me suddenly into Christopher's feelings and helped me to share his shock. Because the lighting wasn't balanced from other sources, it had a very eerie effect.

Nearly all of the lighting was cold white to reflect Christopher's mathematical, ordered brain functions. This simple choice had a huge impact on the look of the production and supported the themes.

The pace of lighting changes was key to making the special effects work seamlessly. At moments, profile spots pinpointed individual actors as they were mentioned by the narrator. These were clean and tightly focused and snapped rather than faded in, which felt very exciting. The lighting contributed to the pace of the show, which suggested the speed of Christopher's brain.

It was the same when we were submerged into Christopher's vision of the stars or maths equations. Projections, pixelated lighting and a low-intensity whitewash of light (used to make the performers visible) were co-ordinated to take us into Christopher's head. The timing of the lighting transitions was crucial and the cues were precise. The overall effect was mesmerising.

Slower, more reflective scenes used lighting for a different atmosphere, such as when Christopher's mum appears for the first time as a memory. Although Christopher is shown in the usual white spotlight, his mother is bathed in a warmer, straw-coloured, softly focused spotlight. This helped me to understand Christopher's warm memories of his mother. By contrast, the use of downlighting to create a clear box of light around Christopher at the flat showed his sense of being imprisoned and uncomfortable there.

My favourite use of lighting was Christopher's journey to the railway station. The ambient lighting pulsed while moving projections of street names and the paths he was following appeared and disappeared very precisely. I was swept up in the journey as all my senses were captivated.

TASK 7.32

Test yourself.

1. Based on the live performance you have chosen:

   > Evaluate how lighting was used to support the themes of the performance and create impact for the audience. **[9 marks]**

   Use the AO4 mark scheme and other tasks to guide you.

2. If possible, ask another student or your teacher to mark your answer. Can you make improvements based on their comments?

DESIGN TIP

Include as much detail as possible in your answers. Highlight your evaluative judgements by using terms such as 'effective' and 'powerful impact'.

FOCUS

How to write as if you are a director.

ASSESSMENT CHECK

In exploring a director's role and how they create impact and meaning, you are demonstrating 'knowledge and understanding of how theatre is developed and performed' (AO3). These notes will help you to study your set text in order to 'offer possible interpretations from the perspective of a director.'

SECTION A: COSTUME DESIGN FROM A DIRECTOR'S VIEWPOINT

To succeed with this question, which asks you to consider a design element from a director's viewpoint, rather than a designer's, you should show your understanding that the two roles are different. In the exam, you will need to give examples that are 'well developed and supported by reasons that fully connect the response to the extract and the chosen design element.'

Thinking as a director for your set text

A director will always consider costume design with a focus on the overall piece. They will be most interested in the way that costumes help to communicate meaning and characterisation, and enhance style and atmosphere, and less concerned with the technical aspects of the set itself.

They will want the costumes to:

- have an impact
- communicate meaning
- convey themes
- help to create atmosphere
- be in harmony with the style of the piece.

Blue Stockings at the University of Windsor, Ontario. How do these costumes suggest the formal, Victorian setting of the university and help to give a sense of the girls setting out bravely on their adventure in education? (Think about shape, length, colour, detail and accessories.)

To do the same, you need to have the whole text at the front of your mind when you answer the Section A question in the exam. You should use your practical experience to help you interpret and analyse the use of costumes.

You will need to comment on the context of the play and its performance. Consider the period in which the play was written as well as the period it is set in and its relevance to a modern audience.

Costume revision for the set text

> ### TASK 7.33
>
> 1. Research and make notes on the historical, social, political and economic contexts of the set text you have studied.
>
>   *Blue Stockings*, for example, was written in 2013 and dedicated to Malala Yousafzai, a young Pakistani activist for female education. The play is set in 1896, during the struggle for academic equality at Cambridge University. For a contemporary audience, the play speaks of the continuing fight for women to gain equal rights.
>
> 2. Use your research to complete your own version of the table below. (An example has been provided using *Blue Stockings*.)
>
> | Character | Garments | Accessories | Link to contexts |
> |---|---|---|---|
> | **Mr Banks** (Lecturer at Girton College who is in favour of women being given degrees. He is sacked in Act 2.) | • White wing-collar shirt
• Black trousers
• Black academic gown, rather untidy to reflect his lack of conformity. | • Pocket-watch
• Wire-framed spectacles. | Mr Banks symbolises the progressive male. He would have been only barely tolerated in the late 19th century. Today, both women and men can commonly be supportive of equality. |
> | **Tess Moffat** (A very able student) | • Ankle-length purple skirt
• White high-necked blouse
• Bloomers. | • Straw boater with green ribbon
• Button boots. | • Purple and green are the colours of the suffragette movement.
• The bloomers are long, so enable the girls to ride bicycles, foreshadowing the trousers of modern times. |

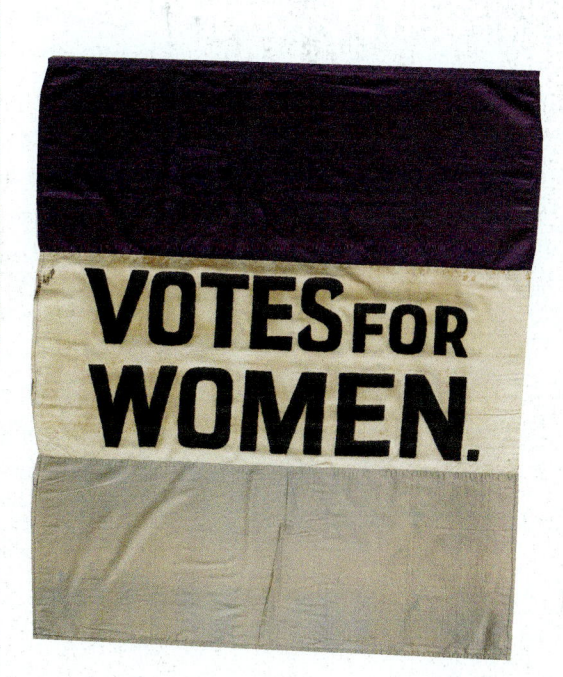

DESIGN TIP

Try to identify and keep in mind the main difference between being a designer and a director.

LOOK HERE

'Introduction to design in the written exam' on pages 202–205 has several tasks and lots of advice. Read it carefully and complete Task 7.2 in particular. You could simply focus on lighting design at this stage.

Exam practice

You need to practise how to respond in the written exam. If you have prepared well, it should not be too daunting.

A potential risk in any exam is running out of time. You need to be ready to write confidently and fairly rapidly as soon as you have understood the question and decided which design option to write about. Completing the tasks above will put you in the best possible position.

Working with an example answer

The following student-style answer is based on Act 1, Scene 1 of *Blue Stockings*.

As a director, discuss how you would use **one** of the **production elements below** to bring this extract to life for your audience. You should make reference to the context in which the text was created and performed.

Choose **one** of the following:

- Costume
- Sound
- Props/stage furniture.

[9 marks]

The first production of Blue Stockings used naturalistic set and costume. I would do the same to emphasise the period in which the piece is set. While the original version used a thrust stage, I would direct my piece in the round, so costumes would have to be accurate and detailed.

As a director, I would use costume symbolically in this extract to show the struggle of the women of Girton College to achieve equality in education. I would want Tess to have a purple skirt and incorporate green and yellow into her costume to symbolise the suffragette movement. She would wear a yellow blouse and have a green band on her straw hat. The costume should be quite cumbersome in terms of the heavily textured, long skirt and white bloomers. Her friends will lift her skirts to 'help Tess assemble herself on the bicycle' – which would have been thought very unladylike at the time. This makes reference to the struggle for women to take part in a patriarchal society, which resonates today.

The costumes of all the girls in this extract would show the constrictions they feel in their everyday lives. Their white blouses would be buttoned high and would contrast with the simple practicality of Mr Banks' costume of trousers, shirt and academic gown. I would want his gown to appear quite tatty to reflect his unconventional nature.

A scene from the original production of *Blue Stockings* at the Globe Theatre. It used naturalistic costume and set items, but on an open thrust stage, giving a range of opportunities in performance.

TASK 7.34

1. Label the example answer with:

   F – Focus on the question

   Ex – Example to support argument or point

   T – Appropriate technical language

   C – The context of the play

   U – Understanding and knowledge of costume in relation to directing the performance.

2. Use the AO3 mark scheme to decide on a band and a mark out of 9.

TASK 7.35

Test yourself.

Select an extract from your set text and use it to write your own response to the question on the previous page.

DESIGN TIP

Remember to focus on how costume reflects themes and artistic intentions as a whole. You **must** refer to context.

FOCUS

How to write as if you are a designer.

ASSESSMENT CHECK

Section A assesses AO3: 'Demonstrate knowledge and understanding of how theatre is developed and performed.' These notes will help you to study your set text in order to 'offer possible interpretations from the perspective of a designer.'

DESIGN TIP

Using specialist design language is one of the most important things you can learn to do.

SECTION A: COSTUME DESIGN FROM A DESIGNER'S VIEWPOINT

The final question in Section A carries 14 marks, which is the highest number of marks for any single question in the paper. What might this mean in terms of how much time you should spend preparing for it?

If you have only worked practically as a performer, the design questions might seem rather daunting. This book is here to support you and increase your knowledge and confidence.

You will have a choice of three design elements to write about for this question. Writing as a set designer might not be an option on the big day, so make sure you have studied and revised the other design skills in relation to your set text.

Thinking as a costume designer for your set text

You will not know in advance what extract you will be given, but you will know which play it will be from.

To start you off, can you think of three ways you could explore the text? Anything that helps you to become familiar with the text on the page and in performance is worth spending time on. The best way to revise, however, is to create costume designs yourself.

How do you think the costumes should look?

TASK 7.36

1. Search the internet for costume images appropriate to your set text. Familiarise yourself with key costume features relating to the period, including fabrics and fashions, and the social and economic conditions of the play's main characters.
2. Select an extract of about 80 lines that inspires you in terms of its costume possibilities.
3. Decide whether the style would be naturalistic or non-naturalistic.
4. Choose two characters from the extract. Complete a table like this for their costume features.

Character	Social/economic position	Fabric/colour choices	Garments	Make-up, accessories, hair and headwear, shoes

5. Sketch each character and annotate it to include detail.
6. Show and explain your designs to another member of the class and answer any questions they have.

Exam practice

You need to practise how to respond in the written exam. If you have prepared well, it should not be too daunting.

A potential risk in any exam is running out of time. You need to be ready to write confidently and fairly rapidly as soon as you have understood the question and decided which design option to write about. Completing the tasks in this section will put you in the best possible position.

LOOK HERE

'Introduction to design in the written exam', pages 202–205, has several tasks and plenty of advice. Try Task 7.2 in particular.

Working with an example answer

TASK 7.37

1. Highlight the key words in the following sample question:

   > Discuss how you would use **one** design element to enhance the production of this extract for the audience.
   >
   > Choose **one** of the following:
   > - Costume
   > - Set
   > - Sound.
   >
   > [14 marks]

2. Now check your understanding of those words, using a glossary.

3. Read and annotate the following student-style response to the question with:

   F – Focus on the question, including context

   Ex – Example to support argument or point

   T – Appropriate technical language

   U – Understanding and knowledge of costume in relation to the performance.

4. The question above and response on the following page are based on Act 3 of *The Crucible* from the entrance of Elizabeth to Abigail pointing with fear.

   Use the AO3 mark scheme to decide on a band for the response, and then a mark out of 14.

In this image of Irene Allen as Elizabeth Proctor, her hair is uncombed and matted. Her face and hands are scratched and streaked with dirt. Her dress is still buttoned up, but it is torn, creased and soiled. These details of costume and make-up clearly reveal the suffering that Elizabeth is going through and indicate her degraded, vulnerable state. (Designed by Michael Taylor for Edinburgh Lyceum.)

Chapter 7   Component 3: Theatre Makers in Practice   239

I have chosen a naturalistic design for *The Crucible* in its stated context of the 1690s.

I want my costumes to show Elizabeth and Proctor's journey as characters. Having been imprisoned for some time in squalid conditions, Elizabeth would wear a distressed, broken-down version of her original costume. Her coarse cotton dress is blue to reflect the coolness of her personality, but it would now be torn and dirtied. Her apron would be gone, to symbolise the loss of her role as a housewife, but she will retain a sullied version of her white puritan collar: the fact that she is a devout Christian will be evident. Her hair will be loose and tangled, and her bonnet gone. She might attempt to secure her hair in the neck of her dress. She would be embarrassed to have her hair uncovered during this Puritan period.

The accuracy of Elizabeth's costume will enhance the audience's connection with the 1690s and draw out their empathy for her situation. She will be barefoot to show her vulnerability. I will use the brown and black shades of a bruise wheel to add 'dirt' to exposed skin. In particular, I will use the bruise wheel's redder shades to reveal the damage done to her wrists by the heavy handcuffs.

Proctor will also wear a degraded version of his original costume. The leather waistcoat will be retained to reflect his physical and emotional strength, but his rough wool shirt will be torn, soiled and bloodied. He has been tortured, so, his face and hands will be bloodied and bruised. I will have ensured that the actor has no allergies to fake blood products. I would mix fake blood with coffee granules to give an authentic textured effect and maintain some shine to the 'damaged' areas of skin so that the marks show up brutally under the intensity of the stage lights. Proctor's work boots will be split and misshapen, encouraging the actor to move with a shuffling gait, demonstrating his pain. The aim is to enhance the audience's empathy with the character.

In contrast, Danforth's costume will be pristine. The texture of his black breeches and doublet will be smooth and fine, to suggest his wealth. I would choose a good-quality cotton with a sateen finish. His black slip-on shoes will be highly polished to reflect his pious attention to detail. In keeping with his Puritan faith, there will be little embellishment to his costume, but I would add a buckle to his tall felt hat to show his sense of superiority. He will have a fine white cotton shirt and starched white cravat. The audience should interpret Danforth's character as being 'holier than thou'. He is correct in his attire, which might suggest his superficial nature. The audience will have an enhanced sense of his stiffness as a character.

DESIGN TIP

You are expected to include technical detail because you are writing from the viewpoint of a designer with subject-specific knowledge and skills. Try to use appropriate technical terms. You might find it helpful to add an annotated sketch.

TASK 7.38

Test yourself.

1. Choose an extract from your set text of around 80 lines.
2. Write your own response to the question in Task 7.37. Remember to focus on the key words you picked out.

SECTION B: EVALUATING A COSTUME DESIGN IN LIVE THEATRE

In this part of the exam, you need to give a detailed evaluation of the costume design in a performance you have seen. You should justify your opinions with examples that 'are well developed and fully support evaluation and conclusions.' You are also aiming to use technical language.

Preparation for a costume design question

Look in the show programme, theatre marketing material and online for information about the costume designer to add to your exam notes. Major productions and tours often have images, information and reviews online. Photographs in particular will help to remind you of details in the costumes and how costumes complemented other elements of the performance, although these cannot be included in your notes.

Remember that you were a member of the audience. The exam will ask you to comment on the impact costumes had on the audience. Share your different responses with your classmates, but aim to write about your own viewpoints in the exam. You are expected to make a critical evaluation.

TASK 7.39

1. Study any costume notes you made after seeing the performance and put them together with production photographs you have found.
2. Use these to draw your own simple sketches of key characters.
3. Annotate them to pick out particular details that created impact or were otherwise important. What do you remember about them? Why? What effect did they have on the audience? Did they contribute to characterisation, context, style or themes?
4. Discuss costuming with other people in your class. Pooling your memories is valid and the discussion will help you to recall the experience of seeing the production.

ASSESSMENT CHECK

Section B assesses AO4: 'Analyse and evaluate your own work and the work of others.' The tasks on these pages help you to:

- 'understand how the meaning of a text can be interpreted and communicated to an audience'
- 'form critical judgements about live theatre'
- 'analyse and evaluate the ways in which different production elements are brought together to create theatre.'

DESIGN TIP

The way costumes worked with lighting or contributed to atmosphere and context would be valuable information to include in your written exam.

DESIGN TIP

A show programme is likely to be a useful source of information.

LOOK HERE

Use Chapter 3 to help you with technical language and period accuracy of your sketches.

TASK 7.40

Read carefully 'Evaluating your costume design' on page 87 and complete Task 3.16 with examples from the live performance. Remember that you are evaluating someone else's costume designs, rather than your own.

SIGNPOST

'Evaluating your costume design' on page 87 gives guidance on evaluative writing about costumes.

DESIGN TIP

Consider including one or two annotated sketches in your notes for the exam.

Evaluation as a skill

Evaluating costume design

The exam question will ask you about a design element of the production as a whole: it will not specify which moments to write about. So, evaluate the moments that stood out for you as examples of how costumes were used effectively.

TASK 7.41

1. If you can, find a copy of the script for the live performance you are writing about. Browse through it until you find a section where you remember the costumes having an impact on you.
2. Try to remember what the costumes looked like at key points in this section. These could be as short as a single moment or as long as a whole scene or more.
3. Write at least two paragraphs of critical judgement, which include:
   - subject-specific language, such as *colour palette, style, silhouette, texture, fit* and so on
   - how the use of lighting changed the look of the costumes and the effect of that
   - how atmosphere or meaning that was enhanced for the audience
   - evaluations supported by detailed examples, such as, 'The use of… was powerful because…' and 'I was impressed by… because it made me feel/think…'
4. Swap your writing with someone else's for feedback. You could use the bullet points above as a checklist.

Working with an example answer

The mark scheme is a valuable tool when you are preparing for the written exam. The following task will allow you to assess a sample answer and then practise one of your own.

TASK 7.42

1. Highlight the key words in the following example question:

   > Evaluate how the costume designer of the performance used colour and shape to create impact for the audience. **[9 marks]**

2. Now check your understanding of those key words, using a glossary if necessary.
3. Annotate the example answer on the following page with:

   F – Focus on the question
   Ex – Example to support argument or point
   T – Appropriate technical language
   U – Understanding and knowledge of costume in relation to the performance
   E – Evaluation in terms of how successful the costumes were
4. Use the AO4 mark scheme to decide on a band for the response, and then a mark out of 9.

DESIGN TIP

Try as many exam-type questions as you can. Your teacher should be able to set you suitable questions. When you feel ready to practise under exam conditions, keep only your 500 words of notes with you. Give yourself a maximum of 20 minutes to complete your answer.

The Woman in Black at the Torch Theatre, Milford Haven. A good example of costume, set, lighting and direction working together to create atmosphere and a sense of mystery and foreboding.

The costume designer of The Woman in Black used shape to firmly locate the period of the piece. This could be seen in the men's costuming where appropriate waistcoats, jackets and trousers presented the professional classes in the Edwardian period. The jacket of Kipps was cut with the correctly sized lapels and cufflinks were used on his shirt, which is in keeping with the period. It could be argued, however, that the use of a wristwatch for Kipps was slightly out of keeping with the period as a pocket watch would have been a more likely choice in that period.

Colour was used symbolically with the character of the woman who was dressed in black to denote her link to death. Black also heightened the audience's sense that she is a sinister and mysterious figure. The use of a coarsely woven lace veil to cover her face which was also black was accurate for the time period and the paleness of her skin tone as it showed under the intense stage lights had a strong impact on the audience as it gave a rather unearthly effect.

The shape of the woman in black's dress was Victorian, which suggested that she was an older woman who still dressed in the mourning clothes of a previous decade. The leg-of-mutton sleeves and strictly demure nature of the collar with its's ties and embellishments added to her imposing nature, helping the audience understand the sense of fear for those who saw her.

TASK 7.43

Test yourself.

Based on the live performance you have chosen:

> Evaluate how costume was used to reveal character and character relationship.
>
> **[9 marks]**

Use the AO4 mark scheme and other tasks to guide you.

DESIGN TIP

Include as much detail as possible. Be sure to highlight your evaluation by using appropriate terms such as 'effective' and 'powerful impact'.

Chapter 7   Component 3: Theatre Makers in Practice

DESIGN TIP

Immerse yourself in the idea of being a designer rather than a performer for your set text.

Exam practice

You need to practise how to respond in the written exam. If you have prepared well, it should not be too daunting.

A potential risk in any exam is running out of time. You need to be ready to write confidently and fairly rapidly as soon as you have understood the question and decided which design option to write about. Completing the tasks above will put you in the best possible position.

Working with an example answer

The following exam-style question and response is based on *Twelfth Night* (Act 2, Scene 5, from 'Enter Maria (with a letter)' to 'Malvolio: It is in contempt of question her hand').

As a director, discuss how you would use **one** of the **production elements below** to bring this extract to life for your audience. You should make reference to the context in which the text was created and performed. Choose **one** of the following:

- Set
- Sound
- Lighting.

[9 marks]

The sound I would use as director of *Twelfth Night* would be largely naturalistic with some use of non-diegetic sound. The original performance would have had very little sound other than music from the gallery. I want to capture the context of Elizabethan England for the audience. At that time, any sounds would have been produced live by the performers. So, this would only be for special dramatic effects.

The extract is part of the comic subplot and is set in the garden of Olivia's wealthy household. The text itself would create location for the original audience, but, I would use a natural soundscape of birdsong and a gentle fountain to set the scene and add atmosphere. This would be in harmony with the set and lighting for the scene and be designed to transport the audience into the garden.

Although it is from a later period, I would use Handel's 'The Arrival of the Queen of Sheba' as underscoring for Maria's speech where Sir Toby and the others hide as Malvolio approaches. This piece has a jolly tempo in a major key, which would suit the bustle and humour of the moment. Any audience member who knew the title of the piece might smile because Malvolio sees himself as an important man. I want the audience to have an enhanced sense of Malvolio's self-importance.

This music would fade out as Malvolio enters and be immediately followed by the loud squawk of a peacock, causing Malvolio to turn and scowl at the interruption to his thoughts. The humorous moment would lead nicely into his first line ''Tis but fortune, all is fortune.'

The following comic dialogue would be underscored by the garden soundscape at low volume so that the voices can be easily heard. Then, as Malvolio's speech slips into his fantasy of being married to Olivia, I would fade out the garden underscoring and fade in a quiet soundscape (previously recorded by the cast) of court voices saying admiring things about Malvolio. This would take the audience into Malvolio's secret world. It would be used very carefully to avoid distracting from the onstage voices and fade out as Malvolio says 'One Sir Andrew.'

As Malvolio starts to read the letter, I would underscore it with a romantic piece of music to remind the audience of his feelings for Olivia.

The National Theatre production of *Twelfth Night*, with Simon Paisley Day as Malvolio, watched over by Charles Edwards as Sir Andrew Aguecheek, Simon Callow as Sir Toby Belch and Samuel James as Fabian.

TASK 7.45

1. Label the example answer with:

   F – Focus on the question

   Ex – Example to support argument or point

   T – Appropriate technical language

   U – Understanding and knowledge of the design skill in relation to directing the performance

   C – The 1602 context of the play.

2. Use the AO3 mark scheme to decide on a band and then a mark out of 9.

TASK 7.46

Test yourself.

1. Answer the example question yourself, using an extract from your own set text. Ideally, try it under exam conditions, giving yourself no more than 20 minutes.
2. Then, if possible, ask another student, or your teacher, to mark your answer. Can you improve it, based on their comments?

DESIGN TIP

Remember to focus on how lighting design reflects themes and artistic intentions as a whole. You **must** refer to context.

Chapter 7 Component 3: Theatre Makers in Practice   247

FOCUS

How to write as if you are a designer.

ASSESSMENT CHECK

Section A assesses AO3: 'Demonstrate knowledge and understanding of how theatre is developed and performed.' These notes will help you to study your set text in order to 'offer possible interpretations from the perspective of a designer.'

LOOK HERE

'Introduction to design in the written exam', pages 202–205, has several tasks and plenty of advice.

DESIGN TIP

Using specialist design language is one of the most important things you can learn to do.

LOOK HERE

'Introduction to sound design' on pages 90–91 will develop your thinking.

SECTION A: SOUND DESIGN FROM A DESIGNER'S VIEWPOINT

The final question in section A carries 14 marks, which is the highest number of marks for any single question in the paper. What might this mean in terms of how much time you should spend preparing for it?

If you have only worked practically as a performer, the design questions might seem rather daunting. This book is here to support you and increase your knowledge and confidence.

You will have a choice of three design elements to write about for this question. Writing as a sound designer might not be an option on the big day, so make sure you have studied and revised the other design skills in relation to your set text.

Thinking as a sound designer for the set text

Do you listen to music? Do you watch television and films?

If yes, you will be able to harness your subconscious knowledge of how sound can be used creatively.

Next time you listen to music or watch something that goes beyond the use of dialogue in terms of sound, concentrate on the meaning and atmosphere being enhanced. This might mean listening out for the diegetic and non-diegetic sounds in a film or identifying the dominant emotion or atmosphere in a piece of music.

You will not know in advance what extract you will be given, but you will know which play it will be from.

To start you off, can you think of three ways you could explore the text? Anything that helps you to become familiar with the text on the page and in performance is worth spending time on. The best way to revise, however, is to create sound designs yourself.

What early decisions about sound need to be made?
Once you are familiar with the whole play, ask yourself:

Will non-diegetic sound work with the chosen style of the production? (A purely diegetic and naturalistic design would only include the sounds that the actors would hear.)

What period of time is the production to be set in?

Creating a mood board
Mood boards help a designer to think about style, atmosphere, sound and artistic intentions in terms of impact and meaning. It could be digital or produced on paper or card.

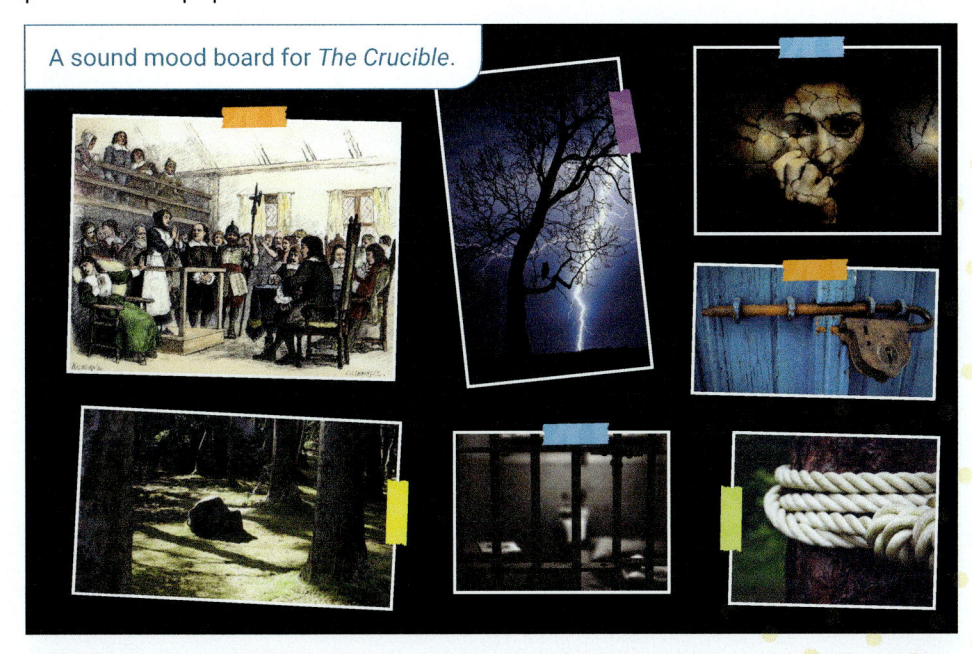

A sound mood board for *The Crucible*.

TASK 7.47
With a partner, discuss what sound effects the creator of this mood board might produce.

TASK 7.48
1. To begin your own mood board, quickly think of ten adjectives for your set text. Words for *The Crucible* might include: *frightening*, *dark*, *secret*, and so on.
2. Gather images that match your adjectives in some way.
3. Move on to think about suitable nouns, such as *witchcraft*, *persecution*, *McCarthyism*, *puritans*, *farmsteads*, and gather images for them with the same 'feel' as those for your adjectives.
4. Now think about how to organise these images onto the page. They could overlap or be grouped in ways that inspire you.
5. You could also add pictures or actual items showing colours and textures, such as bark, rope and wood.
6. With a partner, discuss what sound effects are suggested by your mood board.

DESIGN TIP

Underscoring and soundscapes can add an extra dimension to sound design.

Planning your sound design

TASK 7.49

1. After you have read the whole play, begin your own version of this table with factual, stylistic and atmospheric clues that could influence sound design choices.

Locations	Historical period	Style, genre and atmosphere	Sounds required by the script/stage directions

2. Taking your mood board and the table above as a guide, begin to make some decisions about your design (as much as you can so far).
   - What will the stage configuration be? Where will the audience sit? (This effects where you will place your speakers.)
   - How will locations be suggested?
   - How will the time period of the play be indicated?
   - What are the main moods and atmospheres?
   - How much non-diegetic sound might you want?
   - Do you need your sounds to fit in with changes in lighting?

A production in the round, like *The Crucible* at Cleveland Playhouse, presents interesting opportunities and challenges for a director, designers and performers.

Documenting your sound design

Why is it useful to create sound design for the set text?

LOOK HERE

'Introduction to design in the written exam', pages 202–205, has several tasks and plenty of advice. Read it carefully and complete Task 7.2 in particular, relating it to sound design.

- Working with your design practically will make it memorable when it comes to the written exam.
- If you are new to sound design, you will gain practical knowledge and subject-specific language that will be useful in the exam and in real life.
- It is also fun!

Steppenwolf's production of *The Crucible*. What sound effects and music – if any – might be suitable for this scene?

If you decide to complete your sound design, you will create the documentation that would enable your sounds to be successfully operated during a performance.

Exam practice

You need to practise how to respond in the written exam. If you have prepared well, it should not be too daunting.

A potential risk in any exam is running out of time. You need to be ready to write confidently and fairly rapidly as soon as you have understood the question and decided which design option to write about. Completing the tasks in this section will put you in the best possible position.

Working with an example answer

> **TASK 7.52**
>
> 1. Highlight and make sure you understand the key words in this question:
>
>   > Discuss how you would use **one** design element to enhance the production of this extract for the audience. Choose **one** of the following:
>   > - Costume
>   > - Set
>   > - Sound. [14 marks]
>
> 2. Label the example answer on the following page with:
>
>   **F** – Focus on the question
>
>   **Ex** – Supporting example
>
>   **T** – Appropriate technical language
>
>   **U** – Understanding and knowledge of sound design in relation to the performance.
>
> 3. Use the mark scheme to decide on a band and then a mark out of 14.

> **TASK 7.50**
>
> 1. Select a section of your set text that offers plenty of opportunity for interesting sounds and music.
> 2. Make a list of the sound effects that you want to create and the type of music you think would add the right atmosphere.
> 3. Read sections in Chapter 4 to help you make notes about how you could find and cue those effects.
> 4. Set up a computer folder that contains your effects and music.
> 5. Play your chosen sounds to classmates. Use their feedback to evaluate your work.

> **TASK 7.51**
>
> 1. Try creating a source sheet and cue sheet for your extract.
> 2. If you can, work with actors to perform the extract, so that you can operate the sound yourself.

LOOK HERE
'How to document your sound design' on pages 102–103 has advice on creating a source sheet and a cue sheet.

LOOK HERE
A cue sheet is available on the *Designing Drama* product page at illuminatepublishing.com.

Chapter 7   Component 3: Theatre Makers in Practice

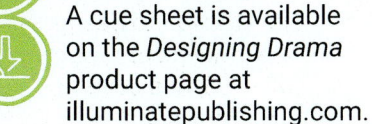

TASK 7.53

Re-create the soundscape described in this example answer by opening three separate tabs and playing crows cawing, the symphony and a drone sound at the same time. How effective do you think it is?

TASK 7.54

Test yourself.
1. Choose an extract from your set text of around 80 lines.
2. Have a go at answering the question in Task 7.52 under exam conditions. Allow yourself no more than 35 minutes.

Use the AO3 mark scheme to guide you.

DESIGN TIP

You are expected to include technical detail because you are writing from the viewpoint of someone with a lot of subject knowledge. Try to use appropriate technical terms.

Richard Armitage and Anna Madeley share a quieter moment as Proctor and Elizabeth at the Old Vic.

The following response is about *The Crucible* (Act Three, from 'Danforth: Look at me' to 'Mary Warren: Abby, I'm here!').

I would use sound design to help the audience's journey through the extract. I am imagining that it is staged in the round.

Silence is an important aspect of sound design and I would use it at the start of the scene to allow the dialogue to build its own tension.

When Elizabeth says 'No sir!', I would fade in a piece of music that is a theme for Elizabeth and John's relationship: a section of Shostakovich's Symphony Number 10 – played on the clarinet. It has a slightly haunting feel. It seems to sum up the warmth that is buried deep in their relationship with a sense of regret running through it. As it is underscoring some dialogue, I would play it only to a low volume level (−15 dB).

Using music as a thread that runs through the play enhances the audience's understanding that the character or character relationship is the focus.

The sound effect of the door closing as Elizabeth is removed from the room would be a recorded source and I would add a little echo to help create the feeling that she and John will not see each other again. The effect would fade over 4 seconds. The music track would fade out under Proctor's line 'She only thought to save my name!' This would allow for the change in pace and focus as Hale's speech begins.

The next sound cue would come with the stage direction where Abigail gives a 'weird, wild, chilling cry'. I would snap in a drone sound mixed with the sound of crows and the Shostakovich symphony at a low level. This soundscape creates the kind of multi-layered feel that would heighten the audience's experience of the moment.

This time, the volume level would rise to 0dB as the actors' voices rise during this moment of hysteria. The sound effect would help the audience to sense the fear in characters such as Danforth and the girls. I would have speakers above the acting area pointing at each of the four audience seating areas and on the back walls behind them. I would want the audience to be fully immersed in the scene.

The volume of the soundscape would be briefly reduced to −5dB when Mary Warren jumps to her feet and pleads 'Abby!' It will rise again later, but I want to mark the moment where Mary becomes involved in the girls' hysteria…

SECTION B: EVALUATING A SOUND DESIGN IN LIVE THEATRE

In this part of the exam, you need to give a detailed evaluation of the sound design in a performance you have seen. You should justify your opinions with examples that 'are well developed and fully support evaluation and conclusions'. You are also aiming to use technical language.

Preparation for a sound design question

Look in the show programme, theatre marketing material and online for information about the sound designer to add to your exam notes. Major productions and tours often have images, information and reviews online. Photographs in particular will help to remind you of details of the sound and how it complemented other elements of the performance, although these cannot be included in your notes. You might also be able to find interviews with sound designers.

Remember that you were a member of the audience. The exam will ask you to comment on the impact sound had on the audience. Share your different responses with your classmates, but aim to write about your own viewpoints in the exam. You are expected to make a critical evaluation.

Christopher Shutt with his Tony Award for his sound design in *War Horse*.

TASK 7.55

1. Study any notes about the sound design that you made after seeing the performance.
2. Make some simple sketches based on your notes and images you find.
3. Annotate them with details of sound and music that created impact or otherwise contributed to meaning and mood. What do you remember about the sound, and why?
4. Discuss the sound with other people in your class. Pooling your memories is valid and the discussion will help you to recall the experience of the production.

ASSESSMENT CHECK

Section B assesses AO4: Analyse and evaluate your own work and the work of others. The tasks on these pages help you to:

- 'understand how the meaning of a text can be interpreted and communicated to an audience'
- 'form critical judgements about live theatre based on your understanding of drama and theatre'
- 'analyse and evaluate the ways in which different production elements are brought together to create theatre'.

DESIGN TIP

A programme from the performance is likely to be a useful source of information.

DESIGN TIP

The way sound worked with lighting or contributed to atmosphere and context would be valuable information to include.

SIGNPOST

'Evaluating your sound design' on page 111 gives guidance on evaluative writing about sound.

Evaluation as a skill

Evaluating sound design

The exam question will ask you about a design element of the production as a whole: it will not specify which moments to write about. So, evaluate the moments that stood out for you as examples of how sound was used effectively.

TASK 7.56

1. Read 'Evaluating your sound design' carefully and complete the task.
2. Remember that you are evaluating someone else's set design, rather than your own. Use examples from the live performance.

TASK 7.57

1. If you can, find a copy of the script for the live performance you are writing about. Browse through it until you find a section where you remember sound having an impact on you.
2. Try to remember the sound at key points in this section. These could be as a single moment or a whole scene or more. Consider soundscapes and the mixing of sound effects as well as the use of music.
3. Write at least two paragraphs of critical judgement, which include:
   - subject-specific language, such as *volume levels*, *soundscape*, *live*, *recorded*, and so on
   - how sound contributed to the style of the production
   - atmosphere or meaning that sound enhanced for the audience
   - evaluations supported by details, such as, 'The use of… was powerful because…' and 'I was impressed by… because it made me feel/think…'
4. Swap your writing with someone else's for feedback. You could use the bullet points above as a checklist.

Working with an example answer

TASK 7.58

1. Highlight and make sure you understand the key words in this question:

> Evaluate how the sound designer of the performance used live and/or recorded sound to create impact for the audience. **[9 marks]**

2. Annotate the example answer on the following page with:

   F – Focus on the question

   Ex – Example to support argument or point

   T – Appropriate technical language

   U – Understanding and knowledge of sound design in relation to the performance

   E – Evaluation in terms of how successful the sound was.

3. Use the AO4 mark scheme to decide on a band and a mark out of 9.

The mark scheme is a valuable tool when you are preparing for the written exam. The previous task and the one on the following page will allow you to assess a sample answer and then practise one of your own.

Joey faces down the tank in *War Horse*.

The sound designer of **War Horse**, Christopher Stutt, has successfully developed a vast and varied design that uses both live and recorded sound to enhance the meaning and atmosphere of this exciting and moving production on a proscenium stage.

Recorded, naturalistic sounds added a depth of atmosphere to the countryside scenes. The specially composed music was greatly enhanced by the sounds of birds and integrated perfectly with the other design elements, particularly lighting. The warm colours of the lights combined very well with the sounds that evoked summer mornings.

One of the sound design highlights in the production was created using recorded sound. It was the moment when the tank comes onto the stage. Specially constructed speakers were worn by the performers operating the tank. Recorded sounds of a tank engine were amplified from these speakers at a very loud volume, which gave me, in the audience, an incredible and overwhelming sense of the horror that the horse and the characters must have been feeling. Speakers at the sides of the stage intensified the sound on stage and all around the auditorium, which pulled the audience powerfully into the action.

Live sound was introduced when the performers used their voices to create, for example, the sounds of Joey. His snorting, whinnying and so on were synchronised with the puppeteers' movements. Recorded sounds could have been used, but the live sounds had much more life and power. Each of the three puppeteers had separate radio microphones, and then the sound was mixed and transmitted live in the form of one sound by the sound engineer. I think this contributed significantly to our sense of the horses being alive.

The most chilling example of this is when Joey is caught in barbed wire. I felt terribly involved and quite upset during this moment. Fortunately, the same techniques created opposite emotions when Albert and Joey are alone together and their communication with each other is wonderfully uplifting.

DESIGN TIP

Include as much detail as possible in your answers. Highlight your evaluative judgements by using terms such as 'effective' and 'powerful impact'.

DESIGN TIP

Try as many exam-type questions as you can. To practise under exam conditions, keep only your 500 words of notes with you. Give yourself a maximum of 20 minutes to complete your answer.

TASK 7.59

Test yourself.

1. Based on the live performance you have chosen:

> Evaluate how sound was used to enhance setting.
>
> **[9 marks]**

Use the AO4 mark scheme and other tasks in this chapter to guide you.

2. If possible, ask another student or your teacher to mark your answer. Can you use their comments to improve it?

The admired, popular and highly successful *War Horse* is a perfect example of a harmonious world on the stage. All design elements – set and staging, lighting, sound, costume and puppetry – complement each other and work seamlessly with the performances to communicate meaning and create a lasting impression on the audience.

GLOSSARY

Accessories
Items such as bags, jewellery and small items that accompany garments.

Allergy
Natural or synthetic products that cause adverse reactions to skin etc.

AML (automated moving lantern)
Operated digitally, these lanterns can swivel and tilt.

Amplifier
A piece of equipment that produces the sound for the speakers, primarily used to increase volume.

Analyse
Examine in detail, thinking about parts in relation to the whole.

Appliqué
A small colourful piece of embroidery – often a picture or pattern – sewn onto an item of clothing.

Artistic intentions
The creative theatrical aims of the production.

Atmospheric
A sound, for example, that creates a strong feeling or mood.

Backcloth
A large piece of canvas or cloth which is often painted with a setting.

Backlight/backlighting
Lighting that comes from the back of the acting area.

Back stitch
A closely worked stitch done by hand.

Barn door
A metal attachment that slides into the front of a lantern, with hinged flaps to control the beam.

Birdie
A miniature lantern ideal for hiding in small parts of a set or along the front edge of the stage.

Blackout
A moment when all the lights are dimmed, often suddenly.

Bruise wheel
Available from theatre make-up sellers, a palette of yellows, reds, browns and cream make-up, excellent for a range of special effects.

Channel
A number given to a lantern that corresponds to a number on the lighting board or desk.

Collaboration
Working with others towards a common aim.

Colour count
A record of the number of gels of each colour required.

Colour palette
A complementary set of colours that belong to a group, such as pastel or dark.

Constant sound
An uninterrupted sound.

Construction
Something that has been built (a set for example); the act of building.

Critical judgement
Analysing the merits and faults of something to decide its worth or success.

Cross-fade
Fading up one lantern or group while fading down another.

Cue
A moment when something happens, and what happens (such as 'Lights fade').

Cue sheet
A list of cues along with timings.

Cue to cue
Going through a play from one sound or lighting cue to the next, missing out the parts in between.

Darting
Sewing small, tapered folds into a garment to provide shape or otherwise alter the fit.

Diegetic sound
A sound that the characters would hear within their world, such as a phone ringing.

Digital
Using computer technology. Digital lighting desks, for example, are programmed using software.

Dimmer/Fader
A way of controlling the intensity (brightness) of the light. These are often manual or digital sliders.

Dimmer rack
The control centre for changing the intensity of each channel.

Downlight
A light that shines from above.

Drone
A constant sound that is often in the background. Drones are often used in non-naturalistic sound effects and are very good for creating atmosphere such as tension.

Echo
The effect that occurs when a sound bounces off surfaces.

Embellishments
Added extras such as lace, buttons, braids and so on; decorative details.

End on
A stage configuration that places the audience on one side of an open stage.

Evaluate
Give an opinion, a value judgement, backed up with examples and reasons.

Exterior (setting/location)
An outdoor space, such as a garden, street or outside a building.

Fabric choice
Considerations such as suitability and effect under lights.

Fade
A gradual increase or decrease.

Fader
A device to control the volume of a sound or the intensity of a light.

Fill light
Working with a key light, fill light is less intense (bright) and is often used to lessen shadows.

Filter/gel
A piece/sheet of coloured plastic/resin that fits at the front of a lantern to change the colour of the beam.

Finish
The surface of fabric – usually shiny or dull.

Flat
A tall, main piece of scenery that, as its name suggests, generally carries a 2D image.

>**Book flat**
>Two flats that are hinged along their 'spine'.
>
>**Free-standing flat**
>A braced, single flat that can stand anywhere on the set.
>
>**Run of flats**
>Two or more flats joined as a length to achieve a wall, for example.

Floating mic
A microphone positioned on the front of the stage.

Flood
A type of lantern that produces a wide spread of light; a broad cover of light.

Focus
Adjust the angle and beam size of a lantern so that it lights the exact area required

Freehand
Drawing something without a tracing or template to guide you.

French doors/windows
A pair of outward-opening doors often fully glazed, functioning as both windows and doors.

Fresnel
A type of lantern that is good for lighting large areas and which blends easily with other fresnels or spotlights to create a wash of light.

Furnishings
Set furniture (sometimes including curtains, rugs and so on).

Gauze
A loosely woven, transparent piece of fabric that can be front- or back-lit to produce different effects (sometimes called a **scrim**, which is made of a different type of fabric, but produces a similar effect).

Gel
See **Filter**.

General cover
Lanterns that provide overall lighting to the acting area.

Genre
A category or type of play (or other art), such as tragedy, comedy, period drama, that has distinctive stylistic or narrative features.

Gobo
A metal cut-out plate that fits in front of a lantern and casts a shadow shape onto the stage (such as a tree outline, window frames and so on).

Hanging mic
A microphone suspended above the performance area.

Illusion
Something that is not as it seems; something that is not real, but often gives an impression of reality.

In the round
A stage configuration in which the audience encircles the acting area.

Intensity
The brightness of lighting. Intensity is generally measured as a percentage (such as 60%).

Interior (setting/location)
An indoor space, such as a kitchen or a school hall.

Intermittent sound
A sound that is not constant; it comes and goes.

Interpret
Express your own ideas about intended meaning; your choice where there are a number of correct possibilities.

Key light
The main, strongest, most intense light, designed to copy the main light source (natural or artificial) in the real world.

Lamp
The technical name for a light bulb.

Lantern
The technical term for a **lighting fixture** that contains a bulb or lamp.

LED (Light Emitting Diode)
Lighting fixtures that use less energy and create less heat than other types of lantern. LEDs are the most popular type of fixture in professional theatres.

Lighting desk/board/console
The means of operating the lighting, with channels, dimmers and faders.

Lighting fixture
A stage light unit.

Lighting plan
The diagram that shows where the lanterns are hung on the rigging.

Lighting state
The term used to describe the way a lantern or group of lanterns is used on the stage. For example, a particular lighting state could create a moonlit effect.

Live sound
A sound that is played directly for the audience.

Location
The place or setting where action takes place, such as a forest, a bedroom or a park.

Manual
Operated by hand as opposed to digitally.

Mass-produced
Made in great numbers, usually in a factory.

Mixer
A device that can change and combine sounds.

Model box
A 3D set design, often presented within a box of some sort.

Monochrome
Black, white and grey only.

Montage
A sequence or joining together of sounds to make a new piece of sound.

Natural
In terms of fabric – not man-made, such as cotton and wool.

Naturalistic
A set or lighting effect, for example, with characteristics of reality; having the appearance of a real place.

Non-diegetic sound
Sound that can be heard by the audience, but would not be heard by the characters (such as atmospheric music to encourage the audience to feel something).

Non-naturalistic
A set or lighting design, for example, that aims not to appear like reality.

Pace
The speed with which lighting or sound effects transition from one to the next.

Par can
A type of lantern that produces a very strong beam of light.

Pattern
A design printed onto or woven into fabric, including tartan, paisley, stripes. A paper pattern is the template pieces that guide sewers as they cut cloth out to make into garments.

Period (of history)
A specific time, era.

Pitch-shifting
Altering the pitch of a sound which, when mixed with other differently pitched versions of the same sound, makes it have a richer, thicker sound.

Playback device
The means through which recorded sound is played, such as a CD player or smartphone.

Plotting
The process of creating a cue sheet to show choices of what sound or light effect happens when (and where).

Practical effect
A lighting effect that is operated or worn by a performer.

Pre-set
Features of the drama onstage that are already in place before the audience enters.

Profile spotlight
A versatile lantern that can be used to create tight spots of light or bigger areas as required.

Promenade (theatre/staging)
Staging that involves the audience walking (a promenade) from one location to another with the actors. Locations are often outdoors, or in large buildings such as warehouses.

Props
Short for 'properties' (suggesting ownership): objects that would be owned by a character such as a torch, phone, set of keys.

Proscenium (arch)
A stage configuration where the audience are where the 'fourth wall' of a room would be – similar to **end on**, but with the addition of a picture-frame effect around the stage.

Radio mic
A microphone that is worn by a performer, often taped to the cheek.

Raked
Sloping. Raked seating is placed on an upwards slope away from the stage.

Realistic
A set, for example, that sets out to be like real life (naturalistic).

Recorded sound
Sound that is captured electronically, such as onto a computer file.

Rehearsal costumes
Practice clothes or shoes that bear some similarity to the final costume.

Representative
Something that represents (stands for) something else: for example, a non-naturalistic set that 'represents' and suggests rather than copies real life.

Reverb
The effect that occurs when sound waves hit surrounding surfaces and we hear the original sound plus its reflections. Adding reverb to a sound makes it longer and weightier.

Rig
The bars that lanterns are hung on.

Run
Either a rehearsal or read-through of the whole play, or the number of times a play will be performed (for example, The Crucible has a three-week run at this theatre).

Safety bond/cable/chain
The metal chain or cable that attaches the lantern to the rigging.

Scale
The size of something relative to something else.

Scenery
Parts of the set that represent locations or surroundings – on cloth or flats.

Seam
The joining of two pieces of fabric on the wrong side.

Set dressings
Accessories such as tablecloths, cushions and other decorative items.

Sidelight
Light that shines from the side of the stage, perhaps from the wings.

Silhouette
The outline shape of a costume, or the dark shape of a person or object against a lighter background.

Snap
A quick and sudden transition, such as from loud to silent or a **blackout**.

Sound desk
The means of operating the different sounds.

Soundscape
An effect made up of several sounds to give the impression of a city street, for example.

Source
Where the sound comes from, such as a computer file. Also used to describe the sound itself, such as a bell ringing.

Speaker
The device that transmits the sound. Its volume level can be altered.

Special effect
A lighting or sound effect that has a specific purpose, such as a colour wash to suggest a flashback.

Spotlight
A type of lantern that can create a tight circle of light or a larger, softer-edged one.

Stage configuration
The shape of the acting area and where the audience are positioned in relation to it.

Stage furniture
Items in the production that can be moved but are not props, for example a chair, table or block. They might be included as part of the set design.

Stage manager
The person who runs and co-ordinates backstage proceedings.

Staging
The use of the stage as a design element, including type of stage configuration, positioning of entrances and exits and performer/audience relationships.

Stalls
Seating on the ground floor of a theatre, nearest to the stage.

Status symbol
A possession that is seen to show someone's wealth, social position or sense of style.

Stimulus
Something that inspires something else, such as an image or object that is used as a starting point for devising (plural is **stimuli**).

Structure
The way that something is sequenced, put together or built.

Style
Distinctive appearance, often typical of a particular person, period or place.

Stylised
Non-realistic, non-naturalistic, where style features are dominant.

Subculture
A cultural trend in society that is not the dominant one, such as goth, punk.

Swatch
A small sample of fabric that gives an idea of how an item made from it would look and feel.

Symbolic use of colour
The use of colour to communicate a certain meaning or represent a particular theme or mood.

Synchronised
Two or more sounds operating at the same time.

Synthetic
Man-made (fabric).

Tacking
A fast, long, hand-made, temporary stitch to hold seams together ready for trying on or for permanent stitching.

Tarpaulin
Large, heavy-duty, waterproof cloth/sheet, usually of woven plastic.

Texture
The surface feel of fabric, for example. Raised fabrics, such as velvet and cord, have a different texture from smooth ones, such as silk, which are flat.

Three-point lighting
A method that shines light from three different directions to give good coverage.

Thrust stage
A stage that extends into the audience area, with seats on three sides.

Transition
A change between lighting states, such as a snap or a fade.

Traverse
A stage configuration where the audience is in two parts that are seated opposite each other along two sides of the stage.

Truck
A wheeled platform on which a piece of scenery is built – to make scene changes quick and easy.

Underscore
Sound (often non-diegetic) that is played quietly while performers are speaking, to add atmosphere.

Upcycle
Taking an existing garment and changing it in some way to make something different.

Uplight
A light that shines from low down, perhaps positioned at the front of the stage.

Wardrobe
The wardrobe department is where the costumes are produced in a theatre. Alternatively, our wardrobe is the collection of clothes we own.

Weight
How heavy or light is the fabric? Does it drape or hang heavily?

White-card model
A simple 3D representation of a set design.

INDEX

3D models 20, 22–24, 48, 170, 186, 194, 214

accessories (costume) 73, 76, 80, 155, 187, 191
aims and objectives 118–119
allergies 77, 79, 240
amplifiers 92–93, 101
analysing 7–9, 18, 29–30, 47, 52–53, 59, 86–87, 92, 94, 111, 115–116, 119–120, 125, 127, 129–132, 135, 137–141, 144, 146–148, 150–152, 154, 157–159, 162–164, 168, 172, 176, 180, 184, 188, 192, 196, 202, 204–207, 218, 230, 235, 241, 253
artistic intentions, agreeing on 118–119
atmospheric 34, 43, 91, 96, 111, 162, 213, 223, 228, 250
automated moving lantern 37–38, 45

backcloth 26, 28, 220
backdrop 12–14, 17–18, 220
barn doors 36–38, 49, 54–55
Beauty and the Beast 123
blackout 46, 53, 56, 110
body proportions, drawing 81
book flats 23
bringing texts to life 9, 206
bruise wheel 79, 240
budget 10, 17, 26, 47, 72–73, 76, 155, 172–173, 181, 189–190, 197

characterisation 31, 44, 59, 70, 79, 122–123, 186, 190, 204, 234, 241
collaboration 63, 72, 77, 114–115, 124–128, 132–133, 135, 137, 141–144, 152, 154, 160, 162, 168, 173, 176, 181, 184, 189, 192, 197, 220
colour count 50
colour filter 37, 47, 142
colour frame 50
colour palette 16, 37, 63, 68, 115, 133, 135, 154, 171, 173, 188, 213, 228, 242
colours, selecting 68–70
console *see* **lighting desk**
constant sound 90
context 10, 19, 44, 56, 63, 70, 78, 87, 108, 110, 168, 176, 184, 194, 208–211, 222–225, 230, 235–237, 239–241, 244–247, 253

cultural 64, 78, 168, 176, 184, 194, 209, 223, 235
economic 19, 63, 78, 209, 223, 235
historical 10, 63–64, 70, 168, 176, 184, 194, 209, 223, 235, 245
social 19, 64, 78, 168, 176, 184, 194, 209, 223, 235, 245
contrast 46, 76, 83–85, 115, 209
costume design
    colour and fabric 68–72
    devised piece 147–156
    documenting 80–81
    evaluating 63, 87
    everyday 62
    health and safety 77
    history 64–66
    rehearsals 86
    research 63
    resources 72–73
    scripted performance 184–190
    sewing 74–75, 83
    shape and style 66–67
    written explanation 166, 191
costume designer 11
costume fitting 82–85
costume, making from scratch 73
cross-fade 39, 46, 145
cue sheet 9, 48–49, 52–53, 56, 102, 106–108, 116, 144, 162, 164, 166, 182–183, 197–198, 200, 251
cue to cue 11, 56–57, 109–110
cyberbullying 122, 140

daylight 40, 224
decibels 106
design
    assessment 116
    in performance 167
    process 11
    role in drama 10
    starting 115
    working in 10
designer's viewpoint 212–217, 226–229, 238–240, 248–252
devising process 114
diegetic sound 91, 94–95, 104, 122, 162, 164, 193, 200, 206, 248–249
dimmer 38, 43, 46, 53–54
director's viewpoint 208–211, 222–225, 234–237, 244–247

drawings 20–22, 49, 80–81, 87, 102, 116, 135–137, 144, 154–156, 166, 172, 189, 214; *also see* **sketches**
dress rehearsal 11, 29, 58, 86, 110, 128

echo 94, 97, 100–101, 163, 196, 252
embellishments 71, 74–76, 152, 240, 243
end-on stage 12–13, 17, 20, 123, 216
evaluating 29–31, 47, 52–53, 56, 59, 63, 86–87, 92, 111, 115–116, 119–120, 124–125, 127, 129, 131, 134–135, 137–138, 140, 143–144, 146–147, 150–154, 156–157, 159, 161–164, 168, 172, 176, 180, 182, 184, 188, 190, 192, 196, 198, 202, 204, 206–207, 218–221, 230–233, 241–243, 251, 253–254, 256
evaluative words 30
evaluative writing examples 31, 59, 87, 111
exam preparation 206–207
exterior location 17, 169, 176–177, 183, 192

fabric choices 63, 70–71, 121, 187
fabric weight/texture 71
fade 34, 39, 46, 56, 58, 90, 93, 99, 106–107, 109–110, 160, 163, 200, 211, 224, 229, 233, 246, 252
fader 106–107, 109
final rehearsals 29, 57, 108, 110, 128
fitting costumes 82–85
flats 17, 20–21, 23, 28, 133, 135–136, 138, 169, 174, 216–217, 219
flood (lighting) 35–37, 45, 145
focus (lighting) 11, 34–37, 39, 45, 50–51, 54–56, 144, 182, 215, 220, 229, 233
follow spotlight 37
footlight 12, 36, 177, 220
form
    costume design 150–151, 153–155
definition of 120–121
lighting design 121, 139–140, 144–145
set design 121, 131, 134–136
sound design 121, 158–159, 162–163
free-standing flats 21
freehand 80
fresnel lantern 36–38, 47, 49–50, 142, 183, 224, 229

Index 261

gels 37–38, 41–43, 47, 50, 54, 144, 180, 223–224, 229, 231
general cover 35–36, 52–53
genre
    costume design 66, 147–148, 150–151, 153–155, 184, 188
    definition of 120
    devising theatre 114–116, 120, 123, 126–127
    lighting design 35, 139–140, 143–145, 176, 180, 228
    set design 18, 129–131, 134–136, 168, 172, 213
    sound design 84, 157–159, 162–163, 192, 196, 245, 250
gobo 36–38, 44, 47, 49–50, 54–55, 139, 180–181, 183, 223–224, 227
ground plan 9, 20–22, 24, 48, 116, 135–136, 166, 172–173, 205, 214, 216–217
group work 124–127

hair 9, 35, 64, 70, 77–80, 152, 154–156, 191, 238–240
health and safety 8–9, 14, 22, 27–29, 39, 51, 56, 77, 86, 99, 116, 126, 134–135, 144, 152–155, 161–163, 166, 172–174, 180, 198
historical costume patterns 73
house lights 34, 35, 52, 55

illusion 18, 28, 45, 170, 224
intensity of lighting 29, 34–35, 40–41, 43, 53, 69, 86, 139, 141–142, 146, 179, 183, 222, 224–225, 228–229, 231, 233, 240
interior location 17, 169, 176–177, 183, 192
intermittent sound 90
interpretation 9, 18, 70, 78–79, 106, 118, 132, 166–168, 175–176, 182–184, 191–192, 198–200, 204, 206, 208, 212, 218, 222, 226, 230, 234–235, 238, 241, 244, 248, 253

key light 41–42, 45, 53, 60

lantern schedule 9, 144, 166
lantern types 36–37
lanterns, taking care of 39
LED 37–38, 42, 44–45, 47, 220, 223, 229

'Lies' 122, 130
lighting design
    angles, colour and intensity 40–43
    devised piece 138–146
    documenting 48–50
    evaluating 59
    health and safety 51
    importance 35
    plotting 52–53
    power 34
    purpose 34
    rehearsals 57–58
    research 47
    resources 38–39
    rigging and focusing 10, 38–39, 48–49, 51, 54–55, 138, 144–145, 181–183, 229
    scripted performance 176–182
    special effects 35, 43–45, 47, 49, 52–53, 58–59, 141, 179–181, 227, 230, 233
    transitions 46
    written explanation 166, 183
lighting, controlling/operating 39, 56
lighting desk 37–39, 43, 46, 50, 53–54, 56
lighting plan 9, 38, 48, 50, 116, 144, 166, 179
lighting plot 9, 116, 138, 144
lighting state 8–9, 29, 34, 39, 44, 46, 49, 52–53, 56–58, 86, 115, 120, 123, 142, 144, 166, 176, 179–180, 183, 231
lighting styles 35–37
lighting transitions 46, 107, 226, 233
live sound 98, 109
live theatre evaluation 9, 16, 63, 207, 218–221, 230–233, 241–243, 251, 253–254, 256
location, creating 17

make-up 9, 62–65, 67, 70, 75, 77–81, 152, 154–155, 187–190, 238–239
mass-produced clothing 65
microphones 92–93, 95
mixing desk 92–93, 97, 101
model boxes 24, 48, 172–173, 205, 213–214

monochrome 68, 115, 126, 133, 137
montage 94, 102
mood 16, 34–35, 40, 42–44, 62, 69, 87, 90–91, 94–95, 97–98, 108, 111, 114, 128–129, 135, 137–138, 144, 146–147, 154–155, 157, 161–162, 167–168, 171–172, 176, 179–180, 184, 188, 192, 195–196, 200, 209, 218, 221, 223–224, 226, 228, 230, 245, 250, 253
mood board 127, 151, 153, 178, 203, 206, 213, 227–228, 249–250

naturalistic lighting 41–45, 140, 144, 226
naturalistic set/style 18, 95, 114–115, 120–121, 123, 135, 144, 151, 154, 162–163, 167, 169–170, 178, 184, 186, 192, 194, 200, 211, 213, 216, 219–220, 236–238, 240, 245–246, 249, 255
night-time 40, 195
non-diegetic sound 91, 94–95, 97, 122, 162–163, 192–193, 200, 206, 246, 248–250
non-naturalistic lighting 41, 45, 140–141, 144–145, 227
non-naturalistic set/style 18, 23, 96, 98, 121, 123, 126, 131, 135, 144, 154, 162–163, 167–168, 175–176, 192, 195, 200, 211–212, 238

online research/resources 6, 19, 39, 73, 80, 91, 93, 95, 97, 142, 218, 230, 241, 253

pace 39, 94, 111, 144, 146, 226, 233, 252
par can 36–38, 49–50, 233
periods, historical 10, 12–13, 19, 62–68, 73, 76, 78–79, 84, 111, 121, 162, 167, 170, 172, 178, 180, 185–188, 193–194, 196, 206, 208–209, 211, 213, 218, 222, 235–236, 238, 240–241, 243–246, 249–250
pitch-shift 100–101
portfolio 8, 30, 48, 51, 56, 63, 80, 95, 99, 102–103, 115–116, 125, 127, 129–134, 136–150, 152–153, 155–159, 161, 163–164, 204
    practical design 9, 11, 25, 38, 48, 102, 114, 126
pre-set 16, 18, 31, 107, 109, 111, 163, 180, 200

262 Index

production meetings 125, 133–134, 153, 161

profile spotlight 36–38, 49–50, 60, 139, 229, 233

projection 12–14, 17, 35, 132, 167, 212, 223, 233

props 11, 13–14, 17–19, 135, 166, 169, 174, 203, 236

proscenium arch stage 12–13, 104, 168, 212, 229, 233, 255

raked 12–13
realistic set 18; *also see* **naturalistic**
recycling 26, 76
rehearsal costumes 63
representative set 18, 170, 216
responding to stimuli 117
reverb 93, 100–101, 111, 163, 196, 200
rigging 10, 38–39, 48–49, 51, 54–55, 138, 144–145, 181–183, 229
run of flats 133

safety bond 38, 47, 51, 54
scale (in drawings/plans) 20–24, 136
scenery 12–14, 16–17, 21–22, 25, 27–29, 138, 169, 221
set design
    creating 28
    devised piece 129–137
    documenting 20–24
    evaluating 30–31
    health and safety 27
    materials 25–26
    rehearsals 29
    research 19
    resources 25
    scripted performance 168–174
    styles 18
    written explanation 166, 175
set designer 11, 16–18, 20, 22, 27, 29, 48, 68, 77, 129–130, 157, 168–170, 175, 179, 186, 194, 212, 215, 218, 220, 238
sewing 74–75, 83
sidelights 52
sightline 12–13, 29, 126, 166, 171, 215
silence 98, 163, 217, 252
silhouette 37, 66, 76, 82, 85, 121, 169, 185, 229, 242

sketches 6, 8–9, 17, 20–22, 29, 38, 40, 70, 80–81, 105, 116, 118, 125, 129–130, 133–134, 148, 151–153, 168–170, 172–173, 175, 178–179, 181, 186–188, 191, 194–195, 197, 203, 206–207, 214, 217–219, 230, 238, 240–242, 253
skin-tones 69
sound design
    devised piece 157–164
    documenting 102–103
    evaluating 111
    health and safety 99
    plotting 97, 106–107
    real world 90
    rehearsals 110
    research 94–95
    resources 92–93
    scripted performance 192–198
    sourcing, creating and mixing 96–97
    special effects 100–101
    stage 91
    written explanation 166, 199–200
sound equipment, operating 108–109
sound equipment, positioning 104–105
sound plan 102–103
soundscape 59, 90–91, 97, 163, 195, 250, 252, 254
source sheet 9, 102, 116, 162, 166, 251
speakers 12, 92–93, 102–105, 108, 195, 197, 250, 252, 255
special effects 35, 43–45, 47, 49, 52–53, 58–59, 78–79, 100–101, 141, 163, 179–181, 195–197, 227, 230, 233
    spotlight 11, 34–37, 44–45, 49–50, 55, 115, 123, 138, 144, 179, 183, 222, 229, 233
stage/staging configuration 12–14, 17–18, 20, 104, 123, 166, 168, 176–179, 184, 192, 194, 203, 213–215, 220, 228, 233, 250, 256
stage furniture 9, 13, 16–17, 19, 21, 135, 166, 170, 203, 219, 236
stage management 11
stage manager 11, 173, 181, 189, 197
stage space 12–14, 18, 132
staging 12, 179, 203
stalls 13
stimulus 8, 114–118, 122, 124, 130, 139–140, 148, 150–151, 158–159

structure
    costume design 120, 150–151, 153–154
    definition of 120
    lighting design 120, 139–140, 144–145
    set design 131, 134–136
    sound design 158–159, 162–163
style
    costume design 62, 64–67, 70, 78–79, 83–85, 121–122, 147–148, 150–156, 184–189, 191, 234, 238, 241–242
    definition of 121
    devising theatre 114–116, 120–121, 123, 126, 128
    lighting design 35, 44, 121–122, 138–140, 143–145, 176, 178, 180, 183, 222, 227–228, 231
    set design 16, 18, 121, 129–136, 168–170, 172, 175, 208, 212–213, 216
    sound design 90, 94–96, 98, 108, 121, 157–159, 161–163, 192–197, 199, 244, 249–250, 254
    stage configurations 12–13
stylised 18, 68, 84, 171, 178, 186, 194, 224
subculture 67
swatch 70, 153, 188–189

tarpaulin 26
technical rehearsal 11, 29, 57, 86, 110, 128, 145, 174, 182, 190, 198
textured fabric 65, 71, 74, 236
three-point lighting 42, 48
thrust stage 13, 18, 213, 236–237

upcycling 71, 76
uplighting 223, 233

visibility 12, 34, 48

wardrobe 10–11, 62, 66, 72
wash 34, 55, 123
white card models 23–24
wigs 64, 77–78, 187

Text acknowledgements

Extracts from *Collected Grimm Tales* by Carol Ann Duffy. Published by Faber & Faber. Copyright © Carol Ann Duffy. Reproduced by permission of the author c/o Rogers, Coleridge & White Ltd., 20 Powis Mews, London W11 1JN.

Extracts from the Edexcel GCSE (9–1) Drama Specification reproduced by permission of Pearson.

Image acknowledgements

pp5 left, **19 left**, **42 centre**, **50**, **55**, **75**, **77**, **103** and **214** emc design ltd
pp6, **45 left**, **51**, **83 top**, **84 bottom**, **97 top**, **114**, **118**, **126 bottom**, **134**, **153**, **154**, **175**, **190**, **191**, **207 bottom**, **226 right** and **249 top** Neil Sutton at Cambridge Design Consultants
p13 Masque Sound; Timothy Mackabee
p14 Simon Annand; Andrew Billington; The Dukes
pp15, **25** and **136** Marmaduke St. John / Alamy Stock Photo
p16 bottom Dan Norman
p17 Craig Sugden
p18 Lara Capelli; Arts at Michigan
p19 right BFA / Paramount Pictures / Alamy Stock Photo
p20 Ali McCaw
pp21, **23**, **24 bottom**, **123**, **172** and **216** Sue Shewring
p22 Juliet Shillingford
p24 top Nan Austin / Modesto Bee / ZUMA Wire / Alamy Stock Photo
p28 Yvonne Arnaud Theatre
p30 Henry So / A Theatre Near U
p31 Craig Schwarz / USC School of Dramatic Arts
pp34 right and **213 bottom** Mark Sepple
p35 Photo 12 / Alamy Stock Photo / Lucasfilm; Photo 12 / Alamy Stock Photo / Miramax Films
p36 (fresnel) Altman / B&H Foto & Electronics; **(birdie)** DTS Illuminazione / Presentation Design Services; **(par cans)** Lourens Smak / Alamy Stock Photo
p37 (profile) XuanFeng Pro Lighting Co., Limited; **(gobos)** EMEA Rosco; **(AML)** Martin Lighting
p38 left Equinox / Simply Sound & Lighting
p41 Stephen Chung / Alamy Live News
pp42 left and **48** Brent Lees @ BCL Lighting Design
p42 right Expolmaging
p43 Netflix
p44 top Winnipesaukee Playhouse
p45 top Matt Murphy; **centre-right** Prop Scenery Lights LLC
pp45 bottom, **145 top**, **203 top**, **232**, **237**, **247** and **252** Geraint Lewis / Alamy Stock Photo
pp46 and **167** Manuel Harlan
p53 Zero88
pp57 and **86** aberCPC / Alamy Stock Photo
p58 Michele Domonkos / Alamy Stock Photo
p63 Joel Stuthman / Alamy Stock Photo
p64 Alanna Sadler MUA
p65 Collection Christophel / Alamy Stock Photo; Pictorial Press Ltd / Alamy Stock Photo
p68 bottom Sueddeutsche Zeitung Photo / Alamy Stock Photo
p69 top Bree Warner / Leviathan Lab
pp69 bottom, **255** and **256** Brinkhoff-Moegenburg

pp74, **186–188** Fi Carrington
p76 top right Pendragon Costumes
p78 left and **116** Robert Workman
p79 bottom Kryolan / Face Paint Supplies Perth
p80 Alice Smith, Designer for *Noughts and Crosses* at Nottingham Playhouse – August 2016
p82 top University of Maryland Baltimore County; **left** mybluprint.com
p83 bottom See Kate Sew
p84 top Modern Millie Shop; **left** Infamous Commonwealth Theatre
p85 DoHope; Fabians Haberdashery & Trimmings; Duluth Trading Company
p87 S R Taylor Photography
p91 Peninsular Players
p94 20th Century Fox
p98 right George Coupe
p108 Helsinki City Theatre / Meyer Sound Laboratories
p121 Scott Kimmins
p129 bottom Brian J Proball
p132 bottom Adrian Sherratt / Alamy Stock Photo
p133 R. Eric Stone (Scenic Designer, *The Complete Works of William Shakespeare (Abridged)*, Melissa Rain Anderson, Director)
p138 Teresa Castracane
p142 bottom Xinhua/Alamy Live News
p143 Loop Images Ltd / Alamy Stock Photo
p147 Bettina Strenske / Alamy Stock Photo
p148 Walter Bieri (Keystone)
p152 John Roberts
p158 Peter Barritt / Alamy Stock Photo
p162 C.L.Gizmos
p168 Foteini Christofilopoulou
p170 Mike Hoban / Glyndebourne Productions Ltd
p174 Bernd Tschakert / Alamy Stock Photo
p182 Tristram Kenton
p183 Johan Persson
p198 top freeimages.co.uk
p200 EFE News Agency / Alamy Stock Photo
p203 bottom keith morris / Alamy Stock Photo
p205 Alicia Dolen
p206 Luis Escobar / Reflections Photography Studio
p207 top T Charles Erickson
p208 Jon Sachs / Leslie Maiocco
p210 Mark Douet
p212 © Philip Carter. Published under a Creative Commons Non-Commercial Licence.
p213 top Free-Photos on Pixabay, Mitchel Lensink on Unsplash, Paweł Czerwiński on Unsplash, Steve Norris on Pixabay, Sebastian Huxley on Unsplash, FeatheredHatStudios on Pixabay
p215 City Theatre Company; Elizabeth Aaron
p218 Keith Pattison
p219 Steven Scott Taylor / Alamy Live News
p221 Bill Kenwright
p222 TU Berlin Bühnenbild Szenischer Raum
p225 Helen Murray / ArenaPAL
p227 David Mark on Pixabay, Dieter_G on Pixabay, Ganapathy Kumar on Unsplash, Sam Lloyd on Unsplash, martinagreen on Pixabay, Markus Spiske on Unsplash
p229 LEE Filters / Dale Photographic Ltd
p230 KEITH MAYHEW / Alamy Live News
pp231 and **244** Joan Marcus
p234 University Players, School of Dramatic Art, University of Windsor
p235 right Birmingham Museums Trust on Unsplash

p239 Drew Farrell / Royal Lyceum Theatre Company Ltd
p241 sjtheatre / Alamy Stock Photo
p243 Drew Buckley
p245 Karl Hugh, courtesy of the Utah Shakespeare Festival
p249 cocoparisienne on Pixabay, Gerd Altman on Pixabay, haalkab (Omar Gonzalez) on Pixabay, Ichigo121212 on Pixabay, Markus Spiske on Unsplash
p250 Roger Mastroianni
p251 Michael Brosilow
p253 WENN Rights Ltd / Alamy Stock Photo.

All other images: Shutterstock:

p5 top untitled; **pp5 bottom**, **126 top** and **164 left** Monkey Business Images; **p8** Iakov Filimonov; **pp10 top** and **11 top** Lakeview Images / Shutterstock.com; **p10 bottom** Anna Jurkovska; **p11 bottom** metamorwork; **p12** posztos/Shutterstock.co.uk; **p16 top** Photographee.eu; **p34 left** John Arehart, **p36 (background)** Matusciac Alexandru, **(floodlight)** Roman Yastrebinsky, **(barn doors)** lapandr, **pp36 (par can lighting)**, **39 bottom** and **181** Oleksandr Nagaiets; **p37 (LEDs)** Rajesh Narayanan; **p38 top** Pawel_Brzozowski; **p40** Mopic; Wan bo; **p44 left** NANCY AYUMI KUNIHIRO; **p47** Africa Studio, veryulissa; **p52** Kolik; **p54** Trikona; **p56** Tennessee Witney; **p61** MJTH; **p62** OlegD / Shutterstock.com, x4wiz; **p66** NeydtStock / Shutterstock.com, onajourney / Shutterstock.com; **p67** Dziurek / Shutterstock.com, Red Umbrella and Donkey; **p68 top** Adil Celebiyev / Shutterstock.com, **left** WIJI; **pp69 left** and **129 top** Tatyana Mi; **p70** Photology1971; **p71** Colin Ridgway-Cole, acidmit, Deep_Mind, Joaquin Corbalan P; **p72** wavebreakmedia, Zb89V; **p76 left** Eddie Jordan Photos / Shutterstock.com; **centre** Mary Long, **bottom** Yuriy Golub, **p78 top** Dreamer Company / Shutterstock.com; **bottom** Pavel Ignatov; **p79 top** AJP/Shutterstock.com, **right** mirdred; **p89** antoniodiaz; **pp90 top** and **146 bottom** Pixsooz; **p90 left** palidachan; **p93** n_defender; tsaplia; **p95** S B Stock; **p96** GoodStudio, Dmitry Galaganov; **p97 bottom** Anutr Yossundara; **p98 left** allstars; **p99** Anrey_Popov; Javier Brosch; **p100** Lebedev_S; **p101** agsandrew; Petr Malyshev; Ching Design; **p104** Kabardins photo; **p105** ALPA PROD; **p106** Andrew Berezovsky; **p107** igor gratzer; **p109** Syda Productions; Sergey Nemirovsky; **p110** studiostoks; **p117** Aleutie; **p122** Andreev105/Shutterstock.com; **p132 top** Have a nice day Photo; **p139** Kateryna Kon; **p141** GN Illustrator; **p142 top** Yannick Martinez; **p143 background** faak; **p145 bottom** Yaroslau Mikheyeu; **p146 top** Trueffelpix; **p149** Degimages, David Tadevosian; **p150** Lara Ra; **p151** Lightfield Studios; **p155** Lenar Nigmatullin, Andreja Donko; **p156** gabriel12; **p157** PrinceOfLove, New Africa; **pp159** and **161** Lightspring; **p160** Bborriss.67; **p164 right** fizkes; **p171** alexasokol83; **p173** DGLimages; **p178** FrameStockFootages; **p179** Independent; **p180** mijatmijatovic; **p189** Oleksii Didok; **p194** panitanphoto; **p195** Dragon Images; **p196** metamorworks; **p197** Jacob Lund; **p198 bottom** Anutr Yossundara; **p199** Rawpixel.com, hurricanehawk, Pressmaster; **p201** michaeljung; **p202** Kiselev Andrey Valerevich; **p204** Terry Murden / Shutterstock.com; **p223** Molotok289; **p228** Kozlik; **p235 left** Ethiriel, **centre** Masson.